THE PRACTITIONER INQUIRY SERIES

Marilyn Cochran-Smith and Susan L. Lytle, Series Editors

(continued)

Raising Race Questions

Whiteness and Inquiry in Education

Ali Michael

Foreword by
Shaun R. Harper

TEACHERS COLLEGE PRESS

TEACHERS COLLEGE | COLUMBIA UNIVERSITY
NEW YORK AND LONDON

Published by Teachers College Press, 1234 Amsterdam Avenue, New York, NY 10027

This research was made possible in part by funding from the Ruth Landes Memorial Research Fund, a program of The Reed Foundation.

Library of Congress Cataloging-in-Publication Data can be obtained at www.loc.gov

ISBN 978-0-8077-5599-0 (paperback)
ISBN 978-0-8077-5600-3 (hardcover)
ISBN 978-0-8077-7341-3 (ebook)

Printed on acid-free paper
Manufactured in the United States of America

22 21 20 19 18 17 16 15   8 7 6 5 4 3 2

To my partner, Michael, with whom I share the joy and work of building a feminist family, an antiracist community, and an antioppressive lifestyle.

To my parents, Bonnie and Terry Michael, who instilled in me a deep sense of empathy, belonging, and fairness— all of which drive my work and practice.

To the six White teachers in this book, who opened their lives, their classrooms, and themselves to contribute to the lessons shared here.

Contents

Foreword

Several derogatory racial epithets have been used to characterize, insult, and injure people of color in the United States. What is the most offensive thing someone can call a White person? Racist. Being accused of somehow participating in the perpetuation of racism scares most White people—they do not like it, it often makes them uncomfortable and defensive, and it rarely leads to increased levels of interracial cooperation and understanding. Conferring the R-word onto a White person is almost always more harmful than helpful. There is much about America's historical record that engenders especially strong reactions to racial labels. Perhaps it is the residual effects of slavery. It also could be our personal investments in or delusions about living in a colorblind, postracial society.

"You are racist" are three paralyzing words, even when evidence supports such characterization. Thus, some skillfully attempt to disentangle actions from their perpetrators by saying something like the following: "I am not calling you racist, but you are behaving in a racist manner." This strategy is intended to put people at ease and depersonalize racial misconduct. Sociologist Eduardo Bonilla-Silva (2013) argues in his book *Racism Without Racists* that one unintended consequence of this approach is that White people oftentimes arrive at the erroneous conclusion that *some* racism exists but they, personally, are responsible for *none* of it. Such sense making exists among educators in many U.S. schools and colleges.

Numerous data sources reveal sweeping and pervasive racial inequities in our educational institutions. Racial differences in test scores and other student performance metrics, graduation and college-going rates, suspensions and expulsions, and special education misplacement are commonplace. And then there is the increasingly popular approach of placing novice, insufficiently prepared teachers in urban schools that are almost entirely Black and Latino, something that White Americans would never let happen in affluent suburban public schools or expensive private schools their children attend. Does this make the well-intentioned White people who participate in Teach For America and programs like it complicit in the cyclical reinscription of racism? Is it fair to attribute durable, complex racial problems to the recent college graduate who teaches at a school only a year or two before moving on to pursue his actual career interests? Is it right to confer the R-word onto the White woman who disproportionately refers African American boys to the principal's office for petty behavioral problems if she does so unknowingly and little is done in her school to raise consciousness about these and other quantifiable racial trends?

These are indeed critical questions, but perhaps more important are some others that are at the core of this book: How and where are these issues talked about, why are they so difficult to discuss, and what are some productive ways to raise race questions in educational environments that are inescapably raced?

Not talking about racial issues—especially those that are hiding in plain sight—sustains racist educational environments and routinely reproduces racial hierarchies in our schools and society. Teachers participate in this, and so, too, do principals and other educational leaders. I honestly believe the overwhelming majority of these colleagues would prefer to work in schools that are racially harmonious, where equity is consistently realized, and all persons are respected. I know that few enter teaching *wanting* (which is different from *expecting*) students of color to achieve at rates lower than their White classmates. Wanting something is admirable, but making oneself vulnerable enough to achieve it is difficult and frightening, especially for those who have not done sufficient self-reflection or had substantive opportunities for rehearsal, racial mistake making, supportive dialogues with others, and deep learning. As Ali Michael makes clear in this book, raising race questions must first begin with self before it can be done effectively with colleagues in school environments. When and where does this self-reflection begin for teachers? Not usually in schools of education, and probably not during the accelerated Teach For America summer institute.

I have spent considerable time at five schools of education over the past 20 years—at two schools as a student, and at three as a professor. I have also visited a couple dozen others for consultancies, academic program assessments and curriculum reviews, and to deliver speeches. In 2013, I spent a day conducting a workshop on race for the entire school of education faculty at a research university in the Midwest; the school had only one African American faculty member and few other professors of color. Moreover, 2 years of my career were spent serving as executive director of a doctor of education (EdD) program for experienced teachers and educational leaders. The range and substance of these experiences lead me to the following conclusion: Too few race questions are raised in schools of education, and faculty who teach in them are often culprits in the miseducation of racially incompetent professionals. These are my colleagues; some are my friends. I know these people well. I am one of them. Therefore, I know for sure that most of us want equitable educational systems. We want to effectively prepare highly qualified teachers of all learners. Many of us would be horrified by claims that we somehow contribute to racial injustice in the schools our graduates enter. But like the students we teach, we are byproducts of our educational upbringing. That is, raising race questions was not standard practice in many of the colleges and universities at which we were schooled. In fact, we likely learned more about racial avoidance. As such, we often teach teachers in ways that fail to permit tough (sometimes painful) yet productive grappling with personal and institutional racism. No one taught us how to raise race questions. Thus, it is unsurprising to me that so few of us do it routinely and skillfully in our classrooms and academic programs.

Raising Race Questions provides much-needed guidance and inspiration for educators who want racial equity in schools. Its author masterfully instructs and inspires readers throughout the text, while also demanding accountability, authenticity, and deeply reflective personal work. Much about this book moves readers, particularly White educators, beyond the debilitating effects of the R-word. Dr. Michael helps us understand that racism; racist institutional structures, policies, and practices; and longstanding racial inequities in schools are not going to address themselves—educators can address them, but we must do so with greater intentionality and less fear. Critical, honest conversations first with oneself and then with colleagues, students, and families are paramount. This work has to be done more seriously in schools of education and other spaces where teachers are prepared and it must continue throughout their careers.

Shaun R. Harper

Acknowledgments

With every word in this book, I am reminded of the knowledge, empathy, and wisdom with which my mentors have taught me about race. I think of all these people now, and the myriad lessons they have taught me.

I think of my parents, who taught me to be proactive, inclusive, empathetic, independent, vocal, and loving. When I came home from college sharing all of my new knowledge about race, they listened. When I told my Dad I thought his viewpoint was racist, he quietly and humbly helped me learn that calling a person racist does not change his or her mind, and that the line between racist and antiracist is very thin indeed. They taught me that antiracist development happens over the long term, that affirmation and information are more effective than competition and shame, and that White people are capable of learning and changing.

I think of Gertrude Sgwentu—Makhulu—my second mother and my best friend. I think of Tetile, Evelyn, Thania, Sipho, and Sitetile. Gertrude and her family shared their life in South Africa with me, helping me learn that the personal is political and the political is personal. Gertrude guided me through the complex process of relationship building across racial and class disparities. She taught me the critical importance of teaching White people to examine our unconscious biases. Evelyn, Thania, Sipho, and Sitetile helped me remember why race and class matter so much in schools.

I think of Carolyn Michael, Michael Ramberg, Aaron Boyle, and Eleonora Bartoli, with whom I spent 4 years in a White affinity group learning about race. The lessons that I learned from that group have shaped this book. The foundation of allyship and friendship that we formed during that time has helped me feel supported and challenged to maintain my ideals in each aspect of my life.

I think of Chonika Coleman-King, with whom I worked very closely during my research process. Many of the ideas that take root in this book were planted by Chonika in the parking lot after meetings, as we continued to discuss racial dynamics well after our colleagues had moved on to other things.

I think of Howard Stevenson, who made it possible to think and talk about race in graduate school in ways that affect people's daily lives and lead to real change. Thank you for inviting me onto your research team, where I learned so many of the tools that I used to do this research and write this book. I think, too, of all of the members of that team: Duane Thomas, Valerie Bass-Adams, Keisha

Bentley-Edwards, Chonika Coleman-King, Gwen Miller, Celine Thompson, and Zehua Li. Thank you for including me, for trusting me, and for teaching me.

I think of Shaun Harper, who introduced me to Critical Race Theory and who constantly innovates new possibilities for antiracism in higher education. Thank you for your ongoing mentorship, creativity, energy, and commitment. It is an inspiration and an honor to work alongside you at the Center.

I think of Kathy Schultz, who never blinked an eye when I said I wanted to focus my doctoral work on Whiteness. Thank you for your thoughtful, thorough, critical feedback and your constant support. Your ideas contributed immeasurably to this work and to all that came before it.

I think of Lesley Bartlett, who taught me how to be a good person, a feminist, a mother, and a friend while being a researcher, an academic, and a teacher.

I think of Barbara Moore-Williams, who mentored me in the fine art of storytelling, question asking, and active listening for the sake of deepening antiracist education.

I think of Mathu Subramanian, my writing buddy and friend. Thank you for always being willing to share your thoughts and ideas about race—and for constantly reminding me to go beyond Black and White.

I think of all of the members of White Students Confronting Racism at Penn: Sue Bickerstaff, Mary Conger, Sarah Burgess, Luke Reinke, Kathleen Riley, and many more. Thank you for holding the space at the Graduate School of Education for White people to grow, learn, and act in antiracist community.

I think of Sarah Halley and Molly McClure, who taught me how to work with other White people, and who taught me to see myself in every White person I meet. You gave me a framework for thinking and teaching about race that structures much of my thinking in this book. I think of Lorraine Marino and Antje Mattheus, our elders and mentors, who taught us that no one can learn when they are feeling shamed.

I think of my cofacilitators at the Race Institute for K–12 Educators: Frederick Bryant and Sarah Halley. I think of our advisory committee and of all the educators who have come through the institute and continue to be involved in the support network we are building. Thank you for helping me continue to learn the value of cultivating an antiracist practice in community.

I think of those who mentored me through conferences and institutes, including Jamie Washington and Kathy O'Bear of the Social Justice Training Institute, who helped me to learn some of the hardest lessons about myself and my own biases. I think of Diane Goodman, whose work helped me move beyond shame when I was first beginning my journey. I think of Eddie Moore Jr., who first showed me what large-scale impact can look like and who challenges me to think big. I think of Elizabeth Denevi and Mariama Richards, who live and work at the very intersection of theory and practice—and who have helped me learn how to navigate that space. I think of Tiffany Taylor Smith, who has challenged me to create educational tools for teens. I think of Courtney Portlock, who has shown me the importance of storytelling for teaching about racism. I think of Paul Gorski, who holds a firm line as a White person who studies race and models the kind of ongoing inquiry and humility that I wish to emulate. I think of Toni Williamson, who is especially amazing at helping every child of every race learn what they need to know and get where they need to go. And I think of Chezare Warren, who is paving new pathways in academia that honor and challenge K–12 educators.

I think of Michael, Erica, Frances, and Mary, who are constantly engaged with race questions of their own, and who support me in my practice. I think of Grandpa Charles, whose spirit is with us in all of these conversations.

And I think of my college professors: Kim Springer, Kenda Mutongi, Steve Gerrard, Grant Farred, and Laura McKeon, who gave me new lenses with which to view this racialized world.

Thank you to all of my beloved readers and editors: Matt Atwood, Keisha Bentley, Sue Bickerstaff, Aaron Boyle, Mary Conger, Pat Fox, Angela Gillem, Shaun Harper, Heidi Hausman, Bob Michael, Carolyn Michael, Bonnie Michael, Terry Michael, Erica Ramberg, Frances Ramberg, Mary Ramberg, Michael Ramberg, Mathu Subramanian, Julie Landsman, and Sarah Halley.

Thank you to Susan Lytle, coeditor of the Practitioner Inquiry Series with Marilyn Cochran. You first saw the value and importance of my work and encouraged me to turn it into a book. Thank you to Brian Ellerbeck, senior editor at Teachers College Press, for your responsiveness, challenge, questioning, and support. The process of applying and preparing for publication made this manuscript so much stronger under your guidance.

Thank you to my family—Bonnie, Terry, Carolyn, Aaron, Mike, Bob, Heidi, Lindsay, and Jason—for building a network of love and support so large and so robust that I live my life with the sense that anything is possible.

Thank you to Michael, Tina, and Sami for reminding me daily why it matters so much that all human beings have the opportunity to be their whole selves.

White Teachers, Whole Classrooms

"Will they never get it? I spend all of this time coming to these meetings, trying to help teachers be more culturally aware, and nothing changes! Will they never understand how much it hurts when they do things like this?"

Nolena, a Black parent of three Black boys in the district, was hurt and dismayed by the book that one of her son's teachers chose to read to his class. *Metal Man* featured a young Black boy who spoke in African American Vernacular English (AAVE). He lived in an apartment with his mom and his little sister. He spent his days with a neighbor who made sculptures out of garbage. After hearing the book read aloud, many of the teachers in the group still weren't sure what the problem was but did not want to say so for fear of further alienating Nolena. The book seemed like a poetic and artistic portrayal of one kind of life that is often not portrayed in schools, especially predominantly White schools like this one. It brought African American Vernacular English into the classroom and taught an important lesson about recycling.

Finally one Black colleague asked the question everyone wanted the answer to but was afraid to ask because they didn't want to further marginalize Nolena with their confusion: *"What didn't you like about the book?"* Nolena explained how her son was the only Black boy in his whole grade and how he battled to help people understand his reality. His teachers, his classmates, and their parents all thought they knew something about him because he was Black, and usually they were wrong. They didn't know that he was middle class, had two parents, lived in a house, and got excessive amounts of presents for Christmas, just like many of his White peers. On a regular basis he was disabusing people of the notion that he was the boy in this book. And now his teacher, in an attempt to offer more characters for him to identify with, had unwittingly reinforced the connection in their minds between Black boys and poverty, single parentage, and African American Vernacular English.

Situations like this are what led me to write this book. Witnessing, in particular, the tragic misalignment of the *intention* of the teacher in this scenario and the *impact* she had on her students and their parents, I wanted to slow down the conversation and look at the questions, the confusions, and the sticking places that come up for White teachers when they authentically engage in questions about race. This particular example may seem too small or fleeting to be significant.

1

However, for teachers, students, and their families, the school year is made up of thousands of moments like this one, which have the potential to either build or erode relationships and trust.

I spent a year working with six White teachers who were all engaged in different inquiry processes about race in their classrooms. *Inquiry*, a process of constant engagement with a question, is the commitment to sit with a difficult query and to keep asking it over time. It is a rigorous and systematic process of research, experimentation, and community building around challenging dilemmas.

Just an hour after finishing my conversation with Nolena in a predominantly White suburban school district, I walked into Todd's school, passing classes of 2nd-graders, many of whom spoke in African American Vernacular English and lived in low-income and working-class Black neighborhoods. I thought to myself, "*Metal Man* might make sense here." It wouldn't tell the whole story of any one child's life, but in a school that is 100% African American, it would give many of the children a protagonist to relate to. And because all the students are Black, it wouldn't create the same obstacles for kids whose realities do not conform to the book. Their peers would not be as quick to make racialized generalizations about them. The book itself was not wrong. But when it comes to race, context matters. For every race question, there are myriad answers.

In conducting the research for this book, I chose to work with inquiry groups in vastly different types of schools because I wanted to remember that race matters on the individual, group, institutional, and systemic level. The negotiations between Nolena's family and her school district played out on the individual level. But the reasons why her family was one of so few Black families in that predominantly White school district, and the reasons that students on the other side of the city line went to a school that was 100% Black, were systemic.

This book is built on two sets of data. The first set includes the questions, realizations, and practices that grew out of the inquiry process of the White teachers with whom I worked. Rather than attempting to find singular or simple answers to their questions about race, I use this space to convey the complex interplay of the intention and impact, the dynamics and context behind each question. The second data set includes the experiences I've had as a consultant and facilitator in schools and workshops. In the years since I originally conducted this research I have had the opportunity to work with hundreds of teachers asking similar questions. Whenever relevant, I include stories from those teachers to illustrate the varied ways that race questions get raised in practice.

GUIDING PRINCIPLES OF THIS BOOK

This book is shaped around four fundamental premises. First, the practice of race inquiry is a practice that is meant to make all of us (teachers, students, classrooms, and schools) *more whole*. Second, you can have a multicultural curriculum and still not have an antiracist classroom. Third, building whole classrooms requires supporting each student to have a positive racial identity; teachers, however, cannot accomplish this unless they have a positive racial identity themselves. And fourth, racial competence is a skill that can be learned. Each premise will be briefly described in the sections that follow and will reappear throughout the book.

Guiding Principle 1: Whole Teachers, Whole Classrooms

The practice of inquiry about racism in our classrooms and schools is a practice that is meant to make us more whole. Racism has a fracturing effect on individuals and communities, and we cannot repair these fractures without really understanding how racism functions, both inside and outside of us. Signs of this brokenness can be seen in the strain of cross-racial relationships, the ways that segregation and inequality begin to seem normal, and the internalization of stereotypes that keep us from understanding one another. The work of this book is not to shame people for what they don't know or for privileges they didn't ask for. It's about seeing how race is a part of all of us and understanding how we have all been broken by racism. It's about learning to understand those fractures so that we, our students, and our classrooms can be more whole and more fully ourselves.

Guiding Principle 2: Positive Racial Identity

Building whole classrooms requires supporting every student to have a positive racial identity.[1] This is work that teachers cannot do unless we already have a positive racial identity ourselves. For the first many years of my teaching career, I did not even realize I had a racial identity, and couldn't envision what a positive White racial identity might look like. "What's positive about being White?" I asked when challenged to think about this premise at that time. Before I learned how to see my "Whiteness," I felt that all I could do in a conversation on race was to listen to the stories of people of color. I felt I didn't have a race, and I didn't have a story. As I learned to name Whiteness and to see the role that it played in shaping my life, I started to see how I fit into the larger conversation about race as well.

I was in a school in the southern United States recently doing a training with school administrators who pushed back against the idea that they could ever feel good about being White. In a state where White supremacists still fly the Confederate flag for reasons that include—but are not limited to—"cultural pride," they felt there was no way to own their Whiteness while being antiracist. White antiracist activist and cofounder of the Whites Confronting Racism workshop, Antje Mattheus, suggests that this feeling is prevalent because White supremacists have co-opted White identity. In mainstream society, it has been true historically that the only White people who identify with their Whiteness are White supremacists (Tatum, 2003). For White people who do not consciously identify with the ideology of White supremacy, there have traditionally been only two other ways to be White: One could either be ignorant of one's Whiteness or one could feel guilt and shame about it. Given these three options—supremacist, ignorant, or guilty—any healthy conscious identification with one's White identity seems impossible. Tatum suggests that in order for White people to be able to take part in antiracism, they have to be able to identify as White in a way that is not psychologically hurtful, requiring a conception beyond those three narrow categories. She suggests a fourth way to be White: the option of the antiracist White (Tatum, 2003). Tatum suggests that the ways to help White people develop a positive racial identity is to give them the tools—and the option—to become and identify as antiracist Whites.

Understanding that we have a racial identity—and that it's possible to have a positive one—is the most critical step in building antiracist, whole classrooms. Such an understanding is not simply another tool—it is the toolbox. The larger, stronger, and more robust my racial identity, the more tools I will be able to carry around with me. If I do not have a strong and positive racial identity, I will not be able to hold any of the other tools that I acquire. Having a positive racial identity—for White people—does not mean feeling good about being White. It means having an understanding of what it means to be White in a society that historically, contemporarily, and systemically favored Whiteness above other races. It means acknowledging one's racial privilege and the history of racial oppression in the United States, while recognizing and confronting the racism that continues today. And—here's where the positive part comes in—it means accepting one's Whiteness as part of who one is and being wholly oneself while refusing to perpetuate the oppressive parts of Whiteness. Feeling badly for being White does not satisfy this tenet, but neither does ignoring or denying racial inequality and racial privilege. Having a positive White racial identity requires the ability to see how one can be simultaneously part of the problem and part of the solution. This tenet will be explored in greater detail in Chapter 2.

Guiding Principle 3: A Multicultural Curriculum Is Not Sufficient for Building an Antiracist Classroom

Because curriculum is so tangible compared to more elusive aspects of classroom life, such as relationships or communication styles, teachers often address curriculum as the first step to creating an antiracist classroom. Although a multicultural curriculum is a critical component of an antiracist classroom, it addresses only one of myriad factors that contribute to classroom life. As teachers develop in their racial identities, they will be better equipped to see the many ways that race affects their classrooms beyond the curriculum, and to begin to make changes in those fields as well. We will explore this concept further in Chapter 3.

Guiding Principle 4: Racial Competence Can Be Learned

I once thought that racial competence was something that people were born with—that people of color had it, and White people didn't. Certainly White people like me, who grew up in the suburbs and never talked about race, did not have racial competence, did not "get it." In my family we didn't discuss race, and we didn't know many people of color, so I grew up thinking I was not supposed to talk about race. When I tried to engage in race conversations, I would leave feeling embarrassed, thinking I had all the wrong answers. Although it's true that there were a lot of things I didn't understand or simply got wrong, it was more often true that what I said was a useful or benign contribution to the conversation. So why did it feel so bad when I talked about race out loud?

I define racial competence as having the skills and confidence to engage in healthy and reciprocal cross-racial relationships; to recognize and honor difference without judgment; to notice and analyze racial dynamics as they occur; to confront racism at the individual, group, and systems level; to cultivate support mechanisms for continuing to be involved in antiracist practice even when it is discouraging or conflictual; to speak one's mind and be open to feedback on one's ideas; to ask for feedback about one's ideas and work; and to raise race questions about oneself and one's practice. Racial competence correlates highly with the characteristics of a positive racial identity status (see Chapter 3). In my observations and facilitation of race conversations over the past many years, I have started to call the gap between the average racial competence levels of people of color and the average racial competence of White people "the arithmetic/calculus divide." It often seems that people of color, many of whom have spent most days of their lives thinking about race or talking openly about race, have a calculus level understanding of how racism works. They can see it at the individual, group, and systems levels and recognize it by its many different forms and names. Just as in calculus, many people of color could picture the three-dimensional graph of racism just by seeing the equation. Many White people, on the other hand, seem to have an arithmetic level understanding of racism. We know some vocabulary words and some basic functions, but we still can only operate in one dimension. If an equation demands subtraction or multiplication, our knowledge of the rules no longer applies, and we get it wrong. We don't believe in the third dimension of racism, and when asked to envision it, we throw the whole concept out the window in frustration. Robin DiAngelo (2012) calls this "White racial illiteracy." No wonder we have such a disconnect when White people at the arithmetic level and people of color at the calculus level try to talk about race together. We would never put arithmetic students in a class with calculus-level scholars. One group has extensive knowledge that they take for granted as they work through equations, while the other is still daunted and confused by basic concepts.

Contrary to what I once believed, I have found that racial competence can be learned. If this wasn't true, I would still be afraid to talk about race, to say the words "White" or "Black" or "Asian" or "Latino" out loud; I would still hesitate to ask questions and reveal my ignorance. Just as with calculus, there are skills and concepts that comprise racial competence, and it's possible to learn them. And the truth is, people of color are not born with racial competence, either; many people of color do not feel comfortable talking about race. And, though unbeknownst to me for much of my life, there are many White people who do. But even the people of color who really seem to have that calculus-level understanding of racism had to learn what they know through practice and, often, many difficult conversations.

It is my hope that individuals of all races will read and discuss this book together with the awareness that they begin with vastly different skills, levels of experience, and background knowledge related to race. Beyond that, they will bring other diverse identities, including class background, gender identity, sexuality, religion, ability, ethnicity, language background, and immigration status—all of which will influence how they experience race. The situations explored here might seem familiar to some readers, whereas others will be hearing them for the first time. We cannot all have the same level of competence in this conversation, and we will always be working and living with people who know more than we do in some areas and less in others. But if we take the approach that the skills required for this conversation can be learned, we can all begin from a place of inquiry and support one another through the process.

That racial competence can be learned is a revolutionary concept put forward by Howard Stevenson (2014) that can be characterized as a "growth mindset" approach (Dweck, 2007). Psychologist Carol Dweck developed the term "growth mindset" to describe people who believe that growth in ability, intelligence, and even relationship skills is possible. She contrasts this to a "fixed mindset," in which a person believes that attributes such as intelligence and ability are fixed and cannot be developed. She has demonstrated through controlled studies that when people believe that they are intelligent and that intelligence is fixed they are afraid to work hard or to ask questions for fear that a failure might reveal that their "intelligence" is actually a sham. They would rather play it safe and avoid risk in order to continue to uphold the image of themselves as intelligent. People with a growth mindset, who believe that intelligence is malleable and can be developed, do not feel the need to prove or protect their intelligence. This, ironically, gives them the space and freedom to develop their intelligence. It is in the best interest of schools to cultivate a growth mindset among students and teachers, to support everyone in a learning community, to see the ways they grow and stretch their abilities by working hard and taking risks, rather than resting on the underdeveloped laurels of innate talent. Stevenson (2014) similarly challenges us to see that racial competence must be learned and that everyone who has it has earned it the hard way. If we maintain a fixed mindset about race, then my childhood notion that people are either born with racial competence or are not holds true. In such a scenario, people spend a lot of energy trying to prove they are not racist but have few opportunities to actually practice or develop their competence. In such circumstances, people don't take risks or ask questions for fear their incompetence might be discovered—and if incompetence is fixed there would be no way to redeem themselves after a fall. But if in schools we can adopt a growth mindset in regard to race, we can create a culture in which we are all learners. I wrote this book to support teachers and faculties to have more successful conversations about race so that people like me, who were raised to be colormute[2] (Pollock, 2004), can gain the tools and skills they need to continue learning, while those with advanced skills can choose how and when to engage.[3] I believe it should be possible for all members of a school community to become more racially competent with every passing year.

IN THE FIELD

The focal teachers featured in this book all identified as White and middle class. Aside from these social identity categories, they were a diverse group. They were in their 20s, 30s, 40s, and 50s. They taught in private schools, public urban schools, and public suburban schools. They were Republican and Democrat, men and women, gay and straight, Christian and Jewish, secular and religious. They taught kindergarten, 2nd grade, middle school science, high school English, and high school special education. Some had classrooms that were 100% Black, and some that were 100% White. Most had classes that were predominantly White, with a few children of color. The teachers themselves, though, had one important thing in common: They all wanted to improve their teaching practice by learning more about race. They had questions about racial dynamics in the classroom, communication, relationships with parents of color, expectations, curriculum, and more that they had never raised, for fear of looking racist or for a lack of time and space to do so. They knew that they could serve their students and their school communities better if they took the time to raise these questions.

The teachers in this book were from three professional development groups focusing on race. Although this book focuses on the experiences of White teachers in those groups, all of the groups were multiracial in composition. One group was from a small independent school in the suburbs of Philadelphia. One group was for teachers who taught in public and charter schools in the Philadelphia School District. The third group was from a large suburban public school district with an upper-middle-class population.

The teachers joined their respective inquiry groups for different reasons. Most of them wanted more community to support them in thinking about racial questions. They had spent time in college or at previous teaching jobs learning about race and wanted colleagues with whom to think and talk about it. One teacher, Sam, wanted to be a part of the group because he thought the inquiry group project was going to lead to the dismantling of Honors English and wanted to stop that from the inside. They all agreed to participate in this book project with me because they appreciated the opportunity to have someone to talk with about race. They also appreciated the chance to be observed and get feedback on their teaching.

Research *with* Teachers, Not *on* Teachers

From the beginning of this project I wanted to do research *with* teachers, not *on* teachers (Reason & Bradbury, 2006). I chose to work with teachers in inquiry groups because inquiry has successfully been used to support teachers in shifting their practice using theory and reflection. The concept is premised on the idea that teachers are experts in their own classrooms, and that by following areas of interest in their own practice, they are more likely to develop their practice in positive ways. This process of change is wholly different from responding to negative criticism or district requirements. Marilyn Cochran-Smith (2004) calls it a "generative way" (p. 46) for teachers to recognize and reconsider their own biases in ways that lead to the creation of pedagogy that is more relevant to all students. Because teaching requires teachers to be able to make hundreds of decisions on any given day, developing an antiracist practice involves considering race with each new decision. The work requires challenging oneself, one's environment, and sometimes, one's superiors. It requires each individual teacher to be critically engaged in thinking about her or his own classroom as well as the larger context of school and society:

> If we are going to prepare teachers to work intelligently and responsibly in a society that is increasingly diverse in race, language and culture, then we need more teachers who are actively willing to challenge the taken for granted texts, practices and arrangements of schooling through participation in systematic and critical inquiry. (Cochran-Smith, 2004, p. 63)

Mandating personal change and thoughtfulness is not particularly effective. But supporting teachers as they participate in inquiry that they initiate themselves can be transformative. Because all of the teachers volunteered to be a part of this project so they could engage more deeply in the questions they were already asking about their classrooms, I openly shared the thoughts and suggestions that eventually became a part of this book. Nothing written here will come as a surprise to the teachers whose stories I tell. In fact, the focal teachers read early drafts of this book and responded to it in writing. See Appendix A for their responses.

Why a Book About and for White Teachers?

Conversations about race in schools can be particularly difficult because racial issues are not only systemic and historic but also localized, current, and personal. Teachers are in the unique position of working one-on-one with individual children and their families, while acting as representatives and gatekeepers of the system. White teachers are finding that racial proficiency is required in every classroom, and yet it is rarely taught in teacher education graduate programs (Zeichner, 2009).

This book focuses on White teachers because they comprise a great majority of the K–12 teaching force (National Center for Education Statistics, 2014).

White teachers comprise over 85% of the K–12 teaching force (National Center for Education Statistics, 2014). As of 2011, White students made up only 52% of the public school population, whereas Black students were 16%, Hispanic students 24%, Asian/Pacific Islander students 5%, and American Indian/Alaska Navtive students 1% (National Center for Education Statistics, 2014). In urban centers such as Philadelphia, the percentage of students of color in public schools is as high as 86% (Pennsylvania Department of Education, 2014). Twenty-one percent of the students in public schools speak a language other than English at home (National Center for Education Statistics, 2014). White, English-speaking students make up less and less of the public school population, while populations of students of color are increasing in public school systems in both urban and suburban areas.

As the predominantly White teaching force teaches increasing numbers of students of color each year, racial competence becomes even more essential for the success of our schools. Relationships with teachers and connections with adults in school communities are central to students' feelings of belonging and efficacy in school. If teachers are unable to connect across races because of unexamined biases or simply not feeling as at ease with students or families of color, students will experience a greater sense of marginalization from the community. Compound this with peers who are similarly marginalized or with a curriculum that feels irrelevant, and students of color are at a distinct disadvantage compared to their White peers. Sometimes the most important antiracist act a teacher can take is to connect with students personally, which requires a consciousness of the racial dynamics that may be affecting each student's daily experience. An antiracist practice includes a daily recognition and analysis of racial dynamics and a constant examination of one's own biases and stereotypes.

What White People?

Studying White people is complicated because there are a great many White people who do not identify as White. If you ask them their race, they might tell you "Caucasian," or they might say they don't have a race at all or that they are "just normal" (Sue, 2011). If they do identify racially as White, very few White people acknowledge that being White has any meaning for their lives (Hamm, 2001; Michael & Bartoli, 2014). People do not have to identify as White in order to be identified as such and/or given the privileges of Whiteness—such is the nature of race. Race informs who we think we are on the inside, but it is also used by others to decide who we are from the outside. W.E.B. Du Bois called race a double-edged sword because it both helps us to define ourselves while simultaneously defining us against our will. This struggle to be who we are in the midst of social structures telling us who we can be, where we can sit, or where we can live is the very struggle that our students engage in daily. Psychologist Dr. Howard Stevenson tells a story about one of his students who refused to play basketball because, as a Black male, he didn't want people to think he got into Penn on a basketball scholarship.

Howard responded that people were going to think that anyway, so he might as well do the things he enjoyed despite what people might think. This student was learning to navigate a world that racialized him against his will on a daily basis.

Being racialized against our will is not a reality most White people have to contend with because Whiteness usually does not get mentioned or recognized. Because Whiteness is seen as invisible or the "norm" (Perry, 2002), White people tend to see themselves as individuals first, unaffiliated with a racial group. And yet being White has had tremendous consequences for White people throughout U.S. history. Until 1952, for example, non-White people were not permitted to naturalize as U.S. citizens, and owning land was contingent upon citizenship. While African Americans were granted citizenship following the end of slavery, it was a second-class citizenship devoid of many rights until the Civil Rights Act was passed in 1964 (Haney López, 2006). Some would argue that African Americans have still never been granted the full rights of American citizenship (Alexander, 2012; Delgado & Stefancic, 2012). Many people who were classified as "non-White" fought in court to challenge their racial classification because they needed to be "White" in order to qualify for naturalization. In those same decades, millions of people who were classified as White immigrated to the United States prior to 1952 without ever recognizing that it was their racial classification as "White" that made their entry and naturalization possible. "Whiteness" could not have been more obvious to those individuals classified as "non-White," whereas for many constructed as "White" it was invisible (Haney López, 2006). White people throughout history and still today in the United States often respond to questions about their race by answering that they are just "normal" (Frankenberg, 1993; Perry, 2002; Sue, 2007; Tatum, 2003).

People in the United States generally think that to have a race is to be a person of color. In the 1700s, that included any person who was not Anglo Saxon Protestant. Even phenotypically pale-skinned blond European immigrants such as Norwegians were considered non-Whites. Over time, the category "White" expanded to include Italians, Irish, Scandinavians, Eastern Europeans, Syrians, and Jews[4] (Haney Lopez, 2006). Immigrants did many things in order to become "White": They learned English, converted to Christianity (or secularized), and shed customs and traditions that marked them as "other" in order to assimilate into "American" culture, which was defined in large part by Anglo Saxon Protestant culture. The category of Whiteness today tends to exclude people who seem "other," even if they are phenotypically White, including Muslims who dress in traditional religious clothing or white Latinos who speak Spanish as their first language. Even when an individual is phenotypically White, other types of difference may "race" them in a way that renders them non-White in their racial experiences. In the minds of many White Americans, to be White means to stand outside the category of "raced" peoples. That's why, out of 12 aisles in the grocery store, there is one labeled the "Ethnic Food" aisle, where one can find traditionally Latino, Asian, and sometimes Jewish food. If this is "ethnic" food, what is in the other 11 aisles? Presumably culturally neutral, "normal" foods.

Racialized inequality exists today precisely because the U.S. government historically gave different opportunities to people based on race. And yet we work hard at not seeing and not talking about these differences. As anthropologist Mica Pollock (2004) writes, "In a society that already thinks racially but hates to do so, as we have seen, people often resist mentioning the very racial patterns they seem most trained to reproduce" (p. 171).

Sociologist Amanda Lewis suggests that the reason Whites are often not seen as a racial group is that racial groupings have been conflated with "social problems" (Lewis, 2004). Because mainstream society does not cast Whites as a social problem, they are not seen as a racial group. In turn, White people tend not to recognize that they have a race or identify as members of a group.

Part of the work of diversity education in schools is to help White people to recognize that to be White is to have a race; to be White is to be just as implicated in the broader racial stratification system as one would be if one were raced as Black-, Asian-, Native-, or Latino-American. In this book, I aim to join other Whiteness scholars in problematizing Whiteness in order to show that White people are just as much a part of the racial hierarchy in the United States as any other racial group. This means that Whites are very much a part of any racialized social problem, even though they are often unnamed or unrecognized as a racial group. One advantage of this reframing is that when we recognize our role in racialized social problems, we open up to the possibility of being part of the solutions as well.

Who Has the Right to Write About Race and Raise Race Questions?

One of my readers told me that I needed to credential myself, to demonstrate to readers why I had the right, as a White person, to write a book on race. And furthermore, I needed to establish who has the right to raise race questions. And I know that they are right. How many times have I picked up a book on race and searched for the evidence that this person had ideas worth listening to? With White authors, I scope out their self-awareness, their humility, their critical analysis, their acknowledgment of their own racism. With authors of color, I want to know if they are going to provide a critical analysis that will challenge me. Whenever I pick up a book, I do look for the author's credentials.

I resist credentialing myself, however, because as a reader I am more apt to believe a White person who is humble than one who touts their "credentials" for talking about race. White people who take a learning stance, who resist self-labeling as an "antiracist," who believe that an "antiracist" status must be earned day in and day out based on actions—these are the White people I want to listen to.

When I was in graduate school, I staged a temporary protest of White theorists and pledged only to read what theorists of color wrote about race. This was probably an indication of a particular racial identity status that I was going through (see Chapter 2). But it was also coming from a genuine struggle I had—and continue to have—over how much White people can ever really understand about racism. Racism is an insidious force in our society, one that denigrates the ideas and lives of people of color while promoting and affirming those of Whites. As a White person, it takes a lot of work for me to see racism at work, and I never would have learned to do so without the support of friends and theorists of color. Often, academic work created by White people is based on or repetitive of work by people of color. I wanted to learn about racism from the people who are most affected by it, and I didn't believe that White people had anything they could teach me.

When I say that this protest was emblematic of a developmental status, I don't do so to denigrate those beliefs that I held. But in abandoning the orthodoxy of that position, I have found much work of value from the pens of racially competent White people. I found White theorists who were furthering the field of Whiteness studies and creating space in dialogues on race for thinking about people who look and act like me. Most important, I found that there just might be space enough in the world for my voice to matter, even though I'm White. Although I don't presume that my voice should matter because I'm White, nor do I assume that it won't matter for the same reason. On the contrary, through my work with White teachers I have found there is a valuable role for me to play in communicating antiracist theory and ideas to other Whites. And still I continue to write and teach with the hope and expectation that colleagues of all races will offer feedback and critiques of my ideas and thus contribute to strengthening my work and my practice.

The second question, "Who has the right to raise race questions?" is easier for me to answer. Everybody has the right to raise race questions; some might even say that everybody has the imperative to raise race questions. But not everybody has the skills. One of the White teachers featured in this book asked during her inquiry, "What right do I have to teach the history of the Civil Rights Movement as a White person?" The answer she came to was this: every right. First, she has the right as a teacher of Black students who have the right to know that history. Second, she has the right because the Civil Rights Movement is everyone's history. It is one of the times in U.S. history that truly shows some of the liberatory potential of democracy, and if people of all races begin to claim it and know it as our history, maybe we would start to think of ourselves differently as a country. Feeling that she did not have the right to teach "someone else's history" was holding her back from teaching her students things they had the right to know. Similarly, racial dynamics, questions, and conflicts are mutually constructed and belong to all of us. If White teachers feel they don't have the "right" to raise race questions, they absolve themselves from aspects of group and relational dynamics in which they play a pivotal role. But in order to raise race questions, they need to gain the skills to do so (see Chapter 1) and a positive racial identity to support the inquiry (see Chapter 2).

Whites Doing Whiteness

Most people do not realize how they unwittingly contribute to the maintenance of racial categories through the choices they make on a daily basis. Most White people, for example, tend to believe that their rational choices, such as choosing to live in predominantly White areas or only dating and marrying other people racialized as White, are just "natural" choices (Bonilla-Silva, 2013). However, even though most White people did not ask to be White and may not even identify as White, they are constantly being racialized in their interactions, their own actions, and by larger racial projects (Winant, 2001). Race is something that we do and that is done to us—it is not just the way we are (Fine, 1997; Lewis, 2004). White people fail to see how they make these choices within a system that has artificially limited the range of their racial reality. And they make these choices to the exclusion of other possible choices, which might interrupt and change the meaning of their Whiteness. "All these 'choices' are the 'natural' consequences of a White socialization process" (p. 276), according to sociologist Eduardo Bonilla-Silva (2013). Most White people assume that the all-White groups in which they are members are completely coincidental. Lewis (2004) argues the contrary: "Their racial composition is not an accident but a result of Whites' status as members of a passive social collectivity whose lives are at least in part shaped by the racialized social system in which they live and operate" (p. 163). Thus many White people understand their lives as unracialized and "natural," when in fact their lifestyles and choices have all been deeply influenced by the fact that they are White.

I know this trend exists because it is a part of my personal experience. Even though I like to think I have a nuanced consciousness of how being White has shaped my life, it continues to do so in ways that surprise me. Although I live in a racially diverse neighborhood, I still primarily socialize with my White neighbors. I have learned that I must go out of my way to counter the forces that would have me be friends with, be neighbors with, send my children to school with, and work primarily with White people. And yet, in spite of my best efforts, those forces still seem to win. It is the overwhelming momentum of these forces of racialization—and our complicity with them—that makes racial consciousness and inquiry so critical in teaching. When we are not conscious about racial dynamics (and often even when we are), they fracture our classrooms and our relationships in ways that are detrimental to all of our students (more on creating an antiracist classroom in Chapter 3).

"You Either Get It or You Don't": Breaking Down the Binary and Respecting the Commitments of the Teachers in This Book

When I finished the first draft of this book and sent it to one of the teachers to read, we agreed to meet at a coffee shop to discuss her reactions. At one point she described one of the other teachers as "The one who didn't get it." This description took me aback because I felt so strongly that each of the teachers in this book "got it" on a profound level. My measure of how much they "got it" was their willingness to look closely at their practice, and to allow me to do the same. They "got it" enough to believe it was important, to raise questions that made them vulnerable, and to allow me to document their process so others could learn from it. Yes, they had all become involved in this work because they knew that on some level they didn't "get it," and they wanted to learn more, but that was how *they* would have described the situation, not me.

In my work with White people, I am aware of how the process of learning about race can often be derailed by fears of being racist or of being one of "those people" who just don't get it. These fears prevent White teachers from deeply reflecting on the messages they have received about race during their lives, and the ways that those messages affect their teaching. My commitment to teachers as learners makes me want to step away from an analysis that perpetuates the binary that some people "get it," and others don't. According to the tenets of Critical Race Theory,[5] and my own personal experiences as a White teacher, I could foresee that White teachers teaching in mainstream schools would not accidentally happen upon antiracist practices. I knew from the outset that they could not completely escape their position as White and privileged, and thus were going to do racist things. I would need to work hard to reassure them that I was not trying to "catch" them in the act of being racist. In order to build the trust required for this process, teachers had to believe that I would not cast in stone the things they said and did. I ask that my readers do the same. As you read this book, take the opportunity to adopt a growth mindset (Dweck, 2007) toward racial competence and leave behind the "get it" versus "don't get it" binary. One skill of racial competence is being able to honor the vulnerability of teachers like those in this book who are imperfect and who share their stories anyway, rather than distancing oneself from them with judgment and fear. It is a practice that one can rehearse while reading alone and that will contribute to building a stronger antiracist community in practice with colleagues.

ROAD MAP FOR THE BOOK

Each chapter in this book is structured around the lessons that I learned in collaboration with teachers, using stories and examples from the classrooms of six White focal teachers to illustrate my points.

Chapter 1 describes the types of questions that the White teachers in this book asked as they engaged in a year-long inquiry on race in their classrooms. As the year progressed, teachers asked increasingly more self-reflective questions, moving from inquiry related to curriculum and teaching to questions about students and then to questions about themselves. The end of the chapter focuses on the inquiry impasse, which is what happened when the questions they were asking or the answers they found prematurely aborted their inquiry process.

Chapter 2 addresses the third foundational premise of the book, which is that building whole classrooms requires supporting every student to have a positive racial identity. As stated earlier, this is work that teachers cannot do unless we already have a positive racial identity ourselves. After describing the process of racial identity development, I demonstrate different statuses of racial identity development with stories from my life and from teachers in the book. Most of the teachers in this book had a similar status of racial identity development, which might also be true for many of the White teachers reading this book. This was true because choosing to be deeply engaged in an antiracist practice comes about during a particular racial identity status. In this chapter I tell stories about the different ways that being in the immersion status of racial identity development affects the inquiry process of the featured White teachers. I close the chapter with a discussion of how White teachers can support their students and themselves to develop positive racial identities.

Chapter 3 explores the premise that a multicultural curriculum is not sufficient for building an antiracist classroom. When teachers start focusing on race in their classrooms they often begin by adding more pictures or stories of people of color to their curriculum. Although this contributes to making schools more inclusive and relatable, it is not a primary or sufficient condition for creating antiracist classrooms or schools. The list of ways race matters explored here is not exhaustive but is rather just a beginning—and an invitation to begin looking at classrooms more expansively. The chapter ends with a description of what an antiracist classroom might look like.

Chapter 4 introduces readers to three primary tenets of race talk: (1) Simply talking about race is not racist. (2) Talking about race is challenging because it breaks the "racial contract" that exists in most White communities. (3) Talking about race with students is not the primary reason to do this work or read this book; similar to a multicultural curriculum, talking about race is not sufficient for creating an antiracist classroom. I developed these three tenets of race talk because of the ways that "talking about race with students" dominates the concerns of the teachers I work with in schools across the country. Although I'm sympathetic to their concerns about how to respond when race comes up in the classroom, there are simply no easy answers. A teacher with a negative or weak racial identity will not be able to sustain conversations about race regardless of how well the instruction manual is written. If a teacher has policies or practices that otherwise alienate or marginalize students of color, the students will not trust that person to lead conversations about race.

In spite of these caveats, I chose to include a chapter on race talk because the teachers in this book were beginning to have these conversations in their classrooms and wanted and needed support in doing so. Choosing to break the racial contract means that we open up conversations in our classrooms that we are often not prepared for. This chapter identifies the ways race might come up in classrooms and how teachers can support or lead the conversations.

Chapter 5 is an inquiry into my own role as a facilitator of race inquiry groups, and a guide to facilitating such groups. I describe my own facilitation strategies that might be valuable to inquiry groups on race. Because most White teachers do not even recognize that they have a race, much less that there is unaddressed racism in their classrooms and schools, it can be very difficult to ask substantive questions about race in the context of inquiry group work without substantial support. For that reason, I include specific strategies for facilitating challenging and supportive inquiry groups focused on race.

I include Appendix B for teacher inquiry groups on race, detailing the different resources used in the teacher inquiry groups described in this book. I also provide a more in-depth description of my methods for data collection in Appendix C. Finally, each of the teachers in this book wrote a response to the book, including where they are now and how being a part of this book has affected their teaching and learning. Through their responses, the teachers have the final word on their own stories. These powerful pieces can be found in Appendix A.

The Endgame

This book is about White teachers learning the salience of race in every aspect of their classrooms: relationships with students and parents, curriculum, discipline policies, classroom culture and procedures, styles of speaking, styles of listening, classroom community, student friendships, seating arrangements, recess habits, expectations, communication, decorations, and food. Race is not simply a benign demographic fact that describes our students; it is a social force that influences everything that happens in school, and that most educators do not know how to discuss (Pollock, 2004).

It is my hope that after reading this book, teachers will feel more equipped to take risks to talk about race and to think in racial terms. I hope that many of the common barriers to race conversations, such as either/or mindsets, the invisibility of White experiences, and the common misperception that talking about race is racist, will be removed by the stories in this book. I hope that both White teachers and teachers of color will come to see themselves as allies to one another in creating an antiracist school environment. I hope that readers who are not part of inquiry groups will recognize the importance of raising race questions that lead to an engaged process of inquiry over time, rather than seeking simple answers. I hope that readers who are not teachers will learn strategies that are applicable across professions and experiences.

For the most part, the teachers featured in this book were not beginners at thinking about race. They had taken courses on race or read books about race or heard talks on race. They already had ideas and questions that prompted them to get involved with their respective inquiry groups. So although this book could absolutely be used as a resource for beginners, my experience with the teachers featured here tells me that many teachers who are experienced in thinking about race still struggle with it and seek ways to sustain growth and engagement. I hope this book will be useful for motivating and sustaining people who already think a lot about race, but don't know what their next steps should be. The book illuminates and connects lessons learned from multiple real classrooms that, when taken as a whole, begin to bring possible pathways into relief.

"Mom, I Can't Believe You Said That!"

Language matters. The choices we make about what to call things, how we name ourselves, and how we presume to name others all influence the way we see and understand the world. I made intentional choices about the words I used in this book, and yet I know that there will come a day when my children read this book and say, "Mom, that's not the right word for _____!" Language is constantly changing as it gets picked up and used for different racial projects. I tend to use the words "Black" and "White" as racial categories. I use "White" because it describes a political category that has been named and privileged in U.S. law. "Caucasian" and "European American" suggest a geographical origin that is not relevant to most White people in the United States today. "Black" is a term that encompasses most people whose ancestors emigrated from Africa or the Caribbean, who emigrated themselves from Africa or the Caribbean, or who are descendants of Africans who were enslaved and brought to the Americas by White people. When people self-identify as "African American" or "Caribbean American," I use those terms, but otherwise I use "Black" because it is more expansive. (I use the term "Latino American" to describe people who can trace their family lines to Central and South America. I use the term "Asian American" to describe people whose families once lived in any part of Asia, while acknowledging that many people from both groups have been in the United States for multiple generations.) I use the term "multiracial" to describe people who do not identify with just one racial group. I capitalize most racial categories to acknowledge them as political categories rather than mere descriptors (i.e., "White" people are not literally the color white; "White" is a political category). I do not capitalize the term "people of color" because it is a broad category encompassing many groups. I have seen the term "people of color" used to refer specifically to Black people. When I use the term "people of color," I am referring to any people who do not identify as White in the United States. I use all these terms imperfectly, knowing that racial categories are not discrete and that most people are multiracial even if they do not identify that way. For all these reasons—and many more—my children's generation will question what's written here. And yet I move forward knowing that if I waited until the verbiage was perfect, these ideas would never see the light of day.

There are a few places in the book when, according to the rules of grammar I was taught, I should use "he or she" (or "she or he") to refer to an anonymous third party. I have resisted that convention and used "they" instead. I do this to protest the gender binary that insists all people must fit into either a male or female identity. Gender is fluid and socially constructed (Butler, 1993), and a great many people do not identify as "he" or "she."

Finally, I use the terms "colorblind" and "colormute" throughout the book. I struggle with this decision because from a critical disability perspective, these terms are ableist as they conflate an unwillingness to see or talk about race with disability, rather than political orientation, ignorance, and lack of skills or experience. Although I do not want to perpetuate this ableism, I use this language here because the terms are so prevalent in the literature on race that I think the use of alternative terms would be confusing. It is my hope that through the extensive exploration of these terms in the context of race by prominent theorists such as Eduardo Bonilla-Silva (*Colorblind Racism*) and Mica Pollock (*Colormute*) that the words today have a unique meaning, wholly different from the words "blind" and "mute" on which they are built.

TEACHERS

The following is a brief description of the six teachers whose experiences comprise the bulk of the material for this book.

Ann

Ann taught high school special education at a predominantly White suburban public high school in a community in which there was a small and vocal Black community that had lived in the area for many generations. She was married to a White man and had two school-aged children. Ann grew up in a rural area of Pennsylvania that she described as "a place where there wasn't anybody who wasn't White, Protestant, Catholic." A sociology major in college, Ann's first job involved working with incarcerated youth. From there, she worked briefly at a prison, and then at the parole board, where her job was to help people find jobs. A lot of people she worked with had been in special education, so she started taking classes in teaching special education, which is how she ultimately ended up teaching special education in this predominantly White, predominantly upper-middle-class suburban school district. She had been teaching there for 7 years (out of 11 total years of teaching) at the time of our work together.

Cara

Cara taught 5th grade at a predominantly Black charter school in Philadelphia, which drew students from working- and middle-class families from all over the city. She grew up in a predominantly White, rural community in upstate New York, but she had more experiences with people of other races than the average

White person in her town. She attended the nursery school at her local JCC (Jewish community center), where she had classmates who were Black and Jewish. She identified her religion as "vaguely Presbyterian." At the time of my research, Cara had been teaching for 4 years. She was in her late 20s and was dating the man who is now her husband, Chris, who was her teaching assistant at the time. Chris was Black and had two daughters who became Cara's stepdaughters when they married. They later had a son together. For all of these personal reasons, Cara's concerns about racial socialization extended well beyond the classroom.

Helene

Helene taught 2nd grade at an independent Quaker elementary school. She was newly married to a White Jewish man and in her late 20s at the time of the inquiry group. Helene grew up in a Jewish family in "a working-class town next to [an upper-middle-class town with a liberal arts college]." The year that Helene and I worked together, she was in her third year at Friends Independent School. She immediately welcomed me as a researcher into her classroom.

Sam

Sam Brodsky was an English and history teacher at a historically and predominantly White Quaker independent school with a predominantly middle- and upper-middle-class student body. Inexplicably, Sam Brodsky was called by both his first and last name by most of his students and colleagues. As the child of Jewish Russian immigrants in the Jim Crow South, Sam felt that he was considered neither Black nor White—he was a Jew. And yet, as he grew older and moved to the north, he noticed that his Jewishness began to be subsumed into Whiteness. He was married to a White Jewish woman, was in his late 40s, and had two children, one of whom attended the school where he had taught for 11 years. Sam had two graduate degrees, one in American literature and one in information sciences.

Todd

Todd taught 7th-grade science at a K–8 public school in Philadelphia where almost 100% of the student body was Black. Most of his students came from poor and working class families and lived in the neighborhood around the school. At the time of my research Todd was not in a relationship. He was open about being gay to his colleagues but conflicted about whether he should be out to his students; the year of our research he was not out to his students. Todd grew up going to a racially diverse Catholic school in a postindustrial working-class neighborhood on the South Side of Chicago. When White flight changed the racial composition of his neighborhood, his middle-class White parents decided to stay. Todd entered teaching through Teach For America (TFA) in Philadelphia right after graduating from college. He had been looking for service-oriented work and wanted to stay in the United States. He was an African American history/Africana protest studies major in college and, when he applied to teach through TFA, he was assigned by the school district to teach 7th-grade science. Todd had chosen to buy a house a few blocks away from his school. At the time of the project, Todd had been teaching at his school for 4 years.

Laurie

Laurie Mendoza taught kindergarten at a racially diverse, historically White Quaker independent school in which most of the families were upper middle class. Though the school was historically White, recent efforts at diversifying had led to the lower school being more racially diverse than the rest of the school. Laurie's classroom had a majority of children of color. Laurie Mendoza was a White woman who took her husband's El Salvadoran surname (he was Latino American). She had two children, both of whom were enrolled in the school where she taught. From the first day I met her, she talked about her multiracial children and her concerns about racism. She grew up in a working-class White family in a rural area nearby and attended a local college. She said that she never thought much about race until she got to college. In one of her small-group meetings, during a discussion of names, Laurie said her name used to be Lauren Marie Smith and imitated her kids' response to her name, "Like c'mon, Mom, could you get any more plain?" Another group member, an Asian American man, said, "Wow, I think I would look at you differently if I knew you were Lauren Marie Smith." Laurie said, "In fact I was really different back then." At the time of my research in her classroom, Laurie had been teaching for about 20 years, 10 of which had been at Friends Independent.

CHAPTER 1

Raising Race Questions and Managing the Inquiry Impasse

"How do we help a negro mother of low socio-economic status to become less punitive toward her children and use less 'whupping'?" (Landes, 1965, p. 27)

This question, like the hundreds of others collected from White teachers by anthropologist of education Ruth Landes, is remarkably similar to questions I heard from White teachers today. In my research, as in Landes's, White middle-class teachers asked about Black hair, motivation, the implications of free and reduced lunch, the social isolation of children of color in predominantly White classrooms, the conflict between neighborhood cultures and school cultures, families who feel marginalized by the all-White PTA, low self-esteem among children of color, physical punishment by families, adolescent sass, and countless other topics. In 1965, as in 2014, they asked systemic questions, such as "Why are there so many dropouts?" and personal questions, such as "As a White male, am I an adequate role model for my Black male students?"

I started collecting race questions with two major misconceptions: first, that all race questions are equal; second, that if I looked hard enough and asked enough people, I could find answers to them. As I observed and interviewed White teachers engaged in race inquiry, it quickly became clear that neither of my beliefs was true. Raising race questions is not just about asking questions; it's about recognizing what one doesn't know, cultivating self-reflectiveness about one's own race, learning about racial subcultures, and beginning to see and name racial dynamics. Raising race questions is a skill to be developed. Some questions build a process of inquiry that is self-reflective, generative, and continuous. Other questions are too imminently answerable to yield growth or change for the teacher or the classroom. This gets to my second misconception: Although some race questions have answers, the ones that are most worth pursuing lead to a process rather than an answer. Because questions are specific to the individuals involved and the localized school subculture with all of its peculiar norms and customs, it would be impossible to answer them without minimizing the complexities of all social interactions, of which race is always only a part.

In this chapter I explore lessons about racial inquiry that emerged from the inquiry process of six White teachers. I have divided the inquiry questions they raised into three types of questions: (1) questions about teaching, pedagogy, and logistics; (2) questions about students as racial beings; and (3) questions about oneself as a teacher. After exploring each of these categories of questions, I explain the "inquiry impasse," which describes the many different dead-ends where race inquiry can wind up. These include the questions that don't get asked because we don't know what we don't know; the perfectly logical explanations and myths we use to explain things we don't understand; and the "untouchable" questions that often don't get asked because teachers don't feel strong enough in their racial identities to ask questions that might seem racist. I end the chapter with strategies for raising race questions.

QUESTIONS ABOUT TEACHING, PEDAGOGY, AND LOGISTICS

Throughout our year together, the questions teachers asked changed as the teachers grew more comfortable with one another, with the inquiry process, and with me. At the start of the year, the questions focused almost exclusively on the logistics of teaching. These included questions about pedagogy (how to teach about race), resources (what materials, curriculum, books to use), instructional questions and knowledge questions (questions that came from a teacher's realization that they had significant holes in their knowledge, for example, often with regard to teaching Black history). When teachers brought up questions in their inquiry groups, they were usually questions that fit into this larger category of questions about the logistics of teaching and of curriculum. These types of questions were also questions about how to teach issues of race in the classroom (or "racialized" topics) and how to talk about race with students. Some examples of questions about teaching include the following:

1. How do I emphasize to my students that there is great diversity within any given population? How do I help them understand that not all Africans are poor? (Helene)
2. How can I create a curriculum to support a healthy development of self and diffuse the impact of bias and stereotypes? (Laurie)
3. Where can I find short essays on race to accompany our discussions of the novels? (Sam)
4. How do I find good resources that are inclusive of many racial backgrounds? (Helene)
5. Where do non-Black people of color fit into the Civil Rights Movement? (Cara)

Each of these questions helped the teachers who asked them build a more antiracist classroom. Finding answers to these questions helped teachers maintain an ongoing process of inquiry and engagement. But at the beginning of the year, just as they were beginning their own inquiry work, focal teachers' questions were almost singularly questions about teaching. As a researcher and facilitator, I loved these questions because I could answer them. I could point teachers toward resources or look up their questions online. But inquiry shouldn't stop with logistical and pedagogical questions like these. It wasn't until I started observing teachers in their classrooms that I began to realize that there were questions that needed to be asked that had not yet been raised.

QUESTIONS ABOUT STUDENTS AS RACIAL BEINGS

As the year progressed, teachers' questions seemed to focus less on instruction and more on their students as racial beings. Teachers' increased willingness and capacity to name race and notice racial trends made it possible to ask race questions that they could not conceptualize at the beginning of their process. These questions were harder, in part because they required the willingness to think about students in racial terms and to ask questions that seemed politically incorrect, if not racist. Here are a few of the questions they asked:

1. How do discussions of slavery affect my students, especially my Black students? How do I explain different types of slavery? (Helene)
2. How do I help 2nd-grade students talk about race honestly and critically? (Helene)
3. Why don't my Black male students want to participate? (Cara)
4. Why are Black males overrepresented in special education? What's wrong with the system? (Ann)
5. When is it appropriate to begin teaching students about injustice? (Helene and Laurie)

Noticing and Naming Racial Trends

The questions about students take the level of inquiry one step deeper than the instructional questions. This type of question tends to acknowledge different racial populations within the classroom. Teachers who have not learned how to break the norm of colormuteness (Pollock, 2004) will usually refuse to acknowledge the different races they have in their classrooms and will not notice (or say they don't notice) racialized trends such as a tendency for White girls to speak up when they are confused about the directions while Black boys do not. In any given classroom such a phenomenon might not necessarily be a notable distinction, but it might be. If we are unwilling to notice racialized trends, we cannot observe further. The following is an example of a teacher being willing to notice racialized trends:

> I want to be more mindful of what being Black in the classroom means. And there's this one White kid who constantly interrupts (a Black girl) all the time and then I'm thinking well maybe all the White kids are . . . (Sam)

Sam's question required noticing a behavioral trend and being willing to superimpose a racial lens to see that it was not just the constant interruption by one student of another, but it was a Black girl being interrupted by a White boy. Again, this phenomenon might not be notable, but it is not unreasonable to suspect (as Sam does) that in fact it is quite common and that it has a significant effect on the experience of both students. What might the school day be like for a Black girl who gets constantly interrupted by her White male peers? And what are the messages received by a White boy, who feels entitled to interrupt and ignore his female and Black peers? How might he respond if he was prevented from doing so? Sam would not be able raise this question—to confirm whether this was a destructive pattern—if he had not been willing to notice and name race.

In schools where a culture of colormuteness dominates, even this one simple question would take a lot of nerve and practice to vocalize. Many teachers at Sam's school were just beginning to be able to talk like this out loud in the inquiry groups. And even though I imagine Sam would have been able to speak in racial terms such as this even before he began the inquiry group, it was new for him to notice trends such as this one in which Black students were constantly interrupted by White ones—and to do so in front of colleagues. It was also a new stance for him to then ask what being Black means in his classroom.

Similarly, Ann's awareness of disproportionality in the special education program required her willingness to see and name race:

> Yeah, I would say, the majority of students that I have for reading are African American and I don't know why that is. I mean I know all the theoretical factors. When I talk with them and I say to them, "What was reading like for you in 1st grade, 2nd grade, 3rd grade?" I want to get a feel for why do they hate reading. Why do they like reading?

In observing a racial trend, Ann was not suggesting that all African American students hate reading. But she was noticing a trend that might be related to the ways that African American students had been treated in her school district. Ann wanted to know who their previous teachers were, what assumptions had been made about them, and why they had not been given extra support sooner. She also noticed a trend of White teachers not recommending Black students for extra help because of a fear of being called racist. In turn, Black students came to Ann in high school with a dislike of reading that had been reinforced over many years of failure. Ann wanted to understand this and couldn't question it without be willing to name it.

Questions That Focus on Inequity

Sam changed his honors and AP level English curricula to make the work much more accessible and engaging to students of color, which he hoped would lead to minimizing the disproportionately low rates of Black students in those classes.

The question he asked was directly related to the curriculum: "How can I change the curriculum to provide more windows and mirrors for students of color?" I wondered how his inquiry process might have been different if his inquiry question had focused directly on the inequity, such as this: "What must I do to achieve a proportionate representation of and success for students of color in honors and AP English?" or "How can we provide a challenging, high-level English curriculum to all students without tracking by perceived skill level?"

All three questions are important, and all three are generative questions for an individual teacher to ask. But if an important goal is the proportionate representation of students of color in advanced classes, that needs to be the explicit question asked. Moreover, if the ultimate goal is how to achieve parity of achievement among students of different races, then that needs to be the question asked. And though changing curriculum is certainly one answer, other possible answers include raising expectations, ensuring that a student of color is not isolated as the only student of color in the honors track, providing honors level curriculum and instruction to all students in untracked classes, encouraging students of color to take difficult but optional courses, educating parents of color that a B in an AP course might be more highly valued by colleges than an A in a regular course, ensuring that all students have access to the resources they need to complete projects, supporting all students (especially White students) to have honest and open conversations about race when relevant to the class discussions, and—in the absence of detracking—ensuring that there is permeability and transference between the honors and regular classes so that placement in one track does not become an unalterable academic destiny.

QUESTIONS ABOUT ONESELF AS A TEACHER

The third level of questions that teachers asked were questions about themselves as White teachers:

1. Am I a racist? How do I come across? How do my students perceive me? (Ann, Cara, and Todd)
2. How do I reach out to Black families? How do I get them to trust me? (Cara)
3. Am I, as a White person, sufficient as a teacher for my students of color?
   a. Can I be a mentor to my students as a White male? (Todd)
   b. As a White woman, how can I connect with the parents of my students in a more authentic way? (Cara)
   c. Can a White teacher be an effective teacher of the Civil Rights Movement? (Laurie and Cara)
   d. I know that racial socialization is good for my Black students. Is that something I can do for them as a White teacher? If so, how? (Todd, Laurie, Helene, Cara, and Ann)

Teachers' questions about themselves began to take into account their own Whiteness and their nontraditional willingness to acknowledge the way that the racial context in which they taught shaped all of their relationships. They acknowledged that, as White people, they had work to do in building relationships with students of color and their parents. They knew that if they left all of the work of crossing this racial barrier up to the students and families, they would not be doing their jobs. They also knew that the White teachers with whom their students had interacted previously might not have had any awareness about race, which meant that they might have negative impressions to undo in order to gain the trust of the students and their families. Finally, they knew that they were stepping outside the boundaries of what was socially acceptable for White people, and they wanted to do so in a way that would be understood as antiracist rather than racist. They feared that talking openly about race or demonstrating any racial consciousness as a White person could be misperceived as racist.

Cultural Mistrust

Some people might read the preceding paragraph and wonder if Black parents' mistrust of White educators is a form of reverse racism. If White teachers are not supposed to make broad generalizations about their students of color, why is it okay for students and parents of color to assume that they should fear White teachers until proven otherwise? What's the difference?

Psychologists have developed a name for a similar phenomenon in therapy called *cultural mistrust* (Thompson, Neville, Weathers, Postin, & Atkinson, 1990; Whaley, 2001). Noting that rates of misdiagnoses of paranoid schizophrenia are high among African Americans, researchers set out to understand why. What they found was that paranoia was manifesting in patients' behaviors in which paranoia was not their presenting problem because it was triggered by the interaction with the White clinician; Black clients had a mistrust of White clinicians that they did not exhibit with Black clinicians. The explanations for why African Americans would demonstrate cultural mistrust vary—these include a rational response to historical and current oppression in the United States, a response to the hypervisibility of Black people in our society, or a self-protective response to widespread mainstream doubts in one's abilities and/or beliefs that Black people are less capable. All of the explanations describe circumstantial behavior that evolved for some members of a group because of a common position in an oppressive society. It is a racial dynamic that White clinical psychologists must understand in order to avoid making erroneous diagnoses that, ironically, breed even more cultural mistrust because Black clients feel further misunderstood. For teachers and schools, understanding cultural mistrust is part of understanding how to teach the whole student and serve the whole family. Cultural mistrust is not a form of reverse racism; it is a phenomenon that arises from real or vicarious experiences in a society that has historically disadvantaged Black people. Cultural mistrust can show up in education in the way that Black children are so commonly recommended for special education testing or disciplinary procedures. As a result, many Black parents have come to automatically question such recommendations. Sometimes Black parents have had such negative personal experiences with White teachers in their own lives that they do not automatically trust the White teachers of their children. Racism is defined as prejudice plus power (Katz, 1978), and teachers have incredible power over the future of the children in their care. Parents recognize this and might be wary of any prejudice that could affect how a teacher wields that power over their child.

How Do Stereotypes Inform Interpretations?

During one of our inquiry groups, I pointed out to Cara that the way she talked about her girls and boys seemed to fit stereotypes of Black men and women.

> *Ali:* I don't know if this is useful, but I want to just notice that in what you're saying there are stereotypes about lazy Black men, and tough, self-reliant Black women. I'm not saying you shouldn't say these things because you're stereotyping.
>
> *Cara:* I might be.
>
> *Ali:* Right, you might be. But there might be a lot of other things going on with it too—like maybe your kids are filling a role they think they're supposed to be playing and maybe you're angry at the boys because you don't want them to play that role.
>
> *Cara:* When we have transitions, especially during testing, the expectation is that you read your independent reading book—boys find 99 ways not to do it, and girls, I rarely have to remind them. The boys, they're lying down, they're pretending to read. A lot of times they're lying down, head under blazer.

In pointing out the stereotypes, I was not suggesting that Cara should stop noting trends that are stereotypical. A fear of falling into the stereotyping trap is part of what makes White teachers loath to make any generalizations based on race or gender. If we are unable to recognize any trends based on race or gender, we might be missing some of the most important dynamics that we need to work on. But I also wanted to point out to Cara that her generalizations did align with stereotypes. When I realize that my interpretation of someone's actions aligns closely with stereotypes of their racial group, this is usually an indication to me that I might have stumbled upon some unconscious racism. And though that does not necessarily mean that the interpretation is wrong, it should certainly merit a second look.

A Black colleague shared that her child had been evaluated by a White counselor at his private school and had been found, in a 15-minute observation, to be "manipulative, inattentive, hyperactive, and impulsive." Because these assessments were so contrary to her experience of her child and so aligned with stereotypes of Black males, she refused to honor the results of the evaluation. One potential inquiry question that could be informed by such a scenario is: Do my assessments of students align with stereotypes of their racial group? If so, are my unconscious biases influencing how I interpret the actions of my students? What are other ways to interpret the behavior I'm seeing?

Todd began to ask these questions after reading about the ways that depression is often misread in Black adolescent boys as aggression. Our inquiry group read this in the work of Stevenson, Davis, Herrero-Taylor, and Morris (2003), who write, "Most of the aggression we see in Black youth is accompanied by depression symptoms, fear of annihilation, loss of family support and psychological distress. . . . Approaches that attempt to understand and address the depression rather than control the aggression are more likely to be successful" (p. 10). This theory resonated with Todd, and he felt that this reframing helped him see the depression in many of his students, just lurking behind their seemingly aggressive actions. In this case, he not only recognized the stereotyping in his inquiry but used outside resources to support alternative explanations for the actions he first interpreted as "aggression."

THE INQUIRY IMPASSE

Inquiry is successful when it leads the inquirer on a spiral path, which continues to deepen in a process of inquiry, learning, action, and reflection. In the process of that cycle, there are a number of things that can stall or stop the inquiry cycle; I call this the inquiry impasse. These include questions we don't ask because we don't know what we don't know, perfectly logical explanations (PLEs), myths, questions we don't ask about students who are neither Black nor White, and questions we don't ask because we are afraid we will look racist if we do.

Questions We Don't Ask Because We Don't Know What We Don't Know

Another type of question that teachers asked was the open-ended request they made to me: "Please tell me anything that stands out to *you*." To describe these questions, I use the *Johari Window,* which is a tool of cognitive psychology for understanding one's own personality and where one's strengths and weaknesses lie (Luft & Ingham, 1950). The Johari Window demonstrates that for all people there are four types of knowing:

1. Things we know we know
2. Things we don't know we know
3. Things we know we don't know
4. Things we don't know we don't know

The last two categories of questions—things we know we don't know and things we don't know we don't know—created paranoia among teachers. In spite of all they had learned (in fact, *because* of all they had learned), they were aware of how much they did not know. This was a concern not only because they did not want to look ignorant but also because they did not want to do things that were hurtful to students. Some examples look like this:

> What aspects of race do I think about, and what aspects get lost? I want to be thinking about it more, but like where . . . does it get lost? It's like, well, what parts of it do I think about? (Cara)

> Sometimes I wonder if I'm racist in the way I'm talking to students. Like I don't know. (Todd)

> Do I come across like that? Do I sound condescending? I don't think I'm condescending, but I've been told I am condescending, but is it based on race? (Ann)

A critical piece of the inquiry model of learning is that it cannot be based solely on our own existing understandings. The model of inquiry research that the Friends Independent School group followed was significantly strengthened by the fact that they scheduled numerous opportunities for teacher learning that pushed teachers past the questions that immediately occurred to them to ask. Without input from outside speakers, workshops, and readings, teachers would have all continued to ask instructional questions, such as those from the very first section of this chapter. They would not have been pushed to ask questions about relationships and unconscious bias; these types of questions did emerge over time because of the targeted support and professional development built into the inquiry groups. Inquiry models of learning cycle through a process of asking questions, investigating answers, trying something new, observing the impact, and asking more questions. My experience suggests that we must place particular emphasis on the investigation phase because this is the point at which we begin to uncover what we don't know we don't know.

This process of inquiry, leading to progressively more self-reflective questions, was particularly evident in the experience of Helene. She began the year asking instructional questions, such as "How do I find good resources that are inclusive of many racial backgrounds?" Although this question is important, it does not push against her practice in any way, nor does it really provide a foundation for going more deeply into a cycle of inquiry. After she and I had developed more trust between us, Helene started to share questions about her students: "I mean, even my one kid who talks, I don't even know how to say it, but, in a Black dialect, if that's the way to say it . . . how much do I correct him?" This is a question that does not have one right answer but that would lead Helene into an inquiry process of reading, experimenting, reflecting, and continuing to ask.

Helene developed another inquiry question in response to a presentation I did with my co-consultant on racial microaggressions. The term "microaggression," coined by Teachers College psychologist Derald Wing Sue, has revolutionized race conversations because it describes a phenomenon that significantly affects the lives of people of color while being practically invisible to witnesses, particularly witnesses of other racial groups. Racial microaggressions are tiny, barely perceptible racial slights that have a significant impact both because of their cumulative effect and the underlying message that is communicated by them (Sue, 2007). There is usually a great discrepancy between the intent of the person who makes the microaggression and the impact on the person affected by it. One example of a microaggression is a well-meaning White person complimenting an Asian American teenager on her English skills. The White person intends to pay a compliment, but doesn't realize that the person to whom she is speaking is third generation American, and does not know any other language but English. The comment is not one that the speaker would make to another White person; they assumed that the Asian American teenager did not speak English as her first language because of how she looked. A key part of microaggressions is the *cumulative effect* of hearing the same comment repeatedly; in this case the teen, and many of her friends and family members, had heard a variation of this comment many times before from similarly well-meaning people. The underlying message that accompanies it is that she looks foreign; she doesn't look American; she looks like she doesn't belong. The especially insidious thing about microaggressions is that they are difficult to confront because they are so subtle to the person making them, who often cannot see the larger patterns of which they are a part.

In our presentation, we used the example of the microaggression: "Why are Black people so loud?" This example reminded Helene of a question she regularly asked about her classroom: "Do I yell at my Black students too much? They make more noise than everyone else." She noticed a red flag in her assessment of Black children when she realized that being loud fit with this common microaggression. This then gave her the opportunity to consider possible explanations for this phenomenon. Was her perception of loudness influenced by her being White? Was it possible that this could be a cultural difference?

We looked together at research that introduced a concept called "verve," which is a predisposition for the presence of multiple and varied sources of noise and stimulus (Cunningham & Boykin, 2004). Psychologists Cunningham and Boykin cite studies in which Euro-American children (their term) perform better in low-vervistic environments, whereas African American students perform better in, and prefer, high-vervistic environments. At first we were both unnerved by this article, cautious of the possibility for research like this to essentialize race and link it to cultural style. Helene didn't want to pigeonhole students or predetermine learning styles without knowing students as individuals. But at the same time, she saw how it might give her insight into what might be happening for two of her students, one of whom was not only Black, but was also the daughter of musicians and had multiple siblings. There was a distinct possibility that she required a high-vervistic environment to help her concentrate. While the article didn't tell Helene how to teach her students, what it did offer was an expanded concept of ideal learning conditions. It suggested that the notion that quiet classrooms are the ideal learning environment might not be an absolute truth for all students, and that preferences are related to many environmental factors, one of which is racial and cultural subculture influence.

"Black people are so loud" is a microaggression because it assumes there is a universal standard for volume and negatively judges anyone who doesn't ascribe to that standard. It is a statement that is constantly being made about people of color in predominantly White spaces. I led a training once at school where some of the teachers were Latino/a. They said that they had to put on their "White voices" for parent night so that they wouldn't scare the parents and grandparents of White children. In André Robert Lee's powerful autobiographical documentary "Prep School Negro," he talks about how embarrassing it was to hear his mother "talking loudly" while he performed on stage at his independent school drama production in the 12th grade. Compared to the parents of his White peers, she probably was "talking loudly." But a difference in volume, like a difference in culture, should be celebrated, not ridiculed. André's shame about this moment was co-constructed for him by a school culture that was premised on White cultural styles and that interpreted alternative styles as negative or inferior. As a child, he did not have the tools to critique that interpretation of his mother, so instead he directed the negativity inwards, where it had the power to alienate him from his family and community.

Being loud is also sometimes a sign that people feel they are not being heard or listened to. In such a case, loudness might be related to racial positionality within a White mainstream but not necessarily an aspect of a particular racial subculture. The realization that "loudness" is relative and can be related to racial group membership forced Helene to pay closer attention to the assumptions she made. In going through this process, Helene modeled a strategy that can help challenge the inquiry impasse: pursuing training and materials that help one realize those things they don't know that they don't know.

Perfectly Logical Explanations (PLEs)

One common feature of the inquiry impasse is our willingness to accept perfectly logical explanations (PLEs) for why a given situation is what it is, without demanding more intentionality of ourselves and our schools. PLEs are explanations that focus on individual intention or logistical circumstances while failing to acknowledge repeated patterns or racially inequitable impact. An example of this is when Cara started to ask the question, "How do I support my male students in developing resilience when faced with adversity in the classroom?"

She requested that I watch for patterns in how she interacted with boys and girls. The first thing I noticed was that all of the table captains in the class were girls. When I told Cara that, she acknowledged that it was a problem but said that her teaching assistant, Chris, chose the table captains, and he usually chose girls. This is an example of a perfectly logical explanation (PLE); there is a readily accessible explanation for gender or racial disparity that is related to logistics or a diffusion of authority, but is not based on conscious prejudice or malice. In this case, all the table captains were girls because neither Cara nor Chris determined that having gender diversity in classroom leadership positions was a priority. I suggested to Cara that in a classroom where you feel the boys are disempowered, it seems essential to achieve parity among the leadership roles in the classroom. Boys should not be given the honor of being table captains if they do not seem capable of accomplishing the task, but surely there must be some boys who could handle the responsibility. Being proactive about achieving such parity requires designing guidelines for whoever is choosing table captains that stipulate that at least one of the captains at any given time be a boy. PLEs are usually given to explain a racial or gender outcome that was not consciously intended. The problem with them is that they shift the blame away from the decisionmakers and stop the inquiry. Once a PLE is provided to explain a situation, the inquiry no longer seems pertinent.

Much of the racial and gender disparity that occurs in schools is not by intentional design. If you ask any principal or teacher to explain a given phenomenon, they will likely have multiple perfectly logical explanations for it. When Ann had to lead a conversation about race during a book discussion with her homeroom, for example, I asked why there was only one student of color in the room. Ann said it was because the homerooms were organized alphabetically, which meant the racial distribution of students was completely random. So when they decided to do book discussions with the entire student body and chose to organize the discussions by homeroom, many students of color were racially isolated for a sensitive conversation about race. This situation was not consciously designed to disadvantage students of color, but it is the natural result of a decision that was not made with a conscious recognition of racial dynamics in mind.

Usually the only way to prevent racial or gender disparities in schools is to consciously subvert them with decisions and systems that take race into account. Perfectly logical explanations should be a trigger to change the question from "Why is this phenomenon happening?" to "How can we change this?"

Myths

Another feature of the inquiry impasse are the myths that we tell to explain racial inequality in schools. I call these myths because there is often no way to determine their truthfulness; in the tradition of myth construction, they are created to provide answers to a phenomenon that is not well understood. In Sam's school, there were myths that answered the question "Why is there a disproportionately low number of Black students in honors and AP English?" Explanations such as "They are here on athletic scholarship" or "They don't get support at home" or "They don't have time to do all the extra work because they have to work other jobs" were floated by teachers and administrators. Sam didn't have to look far to grab one of these out of the air around him. As an outside observer, I had no idea to what extent these things were true, but they sounded to me like the kinds of myths I had heard in many other schools. The myths suggest that the students' inability to qualify for honors classes is a matter of their talent (or lack thereof) or personal circumstances and not in any way related to the experience of being at a historically and predominantly White school with a Eurocentric curriculum. This myth is grounded within a larger narrative that persists in our society about the innate athletic talents of Blacks and the innate intellectual superiority of Whites. And because we have many different myths about Black inferiority, one of which is the nationwide myth that schools (particularly private schools) have different admissions standards for Black students, we can easily use that myth to explain away disparities without interrogating them.

Myths and PLEs align with common stereotypes, which we've already noted as a red flag. It's not that these statements are not true of some of the Black students who were not in honors or AP English. And it's not that these statements were not more true for some of the Black students than for some of the non-Black students. Maybe they were—we don't know. But these statements are not true of all Black students. There are some Black students for whom none of these things are true, and they are still not in honors/AP English. How do we explain that? And, even more important, even if these things were true, we must interrogate whether the statements about a students' status necessarily preclude them from taking part in a high-level, challenging curriculum. If we want to have high expectations for all students, we need to figure out how to challenge and support them to enroll and succeed in high-level classes. We need to challenge ourselves and our students to move beyond the myths and PLEs and inquire into the multifaceted barriers to success—and then remove them.

Leaving out Students Who Are Neither Black nor White

For the most part, teachers did not ask questions about non-Black students of color. This is partly a reflection of the student populations in the classrooms I observed. However, even in classrooms with Asian American students or Latino students, non-Black students of color did not seem to draw much attention. Sometimes this was because they seemed to fit into the classroom norms without any apparent difficulty. Sometimes it was a result of teachers not knowing how to address non-Black/non-White issues, or even how to include them when race was concerned. Other times, non-Black students of color seemed to have notable social difficulties, but they still did not tend to draw much concern from their teachers in connection with race. For the most part, any Asian American or Latino American children that were in the classrooms I observed were the only student of their particular racial background in the class. They did not seem to trigger the same level of stress for the teacher that their Black peers did. And yet I often found my-self wondering whether this apparent ease with which they seemed to assimilate into the racial mainstream (or make their racial "otherness" invisible) demanded a certain cultural occlusion for them, one that they might not be able to consciously recognize until much later in life. Sometimes Latino students are unsure how to identify in terms of race, believing that being Latino is an ethnicity and not a race.[1] They end up choosing to identify as Black or White and yet not quite feeling a part of either group. Similarly, Asian American kids can be unsure where they fit in the world of racial diversity, so associated are they with stereotypes of academic achievement and still so susceptible to racist bullying and racial discrimination. Diversity efforts in schools tend to structure their programming around the per-ceived needs of Black students with the assumption that such programming will accommodate all students of color. This strategy negates the specific cultural ex-periences, values, and perceptions of non-Black students, further reinforces the Black/White binary, and leaves non-Black students of color wondering where they fit—or feeling that they fit better with the White students who don't talk about racism. This absence was notable in our inquiry questions and discussions.

The "Untouchables"

Helene and Laurie both asked questions of me that they did not ask in their in-quiry groups. I call these questions the "untouchables"—they are questions that teachers would not ask without a significant level of comfort and confidence, and that they asked even though the words did not feel right. The asking of "untouch-ables" is a skill in itself—to use words that others might not find appropriate in the interest of articulating a question, rather than staying silent because one believes the words might be racist. There are countless untouchable questions—questions that we don't ask for fear that we will look racist or will be racist for naming ra-cial trends or not already knowing the "racially competent" answer, or for fear of exposing our unconscious biases or using the wrong words. As the following two quotes show, sometimes teachers didn't even know exactly how to frame their question, nor what exactly they were asking:

> How to gain more knowledge to support a situation where perhaps a handful of my children of color, primarily African American/inner-city students, how the culture that they experience in their home and neighborhood may be different than the majority. I've heard from some of these individuals, um, mostly colleagues, who say, "I live two lives. When I leave my neighborhood, you know, I put on this (independent school) face, identity and when I go home to my family I talk different and I walk different and I have two identities." (Laurie)

I mean, even my one kid who talks, I don't even know how to say it, but in a Black dialect, if that's the way to say it . . . how much do I correct him? (Helene)

In these examples part of the reason these two teachers do not know what words to use in asking these questions is that the question itself might be seen as racist because it falls into that category of things that mainstream White culture deems untouchable in polite conversation. Both of these quotes refer to code-switching, which is the conscious or subconscious transitioning from one language dialect to another, typically undertaken when the norms of the local environment shift. Code-switching refers most typically to spoken language, but it can refer to broad range of personal expressions, including behavioral style, body language, dress and hair styles, among other things. The topic of Black code-switching is so rarely talked about in mainstream White society that these two teachers possessed no codes of behavior or vocabulary to support the asking of the question, much less finding answers. In the same way that simply talking about race can lead to someone being called a racist, asking questions about broad differences between a school culture informed by mainstream White middle-class values and a Black student's home culture might be seen as racist too. The idea that Whiteness even has anything to do with a school culture is quite radical because school culture tends to be seen and interpreted more generally as simply "normal" (Ladson-Billings, 1998; Lee, 2005). In reality, it is only "normal" for some of the students, teachers, and parents who make up the majority of the population, who often tend to be White and/or middle class.

Asking the "untouchable" questions required noticing and naming difference, recognizing uncertainty, acknowledging and supporting difference (rather than automatically working to assimilate children who are different), and taking the risk that in asking these questions one might seem racist. In essence, asking these questions requires a positive racial identity, which gives a person the confidence needed to acknowledge when she or he doesn't know (see Chapter 2 on racial identity). These are the kinds of questions that do not get asked in public because they require both racial competence and a sense of safety. Ironically, though these questions are some of the most important to talk about for the sake of students' lives and experiences in school, they do not get asked because of social norms that restrict this kind of explicit race talk. As anthropologist of education Mica Pollock (2004) writes,

Americans are experts at thinking communally about race and achievement problems, but novices at thinking communally about race and achievement solutions—and as the battle between competing explanations of racial achievement patterns rumbles on, the connection between race and achievement remains both an omnipresent presupposition of American educational discourse and schooling talk's most anxious void. (p. 170)

Untouchable questions were notably not raised in inquiry groups, but rather in one-on-one conversations. This suggests another way that race inquiry might be different from other forms of inquiry: Asking untouchable questions may necessitate that teachers work with one another one-on-one in spaces that are even safer than the group itself. Creating such spaces for paired work can raise the level of comfort for all members of the group as a whole. In group dynamics, the best way to create safety in a group is to put people in pairs.

An Inquiry Dilemma

This chapter has explored the many different types of questions that get raised (or, notably, don't get raised) in race inquiry, but it doesn't give many answers. Inquiry is not about finding straightforward answers—it's about engaging in a process of seeking answers and being open to the idea that we might continue to learn the answers well after the time when we first needed to know them. To return to the question quoted to open this chapter, which was posed by a White teacher in research conducted by anthropologist Ruth Landes (1965), I want to highlight the struggle of Helene, the 2nd-grade teacher, who asked, "*How do I address families who discipline their children in ways I see as inconsistent with our school's principles?*" The question is not exactly the same as the one at the beginning of the chapter, but it gets at the same essential dilemma: How do I, as a White teacher, intervene with a family that disciplines their children in a way I disagree with? If I am White and the family is Black, does it prompt a different reaction than if the family was White?

The question is framed from the outset as a logistical question, one that should be easy to answer, as if the asker expects a scripted response or at least a list of talking points or action steps. If we reframe it as inquiry about students and racial patterns, it might look like this: "Why do the discipline strategies of some Black families look so different from what I expect and see as consistent with the school's policies?" If we reframe it as inquiry about oneself, it might look like this: "Why am I uncomfortable with the discipline strategies used by the parents of some of my Black students? What should my role be, as a White person and as a teacher, when I interpret discipline strategies in Black families to be unhealthy?"

I have been asked this question multiple times at different schools but never in large-group conversation. This question comes up one-on-one after I've worked with teachers for multiple sessions. It is one of these untouchable questions that seems to require a great deal of trust before one is willing to ask it. For Helene, this question came up after two Black 2nd-graders in her independent Quaker school wrote in their weekly "weekend update" that they had gotten "whoopings" the previous weekend. By the time we talked about it, we had built quite a strong relationship in which we were both able to share our uncertainty and insecurities about race questions. It seemed that the time Helene had put into building her racial identity supported her to be particularly vulnerable about asking untouchable questions such as these.

Helene's dilemma was that she felt it was her responsibility, first, to protect her students from any abuse that might be occurring at home. Second, she felt it was her job to educate parents to discipline their children in nonviolent ways. She felt that the children involved had poor social and conflict-resolution skills as a direct result of their parents' choices of disciplinary strategies. Third, she personally believed that physical punishment was wrong. She was fortified in this conviction by a speech she had heard by a prominent Black community leader, who said that beating one's children was a practice that had been learned in slavery and passed down through the generations, and that perpetuating the practice perpetuates oppression as well. Helene agreed with this woman but, as a White woman, felt she couldn't tell the families that by whooping their children they were continuing the legacy of slavery. She thought that from a White woman such a viewpoint would be immediately disregarded. Finally, Helene felt particularly moved to intervene after she had intervened with a case of domestic violence in a White family the previous year (after she intervened, the mother thanked her profusely for motivating her to get help).

I related so deeply to Helene's dilemma. I could see how hard she was trying to do what was right for the children in her class while trying not to be oppressive or overstep her bounds as a teacher. As a teacher in the state of Pennsylvania, she was required by law to report a family if she suspected child abuse or neglect (Child Welfare Information Gateway, 2014). And yet the guidelines for what constituted abuse were both vague and subjective: "A report must be made when the reporter, in his or her official capacity, suspects or has reason to believe that a child has been abused or neglected" (p. 3). If I had been in her position, I would have struggled with many of the same questions. I do not know the answer to her dilemma. But as I got to know Helene, the school, and the children, and as I thought more about the question and read more of what others have written about this very point, I came to a clearer understanding of all the parts to consider. My distance as a researcher also made it easier to think about the question in broad objective terms rather than with all the details of the individuals involved. The following points are not answers to this particular dilemma of Helene's but rather considerations for any teacher who is asking similar questions.

First, it is important to recognize that physical punishment is an individual family choice and that this choice is deeply informed by one's own experience in the world. There is a difference between child abuse and physical punishment, and the difference is whether both the child and the parent understand the "whooping" to be a fair response to misbehavior rather than unjustified and random physical abuse. Is the whooping followed by discussion and/or punishment? Is the whooping preceded by verbal warnings that the child repeatedly ignores? When a community has cultural norms about how and when a whooping is carried out, it has a different meaning to a child than if it comes at random times with no warning or explanation. In *NutureShock*, Bronson and Merryman (2011) explore research that shows that if physical punishment, such as spanking, is a norm within a given community, it does not have the compounding castigating shame that it has with-in communities where very few children are spanked. Context matters.

Second, parents of Black children have to prepare them to live in a world that will not always give them second chances. Demanding that they listen to authority might be a way of protecting children from a violent society (Wise, 2011). Physical punishment might be a part of that parenting strategy. The violence of a society that perceives Black males as threatening, for example, is not something that most parents of White children need to think about when disciplining. For parents of Black males, however, raising them to respond immediately when an authority figure says "stop" might later be a matter of life and death.

Third, teachers and schools do not have the authority to tell families how to raise their children. Raising children is a collaborative effort between families and schools in which families should have the final say. In these collaborations, no matter how old the parents, the parents should be respected as the ultimate authority.

Fourth, invoking school norms might have an alienating effect on families. Helene used the nonviolent values of the Quakers to justify an intervention. At first glance, it does make sense to say that Quakers are nonviolent, and therefore so should be all people who attend Quaker schools. But invoking the fact that it's a Quaker school sets up an "us versus them" dynamic that frames the parents as (violent) outsiders rather than members of the community that is shaped by all who are in it. Because Black parents are often framed as outsiders to this historically and predominantly White Quaker school community, it is important for teachers to be aware of how they further perpetuate this dynamic through their judgments about family interventions. After all, the school did not enforce Quaker values on other parents, requiring them to purchase only nonviolent stocks, for example, or to be antiwar.

Fifth, Helene's conviction that the parents were in the wrong was based on a talk that she heard from a Black leader from a different community, which sub-scribed to a particular philosophy. The parents in Helene's class did not necessarily subscribe to that philosophy. It would be worthwhile to ask, "Does the fact that a Black woman said it make it right for all Black people?" This is a place where I have gotten stuck before—at a loss for how to get involved in in-group dynamics (where I am not a member of the group), I try to learn what is right by listening to experts who are members of that group. But then I'm still at a loss as an outsider as to how to intervene, if it all. I mentioned this to Helene during our conversation on this topic when she said that she got her conviction from a Black leader. I responded, "That's where most of my answers come from." We connected over how much we learn by listening to people speak from within the Black community and how we still don't know how to make that knowledge our own in a way that is authentic when communicating with Black parents.

What we both overlooked in our attempt to follow the leadership of Black experts was that we could have just as easily found experts, who were Black, who expressed an opposite opinion. Helene heard the view of one woman from her community, but there are certainly many Black leaders who might suggest that if you spare the rod, your spoil the child. We were both getting in the trap of using the viewpoints of Black leaders to justify our own points of view. Just because one Black person promotes an idea for the Black community, it doesn't mean it should apply to everyone.

Sixth, the issue of social skills is complicated because they are so deeply cultural and contextual. When Black children are found to have poor social skills, it may be more of an indication of a marginalized social position in which they do not share the same context of socialization as their peers, rather than an objective deficiency. In the spirit of using a wider lens to include Whiteness in all of my analyses, I propose that we should also think about the White students in the class who might have poor social and conflict-resolution skills. It seems fair to presume the students that received physical punishment were not alone in these challenges. If a teacher is going to intervene with parents when children have poor social skills, how might she also intervene with the parenting strategies of those that ascribe to permissive or indulgent styles that also lead to poor social skills? And if she decides not to intervene in those cases, that decision might inform how she does or does not intervene in other cases.

Finally, we need to recognize the historical context and the group-level nature of this question. It is clear from Landes's quote at the beginning of this chapter that White women have been asking for a long time how to protect Black children from their own families, with an assumption that Black families are violent and uncaring. Teachers must see this question within this historical context because Black families certainly will. The implication that families are abusing their children has the possibility to drive a wedge between teachers and parents and make it harder for the parents to trust the teacher in the future. The race question to raise in this case is whether children really are in danger, or whether groups simply have different cultural (racial subcultural) understandings of physical discipline. As we consider the possibility of the latter being true, we can see how this one untouchable question takes us from the individual level to the systemic. Individuals ask the question, but the way the question gets answered determines whether the state authorities get involved as well. White people comprise the vast majority of mandatory reporters—teachers, social workers, physicians, nurses, mental health professionals, law enforcement officers and child-care providers (Child Welfare Information Gateway, 2014)—and yet many do not have the familiarity with racial subcultures to be able to differentiate between abuse and disciplinary strategies that do not constitute abuse or neglect.

When Helene and I spoke about this, I truly did not know what to say or how to support her. At the time I could only respond with empathy for what a challenging scenario it is, appreciation for how common a dilemma it is, and admiration for how she chose to handle it. Since then, her questions led me on a process of inquiry for how to support other teachers who approach me with the same question. Even now I feel awkward leaving this analysis so open-ended, knowing that

Helene, because of her conscience and the law, had to go back into school that very week and make decisions regarding whether and how to communicate with the families about what she heard. She did not have the luxury of many months of reading and research to help her decide. In consultation with her division head, Helene chose to talk directly with the parents about what had come up in class and to let them know that she felt their choice to use physical punishment affected their children's development of conflict-resolution skills. She felt that the parents were not particularly forthcoming in the conversations and that things continued to be awkward between them for a while afterward. Still, she felt that if she had to do it again, she would do it the same way.

One important race question that this scenario raises for me is the issue of trust between White teachers and Black parents in particular. While trust is an important issue with all parents, I think that it is particularly so for Black parents, who have been systematically and historically misunderstood and underestimated by White educators. When White educators recommend a Black student for extra testing for behavioral or academic problems, for example, their parents may resist. This is not because they don't like the individual teacher or because they think their child is perfect, but because they are defensive against a system that tends to assume Black children are deficient and inferior. Similarly, in a system that constantly undermines Black people and assumes that they are not fit to be parents, it makes sense that even the question of whether physical punishment is abuse will make Black parents defensive. Family discipline is significantly influenced by family culture and is deeply subjective. Research by my colleague Chonika Coleman-King (2014) has demonstrated that Caribbean American families feel they cannot discipline their children in the United States without being criminalized.

In Helene's case, I admire her immensely for talking directly to the parents rather than employing a strategy that would have been easier for her but harder for the family, which would involve calling Children's Welfare Services and leaving it to them to decide whether abuse occurred. Because she felt so strongly that she could not just ignore the comments from students, she chose a middle ground for her intervention. At the same time, it seems impossible, given the historical context, not to alienate Black parents by doing so. Their parenting is being scrutinized by a person who has power over them, but who does not necessarily have a familiarity with their cultural norms. For a teacher in this situation, a knowledge of the historical context could help the teacher understand the sensitivity of the topic and the work it will take following the conversation to rebuild trust with the parents.

I cannot definitively say what I would do in a similar situation because how one responds must be shaped by the relationships with parents and children, school policies, the nature of the reports from children, and other factors. But I am hopeful that sharing the understandings I came to in my own process of inquiry about the context within which this dilemma takes place might help teachers make those immediate decisions with greater awareness. (See Appendix A for Helene's response to this analysis.)

STRATEGIES FOR RAISING RACE QUESTIONS

Inquiry can be a particularly effective strategy for teachers to change themselves and their practice in a way that is self-initiated and nonthreatening. This is an especially valuable tool for learning about race and racism, which is a process that can be intimidating for White people. However, race learning often involves material that we don't even know we don't know, creating an inquiry impasse. To address this impasse, I have created a number of recommendations for White people engaged in inquiry learning focused on race.

Be Self-Reflective

Your inquiry should include at least one question that invites you to examine your biases and your own cultural style. This process should not just be about understanding people who are different from you, but about the relationship dynamic—the differences and similarities between you. Understanding your own culture (and your own racial subculture) is the first step to understanding others' cultures. Examine your own personal definitions of key concepts in your classroom such as "disruptive," "smart," "leadership," "good student," and "communicative" and question the ways that these terms are culturally relative—and how they might be defined in a culture different from your own. Identify and label perfectly logical explanations (PLEs) or myths when they come up in your inquiry or in your group. These are explanations that make it possible to excuse racist behavior or outcomes. Do not allow inquiry or debate to be ended by PLEs or school mythology, but push past them to investigate more fully.

Build Relationships

Invite antiracist colleagues into your classroom to help you see your own culture and your own biases. Ask them to give you critical feedback, and thank them when they do. Make time to work in small groups (pairs even) with people you trust. Use these opportunities to ask the "untouchable" questions, the questions you are afraid to verbalize because of what they might say about you—and begin to explore them.

Think Racially

Be willing to think about your students and yourself as members of racial and gender groups.[2] How do your questions change when you think about your students as members of racial and gender groups? How do your questions change when you look at students as individuals removed from any groups or labels? Is there any disproportionality occurring in your classroom (i.e., are students excelling, failing, or being disciplined in numbers that are disproportionate to their makeup of the general population)? When you think about your classroom, think about all the racial groups—not just your Black students but also your Asian American students, Latino American students, White students, Arab American students, and Native American students. If a student is the only one of their racial group, they may demand your attention even less—and need it even more. How does your teaching style favor students who are assertive and demanding of attention at the expense of students who do not feel entitled to your attention at the expense of others? Notice how your assessments and judgments of students, parents, and colleagues of color overlap with common stereotypes of their racial group.

Do Your Homework

Place a high priority on the investigation stage of inquiry; seek out resources and be receptive to input from multiple sources. This is the stage of inquiry when you begin to know what you don't know, which cannot happen without outside input. If your inquiry questions can be answered through a conversation with a knowledgeable person (or an Internet search engine), they might not be the right questions for an inquiry process. Questions about pedagogy, instructions, resources, and knowledge are important questions, but they will not lead you on a journey of self-exploration that inquiry is so good at facilitating. Remember that a multicultural curriculum does not make a classroom antiracist (see Chapter 3). Although a multicultural curriculum is an important part of an antiracist classroom, it is not sufficient. An antiracist classroom examines all aspects of classroom life, including discipline, communication, relationships, group dynamics, and cultural styles.

Follow the Agreements for Courageous Conversations

Authors Glenn Singleton and Curtis Linton (2005) present four *agreements* for having a Courageous Conversation, which they say "help create the conditions for safe exploration and profound learning for all" in conversations about race (p. 4). These agreements were used in all three inquiry groups to shape the conversations about race that the teachers in this book engaged in. The agreements are:

1. Stay engaged.
2. Speak your truth.
3. Expect to experience discomfort.
4. Expect and accept a lack of closure.

I suggest that for anyone reading this book with a friend or colleague or group, these four rules are excellent ground rules for shaping your conversation. But, additionally, as I reflect back on the work that teachers did during our year together, I'm struck by how powerfully these rules shape inquiry work as well.

Inquiry is a particularly powerful way to engage race questions because of the way that it constructs a group process around these very ground rules. Practicing inquiry requires that a person stay engaged (1) over a long time period, not just for one workshop or one book group. It requires that a person think about their own perspective and racial identity as a part of that process (2, speak your truth). Finally, inquiry is not considered flawed if one does not develop concrete answers; on the contrary, a successful inquiry tends to lead to more questions than answers. A lack of closure is an inherent part of inquiry (4). As for the agreement about discomfort (3), discomfort is not necessarily critical to inquiry. But it *is* critical to inquiry about race. Discomfort is often the body's way of demanding a "fight-or-flight" response. When we feel uncomfortable, we often abandon the task at hand, especially if it is a conversation about race that makes us feel embarrassed, ashamed, afraid, or isolated. But if you think about the times in your life when you learned the most important lessons, there was likely some discomfort involved. When we spend all of our time in our comfort zones, we miss the chance to do the kind of transformational learning that race inquiry promises. Expecting to experience discomfort is a requirement for race inquiry. And if we know to expect it, then when things start getting uncomfortable we can simply lean into that discomfort and take it as an indication that we might be doing something right, rather than flee from it.

Grow Your Racial Identity

Recognize that racial identity is not just about how you identify racially but also about how you feel about your race and what you understand about your current and historical racial context. Growing and developing a positive racial identity is a critical part of building the foundation for taking any risks with regard to race. The following chapter addresses the development of a positive racial identity.

CHAPTER 2

Racial Identity Is Not Just Another Tool—It's the Toolbox

Building whole classrooms and communities, in which every person can bring their whole selves, requires supporting every student to have a positive racial identity. At first glance, this might seem like an easy task—just throw a few voices of color into the curriculum and check it off your list. That is one standard response. But like with everything else we learned in this year during which six White teachers engaged in race inquiry in their classrooms, racial identity is about more than mere representation in the curriculum. Racial identity scholars say that teachers cannot support their students to have a positive racial identity unless they as teachers already have a positive racial identity themselves. When a teacher has a less developed racial identity than the student, it is called a regressive relationship (Helms, 1984, 1990; Thompson & Carter, 2012). As with anything else we teach, if the students are ahead of us, it is harder to know what they need to keep growing.

How do I develop a positive racial identity if I'm White? In the United States, we have come to associate the mere identification with Whiteness with White supremacist ideology. What's complicated about having a positive racial identity as a White person is that it's not about feeling good about being White. It's about knowing that I'm White in the context of a racist society that favors White people. It's about understanding how being White affects my relationships and opportunities, and how *not* being White affects people of color. It's about proactively learning about and confronting racism outside of us and within us.

Conversely, a negative White racial identity is not about feeling badly about being White. A person with a negative White racial identity holds "unrealistic and idealized notions of one's racial group" (Marshall, 2002, p. 11). In contrast to negative racial socialization for Black youths, which might involve negative feelings toward the self and delusions of inferiority, negative racial socialization for Whites involves delusions of superiority and misperceptions of people of color.

In this chapter we will explore racial identity development and the implications for teachers, students, and schools. The concept of racial identity is not simply another tool for our toolboxes—it *is* the toolbox. The larger, stronger, and more robust my racial identity, the more tools I will be able to carry around with me. If I do not have a strong and positive racial identity, it does not matter how many tools I learn; I will not be able to carry them or use them when needed.

WHAT'S POSITIVE ABOUT BEING WHITE?:
TEACHER RACIAL IDENTITY MATTERS

A number of people have written about racial identity development, which is a model for understanding the developmental process that White people go through as they develop an antiracist identity. Dr. Janet Helms developed the first White Racial Identity model, and Dr. Beverly Daniel-Tatum popularized it in her book, *Why Are all the Black Kids Sitting Together in the Cafeteria?*[1] Helms's model has been criticized because it does not describe all White people (certainly not all White people are on an antiracist trajectory) and because unlike child development, racial identity development doesn't happen in progressive stages; a person can be in all the statuses at the same time or can move through the statuses repeatedly in the course of an hour, day, or lifetime.

While Helms's model does not describe the experience of every White person, I share it here because it does give a sense of what White people who are engaged in race inquiry might expect as they begin to learn about race, racism, and being White. It is a framework that I found incredibly liberating throughout my development in moments when I got stuck. My sticking places typified standard developmental statuses, including being paralyzed by guilt, getting caught up in competition with other White people, feeling like being White means being wrong, or believing I should be colorblind. I have sometimes spent years being stuck in a given place in my racial identity. Helms's theory gave me a way to understand what was happening for me psychologically and to help myself get unstuck. In the following section I share extensively from my own developmental trajectory because I have found that it supports readers to see how these theoretical concepts play out in real life. In keeping with my stance as a facilitator (see Chapter 5), I hope to model vulnerability and honesty through the sharing of my stories here and in doing so model the vulnerability and honesty that inquiry work requires of teachers.

Contact: First Contact with Racism

In Helms's framework, Contact is the first status of development in which one initially encounters racism and begins to get an inkling that White people and people of color don't necessarily get the same treatment in our society. For White people like me who grow up in relatively segregated neighborhoods where they do not know very many people of color, work or college are often the places where they first experience Contact. Not surprisingly, many people of color notice much sooner than college that the world divides people by race and treats them differently because of it. My friend Mathu, for example, who is South Asian, entered the Contact status equivalent for people of color when she was in preschool and her White classmates told her that she could not play their game with them because she was "dark skinned."

In college I took an African American literature class and began to get a strong sense of the ways that racism has shaped the lives of African Americans in the United States. I spent most of the class feeling hypervisible because I was White and trying not to say anything because I was sure it would come out wrong. Contact is generally characterized by this kind of racial shyness, a lack of consciousness of what it means to be White, and sometimes a subscription to colorblindness.

Disintegration: My Idealized Image of the World Disintegrates

Contact is followed by Disintegration, during which one's worldview disintegrates because the reality of racism interrupts one's previously held beliefs about the world being fair. I felt this way for a long time. As a child, people in my community joked about everything, including things like Asian accents or African American names. When I first started learning about racism, I felt I was venturing down a path that might separate me from my community. How could I call myself an antiracist and not confront my family? But how could I confront my family, which is the foundation of all that I love in my life? The stuff I was learning felt like it belonged in another universe, and I didn't feel that I could explain it to my parents without saying, "Just come see this other universe with me—I can't describe it." Fortunately for me, they did, but I will say more about that later. Disintegration is often characterized by this sense of having feet in two different worlds and feeling the pain and sadness of losing a more idealistic worldview as one begins to get a sense of the massive scope of racism—as well as the ways one has benefited from it.

Reintegration: Reintegrating My Image of the World as a Fair and Just Place

Sometimes the process of Disintegration (which is critical for continuing to live with a conscious acknowledgment of the realities of racism) is so painful that people try to reintegrate their former reality in which an awareness of racism was nonexistent (or repressed); that status is Reintegration (Helms, 2008).

I remember going to a conference on race during graduate school and feeling confident that I already knew all the right answers. Yet in two different workshops I received feedback that I was dominating and steering the conversation in ways that felt typical of White women and oppressive to people of color. I wanted to cry, but I had heard that White women crying was also typical and oppressive because it served to refocus the attention on White women rather than on racism. So I didn't cry, and I felt angry about that too. I was there to learn, but this is not the kind of learning I had expected to encounter. By the end of the conference I simply stopped talking and started to wonder if the reason people told me those things was simply because I was White. Maybe being White meant people of color would always find fault with what I had to say. I felt that I couldn't get the answers right and started to feel very uncomfortable around anyone of color. When I mentioned this to my sister, she suggested that I might be "reintegrating." In Reintegration, people turn sadness into anger and guilt into blame in order to protect themselves from feeling the more painful emotions. They are quick to label people of color "reverse racists" and to think that as White people they will never be able to get the right answer to race questions. White people who make fun of political correctness or who make accusations of reverse racism are often in this status. When White people are in Reintegration, their hostility tends to alienate anyone who might be able to help them move forward in their racial identity, particularly people of color. White people who are racially aware will frequently distance themselves from White people in Reintegration status because they don't want to be associated with White people who act in ignorant or bitter ways. But people in this status need White allies to step in and support them to move beyond the Reintegration status so that people of color don't have to deal with these White people who, because of their psychological developmental status, are particularly antagonistic. Knowing that I was reintegrating helped me reassess my experiences and see them as a part of the process of my development rather than a truth about the permanent ignorance of White people (myself included) or the intractability of race conversations.

Pseudo-Independence: I Start to Know a Thing or Two and Think I Know It All

If one is able to get beyond Disintegration and Reintegration, one can begin to build an antiracist White identity. The statuses in this second half of the racial identity development process are Pseudo-Independence, Immersion/Emersion, and Autonomy.

A person in Pseudo-Independence status is aware of racism but tries to fix it by helping people of color become more like Whites, seeing Whiteness and White experience as standard. Such a person focuses on charity rather than solidarity. This person often continues to act out of unconscious bias even while attempting to practice antiracism. I remember taking part in a 5-day intensive workshop in which I was in a small multiracial group of four. Throughout the week, I could tell that my Asian American groupmate had some things she wanted me to learn, and I felt that she did not recognize how much learning I had done already. I finally said, "Listen, do you know how many books I have read on this topic?" She responded, "If you had actually read all those books, you would not have just said that to me." Mine was a classic case of Pseudo-Independence, in which I had learned so much about racism that I thought I knew it all—and was therefore unwilling to hear the perspective of a person of color. This false sense of mastery that belies an insecurity and self-doubt is typical of the Pseudo-Independence status.

Immersion/Emersion: Immersion in Learning and Emerging from My Old Identity

The second-to-last status is Immersion/Emersion, named such to capture the way that people "immerse" themselves in learning about race and Whiteness while "emerging" into an entirely new identity. This status involves actively learning about one's own race and the experiences of others. Sometimes people in this status try to join communities of color and cut themselves off from friends and communities that are White. This status can involve high levels of embarrassment about racism and privilege, which sometimes gets channeled into anger or impatience with other White people. This was the status I was in when I called my dad a racist when I was 20, when I tried to burn my U.S. passport and move to South Africa, when I decided that I could only teach Black students, and when I came up with a plan to adopt Black children so as not to pass my racial privilege on to my progeny. All this might sound extreme, but I have met so many White people who have experienced similar thoughts and feelings. Note how while developing my racial identity and going through this extreme rejection of Whiteness, I still did racist things. By thinking that I must construct an antiracist self-image around teaching Black children or by adopting Black babies,[2] for example, I was tokenizing Black people. When a White person "calls out" another White person using shame and blame, it is often a result of being in this status. That's not to say that White people should not hold one another accountable, but when we do it through shaming or out of a desire to show how much better we are, we often build even more walls. Treating each other badly does not necessarily make the world better for people of color; often it makes it worse. One example of this is when I took a course with a White activist who felt strongly that the White professor was racist. She subsequently took advantage of an anonymous survey given during the second week of class to tell the professor so. When we returned the following week, he confronted the class by saying that he was not racist and that he resented the implication. He took out his anger on the Black students, assuming that one of them had written the comment. In trying to be an ally and intervene with another White person, my White colleague had unwittingly made life much more difficult for all of the Black people in that context. She had not used her racial privilege as social capital for talking with him one-on-one but rather used it as a shield behind which she could bring up issues but remain invisible.

Autonomy: Helping to Build Beloved Community

The last status I have dubbed the "beloved community" (hooks, 1995) status in which White people develop the capacity to be antiracist allies to people of color and to one another. This status is one in which White people can stand with people of color against racism and all oppressions. I know I am autonomous when I am able to seek input, advice, and viewpoints of people of color. I know I am autonomous when I can hear feedback nondefensively and yet be able to have my own thoughts about race even if not all people of color agree with them. In some of my friendships I feel autonomous—able to be honest and vulnerable about the biases I'm still working to dismantle or the things I still don't understand, and yet confident and happy to be myself and a part of an authentic relationship in which everyone can be their full selves. I feel autonomous with my friend Chonika with whom I can talk about pregnancy, babies, pedicures, and health insurance—and when race comes up because of her experience or mine, we can talk about that, too. I can ask her why Black people don't smile at me in my neighborhood, and she can ask me why White people are always smiling at her.

When I first learned about Helms's White Racial Identity Development theory, it was so liberating to learn about this final status in which I could be a part of a healthy community and stand with people of color against all oppressions. I had spent so much of my life having a negative racial identity or experiencing awkwardness or guilt about race that it was a revelation to learn that, if I kept working at it, there was a status of racial identity development that would make all the work worthwhile. And while I don't feel that I get there every day, I can always be comforted by the knowledge that that's where I'm headed when I put in the time and energy to develop my racial identity. Contrary to what I once believed, feeling guilty for being White is not the end goal. The first time I really saw my students of color through the lens of my own autonomous racial identity, I realized how truly transformational it can be to teacher–student relationships. Suddenly I could really see my students of color in all of their wholeness—along with an understanding of the racist subtext that shapes their lives—and my view of them was less clouded by my own guilt, insecurities, and ignorance. The first time I moved through these statuses, it felt like each one took a few years. But now I can see myself passing through all of the statuses in a matter of minutes and, because I'm familiar with the process, it doesn't panic or destabilize me as it once did.

Helms writes that one of the markers of an "autonomous" identity is when a White person no longer feels that they have to rely on people of color to validate their opinions about race. Being autonomous in this way can be especially important for teachers because they often have to make decisions about what resources (e.g., books, movies, and posters) to use in the classroom and they should not have to run to a colleague of color each time they use something new. That does not mean, however, that White teachers should never ask people of color what they think; on the contrary, White people should constantly be checking in with colleagues of color about issues of race. But according to Helms's model, a White person who gets to the point where they don't have to validate their own opinions on race by getting affirmation from a person of color has achieved a measure of autonomy.

Learning about Helms's model was confusing to Cara, in part because she seemed to be looking for answers to some questions that she had been asking for many years. And she seemed to look at the White Racial Identity model (Helms, 2008) as an answer, rather as a general theory. She started to treat it like the list of race rules that she had been hoping to find. In the following example, it seems clear that she was using the model as a guide to how she should behave, rather than as a more general description of her current developmental status. When I asked her, in our final interview, what her plans were for the following year, she said that she wanted to get to know the parents of her students better:

> *Ali:* Would you do anything differently next year knowing how it went this year?
>
> *Cara:* I want to have conversations with my kids' parents one-on-one or whatever before we even get there because I want to know, you know, what do they think is important, what were things that . . . but that's deferring to Black people. That's one of those things I'm not supposed to do.
>
> *Ali:* Well they're very specific Black people. It's not just anybody. They're your kids' parents. I mean that's an important resource.

In this conversation, Cara was referencing Helms's model of antiracist development as a rule that delineated what she was and was not "supposed" to do. The model, however, does not say what an antiracist White person *should* or *should not* do, but rather that a person with a more highly developed racial identity will not rely on people of color to form their opinions about race and will start to develop their own opinions. Cara wasn't just trying to figure out where she fit on the model, but trying to imitate the typical behaviors of an "autonomous" antiracist White person, in order to fit herself into the place on the model where she thought a good "racially aware" White teacher would be.

The model was not helpful to Cara in this scenario both because of how she understood it and because of shortcomings in the ways that models like this consider individuals only in one dimension: race. The model led Cara to begin to think of her students' parents only as Black people and herself only as a White person. She did not want to have to rely on Black people to teach her about racism, which seems consistent with wanting to be at a particular place on the model. However, she was not talking about asking them to teach her about racism. She would be asking for her students' parents to help her better understand her students and the curriculum in her classroom. This is something that any parents should be consulted about, regardless of race.

The model also does not account for the ways in which White people who want to be antiracist White people absolutely must be in relationship with people of color in order to know what racism to fight in the first place. In actuality, in order to be effectively antiracist, White people need to be in constant communication with the people of color in their lives so that they (1) understand how localized racism affects the people of color, (2) check in about what kind of action or resistance is already in place, and (3) consider how any potential action or resistance might negatively affect them. White people working in isolation from people of color risk either disrupting the racial status quo in ways that have negative un-intended consequences for the people of color they work with, or overlapping or undermining the efforts that are already in place. Helms's model says that White people are autonomous when they find that they do not feel they need to be val-idated by people of color in order to express an opinion about racism; but that does not suggest that White people should work against racism without informed support from people of color, or that teachers should refrain from asking parents about their children. Particularly in a classroom, a teacher should constantly be working in collaboration with students' parents.

Helms's model cannot help us qualify the racial identity of the teachers I worked with. No person is ever in only one status. The statuses are fluid and circu-lar. Because the teachers were learning about aspects of racism they had not pre-viously known, most of them found themselves in the Contact status at different times throughout the year. Like the stages of grief, the cycle repeats itself with each subsequent loss; different experiences with racism can send one back through the statuses from the beginning. But all of the teachers had been through the first few statuses enough to be familiar with them and, while each was in a range of statuses at any given time, they tended to generally show signs of being in the Immersion/Emersion status, during which Whites try to *immerse* themselves in learning about race and Whiteness and *emerge* from a prior state of ignorance. This makes sense because they all joined their inquiry groups and my research voluntarily; they had experienced Contact, Disintegration, Reintegration, and Pseudo-Independence, and they were trying to learn more. Because the challenges of the Immersion iden-tity status are likely to affect most White teachers engaging in race inquiry, I will use the rest of this chapter to illuminate them.

NAVIGATING RACIAL ADOLESCENCE

The White teachers in the inquiry groups I observed were all highly motivated to learn about race, both in their groups and on their own, and had already done a fair amount of learning about race on their own. But they were still getting stuck in the Immersion/Emersion status, which is a period of racial adolescence. According to Helms's theory, White people in the Immersion/Emersion status tend to move from trying to help people of color fit into "Whitestream"[3] (Grande, 2003) norms and start trying to change White people and White institutions in-stead. This is partly what the teachers in this book were doing by joining the in-quiry groups. Immersion/Emersion status is a period of identity formation and thus, like adolescence, can be fraught with anxiety, self-image concerns, insecurity, and misalignment with peers or colleagues who are learning at a different pace. The paradox of this status, again like adolescence, is that all of the destabilizing elements of immersion are paired with taking steps toward independent thinking and self-definition.

Fears

I regularly hear from White teachers that they are afraid of making mistakes and thus proving that they are actually racist and thus hypocritical. Their logic is that if they are actually racist, then they have betrayed the trust of people of color who thought they were not. This fear stops people from taking risks that might reveal their racism. In my workshops, when I ask, "Why is it hard to talk about race?" teachers in every school say that it's hard to talk about race because they don't want to be racist. This fear is partially about public image; nobody wants to be seen as a racist. But the fear of looking like a racist is not the whole story; the teachers I work with and the teachers in this book didn't want only to not *look* racist—they didn't want to *be* racist. They love their students and want to protect them. Generally when White people are experiencing Immersion/Emersion, they have developed relationships with people of color to whom they feel accountable about race issues, and have simultaneously developed a personal practice around recognizing unconscious biases. This practice comes with a paranoia that one might easily offend without knowing. It's a continuation of "knowing that they don't know." And so people get awkward—I too get awkward—because they feel that the stakes are higher, that their colleagues trust them, that they recognize the hurt that unconscious bias can cause, and yet they are beginning to recognize the vastness of their inexperience and they fear the harm they might unintentionally cause because of it.

Getting beyond this fear requires a recognition that the work of uprooting unconscious bias is an ongoing, lifelong practice. We can never be finished doing this because the stimuli that lead us to generate such bias are constantly blaring. In my relationships with friends and colleagues of color, I find that they trust me more when I am honest about my process around dealing with unconscious bias. To people who understand the nature of racism, it would be disingenuous to act as though I have no unconscious bias and always act with a pure, antiracist consciousness. The pain and vulnerability that comes from acknowledging these biases are part of my racial story as a White person. People of color often share painful memories of being on the receiving end of this destructive dynamic. My story as a White person involves acknowledging my position in this dynamic that is either causal, or passively advantaged by it. The mutual acknowledgment that I am susceptible to racial bias, a sense of superiority, or acts of entitlement helps me be more open to feedback when it comes out.

Self-Image Preservation

In Immersion/Emersion status, people begin to identify with a new self-image as an antiracist White person, or a person who "gets it." They have joined a group or read a book or generally carved out time in their lives to engage with issues of race and racism. They begin to see themselves as antiracist. This is a point in

White Identity Development that can be particularly frustrating for people of color.[4] White people can get so caught up projecting and maintaining an antiracist self-image that it can be hard to take feedback that threatens that self-image (as my story about reading so many books demonstrates). Authentically *being* antiracist requires a humility and an ability to take feedback that can be incompatible with the self-image maintenance that goes along with *projecting* an antiracist identity.

This would not necessarily be so difficult if we didn't create such a binary around race understandings. In many schools, teachers often put one another into one of two camps: those who "get it" and those who "don't." In Sam's case, for example, he grew into his identity as a White person throughout his time at his school; twelve years after starting to teach there he was not the same kind of White person that he was when he first started teaching there. The following story demonstrates how that binary made it hard for Sam to access support and community around his transformative learning.

Break Down the Binary

As mentioned, when it comes to race issues, the faculty at many schools tend to break into two camps: those who "get it" and those who "don't." This binary freezes people in one camp or the other while preventing people who "get it" from taking risks for fear they will lose their spot. This dynamic negatively affected teachers like Sam, who, by virtue of the work he did in his inquiry group, was increasingly "getting it" but was unable to find support for his new learning in his old camp.

Unlike many Whites, including most of the other teachers in this book, Sam's membership in Whiteness was not implicit or taken for granted. As a Jewish child growing up in the South—where the rules governing membership in Whiteness tended to be more explicitly enforced—he had to work at becoming White through a process that was largely unconscious and that he recognized only in hindsight. I did not realize it until our work together ended, but Sam started identifying as a White man only in the year that we worked together. Until then, he would have identified as Jewish, not White.

> I've been busting my ass to—not get where I'm at because I'm just a high school teacher—but like I mean like I studied what it was like to be a White person like I'm sure a lot of Black people do . . . it almost feels like it's a different language and there are times when I'm reminded of that.

In elementary school, Sam was friends with Jewish kids from Hebrew school and Black kids from public school. He felt closer to the Black kids than the White kids at his school because the White kids were so anti-Semitic. For a few years in middle school and early high school, he was friends only with Jews, as he felt the anti-Semitism "coming from both sides, the Black and the White." With the terrain of Whiteness shifting underneath him in the 1960s and 1970s (Brodkin, 2004), it stands to reason that he did not feel that he fit neatly into any racial category. As he got into high school, he started distancing himself from both his Black friends and his Jewish friends, and started to become friends with White students, dating only White girls. In hindsight, he realized that he had actually started studying how to be White and found himself "code-switching," as he put it, in order to fit in:

> I spent massive amounts of time learning what it meant to be a Southern White person. . . . And my mom even said that I would choose these girlfriends with dads that like knew how to be Southern White men and I would try to learn from them.

Even as an adult, Sam was regularly reminded of the ways that he did not belong within the White mainstream. However, as a teacher in a Quaker school in 2011, he felt pressure from other teachers at the school to recognize that he did receive privileges because he was seen by most people within the school as a White person.

As we began interviews and observations, Sam reserved many of his thoughts and questions for discussion with me, rather than with his inquiry group. He did not find the inquiry group useful and preferred to be challenged by colleagues outside of the group. There are many possible explanations for this, but at least one has to do with racial identity. Sam went through so many changes in his racial identity during that first year of the inquiry group that he was significantly changed by the time he and I worked together in the spring. And yet, especially at the beginning, Sam slowed down the inquiry process for other teachers, sometimes deliberately. As he said himself, he joined the group to find out if they were going to try to abolish honors English—and to protect it. Early in the process, he positioned himself as an outsider to the race inquiry group, or as an irritant within it. He had a real transformation over the year, but many people who worked with him were not close enough to his process to see this transformation and had already written him off because of past interactions. The following quote demonstrates how much Sam valued the one-on-one interactions we shared outside of his inquiry group: "I feel like I can say whatever I'm gonna say and it's like, it's not just me being a Southern racist or blah blah blah."

Sam was joking when he referred to himself as a "Southern racist," but it was true that he did seem to be perceived as "less racially aware" by people who were known within his school to be the "more racially aware" teachers. I put that phrase in quotes not to mock the distinction, as the "more racially aware" teachers that he referred to were teachers for whom I had great respect, and who moved the entire race inquiry process forward with their persistence, knowledge, and experience. But I want to denote it as a classification that creates a binary in which some people are seen as "racially aware" while others are deemed "unaware," or in the language that I usually hear in schools, those who "get it" and those who "don't." In actuality, even those teachers who "get it" still have a lot to learn and others, like Sam, may have racial epiphanies that go unsupported because they have been pigeonholed as the "racist" or the one who "doesn't get it, can't get it, and won't ever get it." Understanding Racial Identity Development theory helps us remove the binary from race learning and begin to see ourselves and our colleagues on a spectrum instead.

During inquiry processes like this one, we have to expect people to change incrementally, and we have to learn how to relate to them anew when they do. In Sam's case, he had offended his "racially aware" colleagues at different points in the past so that they were unavailable to him as allies in his newfound learning. How do school communities allow for growth among colleagues, and accept that they might be different people (or might be trying to be different people) from year to year, even when they have previously offended us? This is especially difficult to do given that White people tend to get outsized recognition for minimal efforts to learn and change with regard to race. That kind of racial and social flexibility tends to be simply expected of people of color, while White people tend to get (and want and need) recognition for even the smallest changes. However, if we don't allow space for change, people like Sam end up being isolated in their change efforts. As a result, they get stalled or regress in their racial identities.

Antiracist Republicans

In a similarly dichotomous framework, I erroneously tend to assume that people who are politically liberal are better equipped to be antiracist than people who are politically conservative. Thus I was surprised when, in our last interview, Ann outed herself as a Republican. Very nonchalantly, she said, "I think that for our faculty we are a pretty educated group and mostly liberal. I know of two Republicans, and I'm one of them." By this point in our time together, she had shared so many of her thoughts about race and education that I had definitely typecast her as a liberal Democrat, like the other teachers in this book. Antiracist beliefs like hers did not seem congruent with my perception of Republican politics. Looking back on her interviews, it became clear that her values differed in slight but significant ways from those of the other participants. Ann was aggravated by the fact, for example, that her school did not say the Pledge of Allegiance—"there's nothing that unites the students." Also, in bemoaning the fact that the school did nothing to observe events such as Black History Month, she mentioned they did nothing for Veterans Day or 9/11 either. She expressed outrage that the one speaker on racism brought into the school was a guy from a rural area, who suggested that people from rural areas are all racists. She said, "It misrepresents people from rural areas." In discussing affinity groups for Black students, she said she understood that need because of her own experiences with affinity groups, but she still struggled with it:

> (B)elieve, me I totally get it. I belong to groups that are just for women, you know what I mean, Daughters of the American Revolution. Girls night, I get it. I'm a Girl Scout leader.

At the time, I thought little of these comments, seeing them as mere examples, albeit examples that I would not have immediately chosen; I do not necessarily believe that 9/11 or Veterans Day should be observed in schools, and I tend to see organizations such as the Daughters of the American Revolution as both elitist and observant of a colonial history that I do not want to celebrate. But I did not realize that some of her examples were reflective of some very real differences between us politically. After learning she was a Republican, I began to see all of these parts as reflective of a whole person who differed in substantial social and political ways from me and from the other teachers in the book. And yet she had more fully integrated her race learning into her teaching than any other teacher I worked with. Indeed, my own stereotypes of White people from rural areas who are patriotic, support the military, and lead Girl Scout troops inexplicably precluded being racially competent. Ann's case helps demonstrate, once again, how complicated and diverse antiracist White people can be.

> Like I'm very proud of the fact that in my Girl Scout troop I have two children of color. I'm very proud of that because, um, when . . . the (Black) mom of the one girl is so involved and she and I are more like co-leaders . . . she's a single mom and she works at a prison. . . . My other mommies are not really happy. They were like "well . . ." the first 2 years they didn't speak to her at meetings and stuff. They didn't know what to say to her.

Ann's case demonstrates that racial awareness is not necessarily a political stance, even though it is frequently conflated with liberal politics. This is a misconception on two points. First, as Ann's case illustrates, White people who vote Republican can be strong teachers, colleagues, friends, and Girl Scout troop leaders to people of color. Second, many liberals who are White believe that their liberal politics disqualify them from being racist. In fact, the two matters are largely separate, yet this misconception often hinders White liberals from seeing their own racism. Steve Biko, W.E.B. Du Bois, James Baldwin, and Richard Wright all warned against the insidious danger of the racism of "White liberals" who are not trustworthy allies because they believe that a liberal political agenda will right racial wrongs when, in reality, racial justice requires a consciousness of the inequities on which the entire society has been built, and a willingness to restructure that foundation. Our schools are actually full of liberal White people who believe they are not racist, and who do very little to intentionally support children of color. At times in my own development, I have been so tied to my self-image as an antiracist that I was less receptive to feedback or indicators that I might have room for improvement. Because her self-image was not tied to being an antiracist White person, Ann was particularly receptive to feedback, making her a more responsive antiracist White ally.

Not Trusting White Colleagues

A common trend in the Immersion/Emersion status expressed by many of the teachers was a general mistrust or critique of White colleagues. Many of the teachers I worked with seemed to feel that other White teachers would not have anything to teach them about race or that they would be called on to educate their White colleagues and they would not know how to do so. Their colleagues' ignorance threatened their own precarious new learning and growth. In the Immersion status, it is common for White people to rely on the perspectives of people of color and to be extremely judgmental of themselves and of other White people. A White person in Immersion might be just beginning to see other White people as potential antiracist colleagues.

When Helene's White colleague offered her support on developing her curriculum about Africa, it intimidated her. She said:

> And even Diana, who is in our group . . . she emailed me, like, "If you ever want to think about the Africa unit, let me know." And I've been like nervous to actually, before I knew her I was really intimidated by her. . . . What are we gonna do, like have coffee? And talk about . . . I mean what? . . . But I'm like, "I really should!" I mean, she's White but she's really thought about this.

Note how Helene suggests that Diana's Whiteness made her *a priori* less qualified to teach her about Africa, by saying, "She's White *but* she's really thought about this." This is not an altogether misguided hesitation; Whiteness remains a reliable indicator that a person likely has not thought or learned very deeply about racial issues. However, there do exist White people who have thought extensively about race and how racial issues manifest in schools.

Sometimes the White people who had thought the most about race were in competition with one another over how best to move the school and their classrooms forward with an antiracist agenda. Teachers in the inquiry groups often seemed to feel that the role of antiracist White teacher had already been taken by someone who had gotten there first or had been around longer. This kind of competition is not uncommon in antiracist White circles; it is a conceit I know from personal experience. I see this as a manifestation of White cultural values, such as individualism and competition, which lead to an expectation that I should be the best at whatever field I am in, even antiracism. This type of White group-level behavior (competition rather than collaboration) can be extremely destructive and is one of the ways in which White people sabotage our own antiracism efforts. Such behavior can stand in the way of productive collaboration with other White people and shift the focus away from working toward racial equity to simply attempting to highlight the White person who is acting in antiracist ways. As a White facilitator in our Philadelphia inquiry group said, "Sometimes I forget that it's not about me being the best White antiracist in the room, but that it's about ending racism. And that requires that we have as many competent antiracist White people as we can find." Becoming effective White antiracists means not only working to create antiracist classrooms but learning to collaborate with (and not alienate) our White allies and potential allies who make up the majority of the teaching force. This competition can also manifest as a tendency to monopolize antiracist initiatives and spaces, which can lead to a competition with people of color in our institutions, ultimately defeating the purpose of being an ally.

Knowledge of Racism a Surprising Barrier

Todd encountered points of "stuckness" that, surprisingly, were directly related to his extensive knowledge of African American protest history and the history of oppression in the United States. Because of this, he often readily excused bad behavior on the part of his students, all of whom were Black, because he felt they should not have to be held accountable for behavior that was shaped by such inconsistent and unfair circumstances. He had not yet learned how to apply what he knew about racial inequality to teaching in a way that would empower his students by giving them the tools they needed to be successful, rather than further punish them by keeping them, and their peers, uneducated. This made it difficult to hold students to high standards or to reprimand behavior that was detrimental to their or others' learning.

Impression Management

Cara seemed to get stuck in how to communicate her antiracist identity to Black parents. She wanted them to trust her and believe she had their children's best interests at heart. One of her greatest challenges was her sadness about the possibility that Black parents might see her as White first and not get to know her well enough to see her antiracist practice. One of Cara's main questions was, "As a White woman, how can I connect with the parents of my students in a more authentic way?" In the following quote, she explained how she struggled to have one parent trust her without coming right out and saying, "I'm trustworthy!":

> I'm really sensitive to the presumptions they might have about me and how I'm treating their children and the idea that maybe on some levels they could be right. . . . I think that's when I'm communicating with parents or preparing to communicate with them, and I'm getting the sense from this parent already that she has some trust issues about me as her child's teacher. What do I do with that? [laughs] And I don't want to be lumped with other teachers and I am lumped with all the teachers this kid has ever had (or

this parent has ever had) and I understand that. And I don't want to be apologetic because I think I'm trying to do a good job here and I'm trying to be cognizant about all these things. . . . But I don't feel like I could openly have a conversation like that that I'm different or that I think about these things at least, you know.

Cara wanted to be seen as an individual and not just a White person, and yet she understood why her students' parents might not be able to see past her race at first. I have heard White teachers who cannot understand this say such things as, "If Black parents are just seeing me as another White teacher before they get to know me, then they're being racist toward me." I do not agree. For White people living in a predominantly White world, many of us have been allowed to think of ourselves as "normal" or without race for most of our lives (Perry, 2002). It is only within a multiracial context, such as a classroom, that White people cannot escape reckoning with some of the uncomfortable realities of racialization, such as the fact that skin color is one of the first things we know about a person. When our students of color and their parents walk around in the world, most people likely see their race before they see anything else. And even though this can be hard for White teachers to reckon with, we have to acknowledge the reality of living in a world where race has so much power over the way we see one another, which is the experience of most people of color.

Cara understood all of this and wanted to know how to demonstrate to parents that she was not like all of the other White people they had met. During one of our inquiry group meetings, Cara sheepishly admitted that she sent the information about a Black Male Symposium at a local university to teachers and parents at her school. She said that she felt awkward about it because at some level she knew she was just doing it to let them know that this was a field that she was interested in learning about and that she was knowledgeable about some resources on Black boys.

Rather than see this as a cause for shame, the group supported her to see this action as a form of signifying/distinguishing behavior. Signifying behavior is a way of breaking out of the typical behavior of White teachers and indicating to parents that you might be a little bit different. Cara wanted to be a teacher that taught the whole child, and she wanted her students' parents to know that she understood that their children's needs, as Black children, were unique. Clearly, if sending out an email about a Black Male Symposium was the only thing that Cara did that differentiated her from the mainstream majority of White teachers, then parents might have put little stock in it. But to the extent that this gesture encouraged parents to watch for other signs of knowledge and understanding she had about race, it might have been a window that helped parents start to see a little bit more Cara and a little bit less "stereotypical White woman." The faster this can happen in both directions, the sooner the teacher and parents can build authentic relationships based on who they really are rather than on preconceived notions based on past experiences. Sending a notice about an event focused on race is a way of breaking the norm of colormuteness that is upheld by most White teachers. Listening nondefensively when a parent of color shares an experience they interpret as racism is another.

There is no easy way for antiracist White teachers to signal to parents that we might be different from other Whites. There is indeed no way to actually know whether we *are* qualitatively different from other Whites. But given that we think we might be, as Cara suspected she was, signifying behavior requires knowing the common, unthoughtful White reaction to a given scenario, and intentionally reprogramming in order to have a different response. For example, a common reaction from White teachers who think they are not going to be trusted because of race might be to blame the parent (maybe call the parent a racist or talk about them behind their back), to build up anxiety and resentment when talking to that parent, or to try to say explicitly, "You can trust me." But if the teacher knows that these are typical behaviors of Whites, and one understands why a Black parent might have trust issues with a White teacher, signifying behaviors might include respecting the parent's space while not taking personal offense to behavior indicative of a lack of trust. In the meantime, one might try to assert oneself in ways that help build trust, realizing it might take longer to build a relationship across racial difference.

STRENGTHENING THE TOOLBOX: BUILDING A POSITIVE WHITE RACIAL IDENTITY

Racial identity is about how one feels and what one understands about being the race that one is within a society that is structured by racism. It is not a political position or a stance one takes for work—it is a profound aspect of one's personal identity. It is a psychological process that does not happen immediately. When I was in the "Disintegration" status and I questioned whether I could continue to learn about racism given that I thought it meant a separation from my family, it was a crisis of identity for me. I was fortunate that my sister and I found ourselves in the same position at about the same time and we began this journey together. Our parents were ultimately receptive to hearing all that we were learning, and I'm not sure why. But I do know that after I told my dad I thought his viewpoint was racist when I was 20 years old, we didn't talk about race for a very long time. And by the time we began to talk about it again I had learned not to call people racist. I learned that families tend to keep showing up in our lives no matter what kinds of fights we have, so it doesn't make sense to argue about race every time we see each other, but rather to constantly engage, or offer engagement, to be open to questions, and to allow people to get comfortable talking about race. The lessons from my family are the same lessons I apply in my work. If people have anxiety attacks when they see me coming because I challenge their views each time we talk, I'm not going to be a great resource for their learning. But if they know that I will listen to their thoughts and questions, meet them where they are, identify with them, encourage them to keep noticing their biases and assumptions, and give them food for thought, they might be more likely to continue to engage with me in this process, which is ongoing. Fifteen years after that conversation with my dad when I used the "R-word," we have great conversations about race. We exchange books on the topic, and he asks me questions like, "So if race isn't biological, why are most basketball players Black?" I don't always know the answers to his questions, but he knows that I will explore them with him. And in doing so, not only has his racial identity shifted, but he has helped me to create a space within our family where my growing racial identity is welcome and safe. Building allies is not just about spreading a movement; it is also about recognizing that racial identity is a part of who we are and that we need a support network to help us sustain positive growth.

In one of my workshops I ask teachers of all races to share what people have done for them to help them develop their racial identities. For many teachers of color, developing a positive racial identity has been about having inspirational mentors of the same racial background, being taught about people of their race who have done great things throughout history, being given positive messages that directly contradict mainstream racist messaging (as in an Asian American mother telling her daughter, "I love your eyes because they are shaped like almonds" or a Black teacher telling Black students, "Look at all these beautiful brown faces I get to see every morning"), spending time with peers who look like them, and getting to read about people who look like them without always having to read about oppression. White people say they develop a positive racial identity by being taught about race and racism; learning the reality of American history, including examples of antiracist White people; having people they trust (both White people and people of color) point out their racial biases and disproportionality in their environment; being around racially diverse groups of people; and spending time in affinity groups with other antiracist White people who can challenge and relate to them in their learning. Both groups say that time to learn about racism in a concerted way, such as in inquiry groups like these, has contributed to their positive racial identity development.

CHAPTER 3

A Multicultural Curriculum Is Not Sufficient for Building an Antiracist Classroom

A team of consultants I worked with was asked to visit a school where a White 8th-grade English teacher had encountered problems teaching a book about Langston Hughes and the Harlem Renaissance in the 1920s. The school was a suburban public school just over the city line. It had historically been a predominantly White district and had recently become about 30% Black and 30% Asian American, leaving Whites in the minority for the first time in its history. That's part of the reason our team was working with the district to begin with; many of the White teachers who had started teaching there 20 years before had little training for or experience with teaching kids of color.

In this classroom, the teacher had chosen to teach the Harlem Renaissance in an attempt to provide "windows and mirrors"[1] to her students—"windows" to those who know very little about the history of African Americans in the United States and "mirrors" for Black students to see themselves in the curriculum. Thinking she was doing a good thing, she was unprepared for the resistance she encountered when a few Black boys in her sixth period class were outraged by the book and refused to read it. They took exception to the author's use of the word "negro."

The teacher tried to explain that "negro" was not *the* N-word. She said that the author of the book was Black. She cited the historical context in which Black people referred to themselves as "negroes." She was beside herself with frustration. The boys would not let it go. She felt they must be trying to stir things up. Her positive attempt to create windows and mirrors was being thwarted by what she saw as Black students playing the race card. She thought they were trying to humiliate her, and they were succeeding. If only she had not tried to read a book dealing with race, she thought, she would not be in this situation. The boys brought their parents in, and they insisted on outside mediation. That's how our predominantly Black consulting team got involved.

When our team came in, we did a workshop with the students. Among other activities, we asked all of the students to draw a picture of what they thought of when they heard the word "negro." Many of the Black students drew pictures of Black men being lynched. Frankly, everyone was taken aback. The boys had been picking up on an image that was in the minds of their Black classmates but that hadn't been spoken in the classroom. It was an image that made them feel victimized, threatened, alienated, and scared. And they did not trust this particular White teacher with their vulnerability. As they withdrew and refused to participate, their teacher saw only disturbance, aggression, and resistance. When they cited their discomfort with the word "negro," she saw only a lack of historical knowledge and ignorance. She blamed the students for this conundrum. Her repeated attempts to rectify the situation had involved further justification, self-defense, and accusation. She could not see how every time she misinterpreted the behavior and feelings of her Black students, she confirmed their fears that she could not be trusted to teach material about Black people. Every time she reiterated her intent, rather than listening to the impact on them, she added another brick to the wall between them.

Windows and mirrors matter. A multicultural curriculum is a critical part of any antiracist classroom. But it is not sufficient. As I have said, although a multicultural curriculum is a critical component of an antiracist classroom, it addresses only one of a myriad of factors that contribute to classroom life. Because curriculum is so tangible compared to more elusive factors such as relationships or communication styles, teachers often address curriculum as the first step to creating an antiracist classroom. But if a teacher does not have a strong racial identity, which includes a comprehensive understanding of racism and racial dynamics, they may not be able to teach windows and mirrors effectively. As teachers develop in their racial identities, they are better equipped to see the many ways that race affects their classrooms beyond the curriculum, and to begin to make changes in those areas as well. The teacher in our example still had so many unconscious biases toward Black boys and their families that she was unable to sympathize with them or hear their concerns; she immediately made wrong assumptions based on her biases and her fears of being seen as a racist. When she saw the pictures of lynchings that students had drawn, she realized how much she hadn't understood.

This chapter highlights just a few aspects of classroom life that must be considered when building an antiracist classroom. This includes—but is not limited to—group dynamics and the unwritten rules of behavior, the invisible (to some) ways that privileged students may enjoy disproportionate access and belonging in the classroom, communication and discipline styles, relationships with families, racial disparity, the implicit privileging of Whiteness, seemingly neutral but culturally loaded norms, and the home cultures of all of one's students. In this chapter we look closely at a kindergarten classroom and an AP English classroom to demonstrate that curriculum alone is insufficient for creating an antiracist space.

THE STUDENTS HAVE WINDOWS AND MIRRORS, BUT THEY STILL DON'T FIT IN . . . BUILDING AN ANTIRACIST KINDERGARTEN

Racial disparities in education start early. A recent report from the U.S. Department of Education Office for Civil Rights (2014) showed that while Black children make up 18% of preschool enrollment, they represent 48% of students having received more than one out-of-school suspension; White students make up 43% of preschool enrollment and 26% of children receiving more than one out-of-school suspension. What happens in preschool or kindergarten can have a significant impact on a child's experience of education, as well as a family's willingness to trust teachers and schools with their child.

This section grew out of Laurie's inquiry process in her kindergarten classroom at a Quaker Independent School. While her primary inquiry questions focused on curriculum, Laurie also asked the question, "How do I support students whose home cultures vary greatly from the school culture?" Given Laurie's intentional work in creating a multicultural curriculum, both of us were baffled by some of the ways in which certain Black students seemed to struggle in her classroom. She had an incredible library of books depicting protagonists and authors of all races, as well as posters on the walls reflecting faces of all hues. Yet there were two Black students who seemed to be excluded or demonized by their classmates at different times throughout the day. Additionally, within the first semester of school, three different Black families told Laurie that they were going to transfer their children to a different school the following year. What was going on that created these racially disparate levels of satisfaction and comfort in the school and in her classroom?

I am so grateful to Laurie for her contribution to this chapter and for asking such a wide variety of questions. As a researcher, I was as baffled by this dynamic as Laurie was and wanted to help her understand it. How and why does racism still manifest itself in the classroom of a racially conscious teacher with a multicultural curriculum? Laurie's kindergarten classroom seemed to be an incredible place for children. She had a great mix of exploration and instruction. She was loving to all of her students. The class was small and diverse; in her class of 13 students she had more students of color than White students. She infused the curriculum with great multicultural literature and led interesting conversations about that literature. When the topic of race came up, she did not shy away; rather, she engaged students fully. As the year progressed, we noticed things outside the curriculum that might have contributed to the negative experience her two Black students were having. I explore these in the sections that follow.

Group Dynamics and Unwritten Rules

There seemed to be a group dynamic that was punishing or excluding certain students in Laurie's loosely structured, experiential learning–based kindergarten classroom, one that Laurie did not seem to be causing. The group dynamic seemed to be reflecting our society at large. The lack of guidelines around free play in the classroom allowed unhealthy aspects of the group dynamic to persist unchecked. In other words, in order to make the group dynamic antiracist, Laurie would have to approach it as consciously as she did her literature curriculum. Because we live in a racist society, something as simple as free play can be a place where racism manifests itself. Here is an example:

> At 8:35, Franklin, a Black boy, entered the room and looked around at all the students. He briefly wandered over to the where the girls were lying down, but quickly got up to look at other options. He asked loudly of no one in particular, "Can I play at playhouse now?" Laurie said, "First come over here." Franklin had not yet started the moon craft project, whereas most of the students in the room were already finished. Franklin asked Laurie, "Was I late?" She responded, "Yes, you were." He looked down at the table in front of him.
>
> Another Black student, Celine, came into the classroom shortly after Franklin and lingered at the doorway, seemingly unsure where to go or what do.
>
> The girls in the house corner went up to Laurie to tell her there was a stinkbug in the corner. Laurie looked at me and said, "Stinkbug attack," and then captured it and flushed it down the toilet. "Most insects we release out the window, but not the invasive species."
>
> Laurie saw Celine and asked her to go to the crafts table to work on her moon project with Franklin. At 8:50 both students finished their "morning jobs" and left the crafts table. Franklin seemed to be frantically trying to find somebody to play with, darting from one group to another, while Celine seemed to wander around the edges of the classroom, unsure what to do.
>
> Mitchell, who was biracial, invited Franklin to play with spaceships. Celine finally found her way to the crafts table, where she chatted with the three girls who were working on their "Hamsa" bead projects.
>
> A Black student named Ava turned off the light. Laurie said, "Please freeze. Time to clean up and put everything back where it belongs. When you are finished, please meet me on the rug for morning meeting."
>
> Rather than beginning to clean up, Franklin picked up a spaceship and flew it over the tower that another student had built. Laurie told him not to frustrate the girl who built the tower and to find something else to do. He said he didn't want to play alone. She said maybe if he went into the playhouse corner, someone would join him. The rest of the students were putting away the toys and games they had been playing with since they arrived a few minutes after 8:00. Franklin started to cry as the other students tore down the structures they had built.

Laurie understood the notion of active and conscious antiracism when it came to literature. She demonstrated the belief that as teachers it is not enough to avoid being racist—we also have to act in ways that are intentionally antiracist to explicitly eliminate the racist impact on students. But applying this belief to the classroom dynamics was difficult, especially because her classroom was already structured according to a particular philosophy—one that valued free and unstructured time for kindergartners. The challenge for Laurie was how to continue to have a kindergarten classroom that was based on an experiential learning model yet still had enough rules to help students feel a sense of safety and belonging.

Formal instruction in Laurie's classroom began at 9:00 a.m., when students cleaned up from their informal playtime and the group convened as an entire class for the first time of the day. Students started to arrive as early as 8:00 a.m. and they had time to play freely with whatever or whomever they chose until 9:00 a.m. During free time, Laurie called them over to the worktable one or two at a time so that they could finish projects that they started the day before. Students tended to trickle in slowly between 8:00 and 8:15, and almost all of them arrived by 8:15. Many days, two students came in after 8:30 and sometimes closer to 8:50, leaving them only 10 minutes to play. These two students, Celine and Franklin, were both Black, and while they were not the only Black children in the classroom, they were the darkest skinned children in the classroom. While Franklin came from a middle-class family, Celine's family was working class, a part of her identity that further marginalized her among her middle-class and even wealthy peers. When they arrived, they often skirted the edges of the playgroups that formed in the first 30 minutes of free play before they arrived, and whatever they ultimately chose to do was cut short by the need for them to finish their work, as the other students had already done earlier in the hour.

Technically the students were not "late," but they missed out on important time to finish their projects and play or relax with peers before the day began. This might be one of the reasons that these two particular students didn't fit into the class socially the way the other students did. They tended to bounce from playgroup to playgroup and were often reprimanded by the other children who told them their behavior was not appropriate. They also missed out on the time meant to help them catch up on work. Part of the culture of the school seemed to be that arrival time was not strictly enforced. However, these particular children suffered big consequences as a result of their "tardiness." Not having a hard and clear rule about what it meant to be on time was hurting the children who did not get to school by 8:15.

Independent schools tend to have a long history of traditions and ways of being that are both explicit and covert, both articulated to the school community and unnamed as part of "how we do things around here." There are often ways of doing things that the entire staff and faculty understand but are never stated explicitly as a rule or expectation. Families are then left to rely on social networks with other families and with teachers to learn how things are done. Part of the culture of this school seemed to be that they did not enforce a strict arrival time.

The Alienating Effects of Privilege

The following example shows how privilege manifested in group dynamics during snack time in Laurie's classroom, as it is likely to do in any classroom:

> Franklin got the cookies first and took them one at a time, but then put one back and took a different one. The students at the table were already mad because he served himself first and they were then even more outraged when he put one back and took a different one. Laurie had already told them that he could take cookies first: "There's no reason why he shouldn't be able to take the cookies first," she told the other children.
>
> Celine took five cookies, and the other girls told her she couldn't take five. She put two cookies back and then the other girls told her people are going to get her germs. Bria, a Black peer, told her to throw the extra cookies away. Celine was clearly unsure what to do. She looked at me; she looked at the other girls. They said she had to throw them away because she already touched them, but she was not allowed to have five. She threw two away. She continued to stand throughout snack, not sitting down at the table with the other children. I wondered to myself how it must have felt for a child who came from limited economic means to be told by her wealthier classmates that she had to throw a cookie in the garbage because she touched it.
>
> Snack was Nilla Wafers and tortilla chips. Some of the same children who had sanctioned Celine about the extra cookies asked Laurie if there was any salsa. She told them no. Halfway through snack, the same students (two White and one Black) got up from the table, went to the refrigerator, and found salsa in the refrigerator to eat with their chips. This was striking to me after Laurie had already told them there wasn't any. When they found it, Laurie put out salsa for all the kids on individual plates. Their action struck me as a demonstration of their sense of belonging and ownership in the classroom, both also a possible consequence of social privilege (both class and racial).

In this example, the actions of the two children who were most excluded in the classroom were highlighted and derided by their peers. They both got in trouble for touching the cookies, and they both seemed alienated and alone during the rest of snack time as a result of their interactions with peers. When the antagonizing students sought out salsa, the teacher not only allowed them to get out the salsa once they had located it but proceeded to pour it onto their plates for them despite the fact that the snack had been set out for them and she had already told them there was no salsa. It was not clear what was and was not permissible. In Franklin's case, a teacher reprimanded the students for correcting him. But no adult noticed when the girls corrected Celine. How did this scenario help her understand what was right and wrong, or whether she belonged in the classroom?

Because the rules were not clear and the classroom was generally permissive, both Franklin and Celine were heavily monitored by their peers. Whenever I visited, they would either get told on by their peers for a minor infraction, or they would be reprimanded by their peers. I wondered how the flexible rules of the classroom exacerbated their marginalization. Again, there is nothing that Laurie was doing to purposefully exclude them; if anything she was going out of her way not to reprimand them in order to minimize their alienation. However, the lack of explicit boundaries and expectations seemed to lend power to certain students over others. I wondered if Laurie's defense of Franklin ultimately meant that the students felt that they needed to watch him with more scrutiny. I also wondered if more explicit boundaries might help Franklin understand what was expected in this classroom.

Culture Impacts Communication and Discipline Styles

Lisa Delpit (2006) writes about how some Black students in White teachers' classrooms can misinterpret directions because they may be more accustomed to direct, authoritative instruction. A White middle-class teacher who believes that her authority is derived from her role as a teacher might give directives in the form of a question, such as "Do you think it's time to start working now?" rather than giving direct instruction, such as "It's time to start working now" or even "Get to work now." This might make it difficult to communicate actual intentions to students who are accustomed to instructions that are more direct. Laurie might have been giving instructions in a way that minimized her authority in the classroom. One morning Laurie asked, "How about if everyone sits right?" Most of the students in the classroom crossed their legs, and Franklin laid down on the ground. She did not correct him. This difference in cultural styles might be particularly pronounced in early grades such as preschool, kindergarten, and 1st grade because students are often accustomed to spending more time with parents, extended family, or in neighborhood preschool programs that reflect their families' cultural styles. In older grades, on the other hand, students have often learned to assimilate over time via the peer and teacher sanctioning they receive when they do not conform.

Once a week, the health teacher, who was African American, came into Laurie's room to teach wellness for an hour. As soon as Craig came into the room, students scrambled for his attention, and he said, "Oh no, we're not calling out, we are not going to do that today, raise your hand if you want to speak." Students then sat cross-legged and upright on the carpet, hands raised, waiting for him to call on them. He would then go on to demand specific behavior from students. He said, "I'm looking for students who are sitting quietly. I don't see everyone's eyes." When all children were sitting according to his expectation, he would say, "Now I have a group where everyone's ready." He would then begin his lesson with a whisper. He stopped talking when Mitchell called out, and Mitchell put a hand over his mouth. He would not continue the lesson if all of the children were not following the rules. His style was consistent and firm. Laurie routinely asked her students to do things in a way that is commonly perceived by White people to be polite and gentle but could be perceived by people with a different style of communication as passive and indirect. This is not wrong—it is a difference in cultural styles. But it does lead to a communication breakdown, which disproportionately punishes the children who are accustomed to a different cultural style. When Black children perform well in the classrooms of Black teachers and struggle with White teachers, there is a good chance that some form of this communication dynamic is at play.

Relationships with Families

Another of Laurie's inquiry questions was why Black families were leaving the school. Three Black families had shared that they might leave the school, and she wanted to know what she could do to make things better for her students and their families. She was generally great at communicating with parents and welcoming parents and grandparents into the classroom as volunteers. But she felt really limited in both her understanding of the parents who wanted to leave and her ability to help them. When she talked to one family about this, she found that the family wanted there to be more structure in the kindergarten classroom. They wanted worksheets, homework, and more structured learning; the experiential play–learning model did not look like learning to them. She was caught in a double-bind in which she felt she was responsible to her stated pedagogical philosophy, the norms of her school community, and the expectations of other parents. She didn't feel that she was in a position to honor their requests, and ultimately she felt that this mismatch of expectations suggested the school might be the wrong fit for the families, as most other teachers probably would.

This is an institutional issue that was really beyond Laurie's control. Her answer to this dilemma was likely the same answer her head of school would have given in this scenario. But I believe there is room to challenge this longstanding way of doing things. When schools are actively trying to recruit families of color, it might be worth asking in a situation like this, "What would it look like to honor the requests of families who want the classroom and the schoolwork to be more structured? How much would it compromise our progressive values to honor their requests? Is there a way in which it is in line with our values of inclusion to sacrifice certain teaching methods in order to accommodate methods preferred by some families of color?" For progressive schools in particular, it seems critical to ask, "To what extent is the school open to changing in order to accommodate the values and beliefs of the families that comprise the school?"

Laurie felt that Black parents' requests for worksheets and homework, in particular, were contrary to the educational philosophy of the school and that they were emblematic of a bad match. She might not have felt she had the agency needed to make the necessary changes they desired. In observing her struggle with this dilemma, it occurred to me that the educational philosophy of the school should be dynamic: a synthesis of the school's resources and the family's expectations. Certainly many White middle-class parents made demands on this school regularly. Teachers frequently shared examples of how White parents got what they wanted from the school, regardless of how incompatible it was with the school's overall philosophy. White students who didn't qualify for honors classes in high school, for example, were sometimes placed there anyway with enough persistence from the parent. In another elementary classroom, parents who were afraid of letting their children go into the city during a unit on local geography managed to get that trip canceled. It might be useful to question why it is that when White parents complain, they often get what they want, whereas when Black parents complain, the school assumes it is a bad match rather than working with them to honor their requests. A race question to raise in this context is, "How can I honor each family's values about education in my curriculum each year?" This question takes multiculturalism a step beyond the inclusion of artifacts and holidays, and acknowledges the deep connections between culture, learning styles, and educational values. Additionally, families need support adjusting to a new school culture. When a given family does not seem to fit in with the school culture, this might be an indication of a communication breakdown (including confusing or unstated rules) rather than an inherent mismatch. The more explicit a school can be with school and classroom philosophies, expectations, and procedures, the easier it will be for families and children to make informed decisions about how to participate.

Inquiry Impasse

Laurie's original question, "How do I support students whose home cultures vary greatly from the school culture?" was a great question, and yet it led her to an *inquiry impasse* because it was impossible for her to see the many different answers just discussed. Laurie could only answer her questions with what she already knew, and so the answer to how to support students with a different home culture became "multicultural literature." This was the answer to most of her questions because it was the answer she already had access to. And while it was part of the answer, it was not all of the answer. Neither of us could see from the outset that the questions she needed to ask included "How does my communication style contribute to the marginalization of some students?" and "How does the group dynamic exclude some children while including others?" These questions are questions about who she is, how she communicates, and what assumptions she has about how classrooms should work; these are taken-for-granted aspects of the classroom that are difficult to recognize, much less change for any teacher. For teachers engaged in race inquiry, it can be important to ask oneself about these aspects of one's practice and to work with a partner who can act as an outside observer. Rather than thinking about "windows and mirrors" exclusively in relation to curriculum, we could start thinking about them in relation to observation relationships with other teachers. Observation partners can hold up mirrors for us to see what we look like from the outside and, in observing others, we get windows to other ways of teaching and relating to students. Observation windows and mirrors can help us raise the race questions we might not otherwise know to ask.

This section looked at some of the things Laurie could do to counter some of the more subtle effects of racism in her classroom as she worked to create an antiracist space. But there is so much more that affects a child's experience that we did not address, including interactions with other adults in the school beside the classroom teacher, such as other parents, administrators, administrative assistants, nurses, counselors, and coaches. We did not include admissions and recruiting practices (relevant to independent schools), schoolwide events, or community traditions. I mention this in closing this section to highlight the limited nature of a teacher's influence. Laurie did not have control over her students' experience of the school outside of her individual classroom, and sometimes it is the larger school culture that determines whether a family and a student feel that a school is the right fit for them. (See Appendix A for Laurie's response to this analysis.)

THE CURRICULUM IS MULTICULTURAL, BUT THE AP CLASS IS NOT

I now turn to a high school classroom to look at this same idea, that a multicultural curriculum is not sufficient for building an antiracist classroom. During one day of observations, I sat in on Sam's Advanced Placement (AP) English class in the upper school of a Quaker Independent School and I noticed, with some surprise, that the class was entirely White. Especially because of all that Sam and his colleagues were changing and analyzing in their English program with regard to race, I was surprised there were no students of color in the AP class. When I first asked Sam about their absence he seemed, understandably, defensive. I was putting him in the awkward position of having to question a program that he had not only worked hard to develop but also to make racially equitable. I also doubted my own question. I knew that if the department could find Black students they considered "qualified" to be a part of the AP program, they would place them there in a heartbeat. The fact that one small AP class at one small independent school had only White students is probably not statistically significant. And yet, given all of the ways that Sam was discovering how his curriculum, questions, class discussions, and assignments privileged White students, it seemed appropriate to question whether the disproportionate representation of White students in AP English was possibly related. In this case, creating an antiracist classroom required seeing the racial disparity and working to change it.

After his initial defensive reaction, Sam said to me, "No, I want to hear what you think. Be honest with me. Let me know if I'm way off base here. I want to be honest with you, but I want to hear what you think."[2] I include Sam's response verbatim because it demonstrates such an important skill in raising race questions. It is only natural to react defensively when outsiders help us critically analyze our teaching. And yet, if we want help thinking about our classrooms, we need to find ways to override our initial defensive reactions, as Sam does here, so that we do not shut down the very people who we have asked for support. Sam's reaction, which was to acknowledge that he had not heard my whole point and to invite me to share, models this kind of openness.

I told him that when I see only White kids in a higher-level class within a school as racially diverse as his, I perceive it as an indication that something might be wrong in terms of how they prepare, screen, and admit students to those higher-level classes. I compared race to gender and said that if they had AP math or English classes with only boys in them, they would recognize that as a problem and try to figure out what was going on. They would be asking the girls why they were not signing up or why they were not interested, or they would be asking why they or others might think they were not qualified to be in such a class. Most important, they would name the problem: There are no girls in AP math. Because talking about gender disparity is more widely acceptable in U.S. society, they would not be afraid to name it. The absence of students of color from AP English is just as important. But because we are afraid to name racial dynamics, it is often easier to let a problem go unacknowledged and unaddressed rather than say, "I noticed there are no Black students in AP English. Why is that?"

Raising Questions About Disproportionality

By the time of my next observation in Sam's classroom a few weeks later, he had changed his action research question to investigate how to get more kids of color into honors classes, as those classes were the pipeline to AP English. "I'm a gatekeeper," he said. And he wanted to change that.

Because Sam was focused on the question of how to get more Black students into honors English, rather than whether to abolish honors all together, he eventually developed more questions about how to support Black students without marginalizing them.

> And then I started reading that Ted Sizer [Sizer & Sizer, 2000] book, the yellow book, the new one. And in that one there's a chapter about kids who want to get into honors and he didn't say you can't get into honors, but he said you sit down with your advisees and you say, "This is what you really need to work on and we're gonna spend this year trying to help you work on it."

Rather than abolish honors, Sam wanted to diversify honors by giving increased support to students of color who wanted to be in honors English. But he struggled with whether a support class that primarily targeted Black students would be too controversial or bad for the students themselves.

> See we're always leery of a room full of all Black kids, you know, especially if it is like trying to help them all write better multiparagraph essays or whatever it is, right, because then they could be labeled or something like that instead of saying it as, which I think I heard you say, you don't need to look at it like that, it's like how can we enhance their opportunities, I guess.

It seems there are three critical points to consider in this scenario: First, if Sam does not give students support because he is afraid of implying they are remedial, they will not advance. According to Lisa Delpit (2006), liberal White teachers are often afraid to give students the support they need because we do not want to suggest they are less capable. As a result, we do not give them support and the students, in turn, are indeed less capable. In the words of anthropologist of education Mica Pollock, "Our very confusion over when to talk as if race matters helps recreate a world in which it does" (p. 17). If indeed there are more students of color who need extra support in order to qualify for honors English, it would be wrong not to provide opportunities for that support simply because it would be disproportionately accessed by Black students.[3] Ironically, while the presence of only White students in a classroom was barely notable, the school took pains to avoid creating a classroom that was predominantly Black.

That said, the second critical point in this scenario is that if Sam did create a support group for students interested in gaining the requisite skills to join honors English, he might find that non-Black students choose to access it as well. The program will also probably be more successful if students do not perceive it as the sole territory of one racial group, as they might see AP classes.

The third point to consider here is that a seeming lack of preparedness for honors level participation might be at least as much about the school, the curriculum, the assignments, the classroom dialogues, and students' identities as it is about the students' actual preparedness. It might not be about the students' skills at all. Finally, programs that are framed in terms of challenge and enrichment, rather than remediation, are almost always more successful. Academic improvement is not only about skill building, but about identity formation, and support programs must therefore be designed with the intent of creating and encouraging scholars rather than playing "catch up."

It's Not Just What We Teach But How We Teach It

In Sam's case, he began to realize that students of color were disadvantaged not just by *what* he taught but *how* he taught. Over the course of our time together, he shared three examples of realizing that by not being intentionally and consciously antiracist, he was inadvertently gearing his lessons and questions to his White students.

> At the end of the *Great Gatsby* test, I said, "Now who would you like to date or eat lunch with from *Great Gatsby*?" And I was thinking maybe the three

Black guys don't want to eat with any of those people. Where I'm at right now, I just feel like I don't have to teach the same old shite anymore. I love the classics, but it doesn't make sense that they could come in my classroom and not feel like they're connected to it.

Seeing his classroom through a racial lens, Sam began to see the ways that White students avoided talking about race, even when it was very obviously an appropriate, and sometimes critical, point of discussion relative to the literature they were reading (see Chapter 4 for more details on talking about race in the classroom). In some classes the students ignored any reference to race. In others, the conversation about race stayed between Sam and his Black students. The rest of the class did not run with that topic. This is understandable, given that they live in a society—not just their school and classroom—in which colormuteness is the dominant approach to discussions of race. But it is so obviously counterproductive when a literature class is reading a book such as Toni Morrison's *Beloved* or Zora Neale Hurston's *Their Eyes Were Watching God* in which African Americans are the primary characters, the author is African American, and the exploration of race is a primary part of the plot. This reluctance or inability to engage the conversation is a way in which colormuteness renders all students, including White students, less capable and less competent in a racially diverse society. If a teacher includes multicultural literature in the curriculum, but White students' views on that literature are the only views that count or come up in class discussions with peers, then the multicultural literature has only reinforced the status quo—it has not led to an antiracist classroom. (See Appendix A for Sam's response to this analysis.)

BUILDING AN ANTIRACIST CLASSROOM

Teachers are sometimes taken aback when told they are going to have professional development that focuses on "antiracism training," saying, "But we're not racist." I respond that the training does not assume they are racist. But it does assume that in order to create an antiracist classroom, it's not enough to not be racist. Anthropologist Ruth Frankenberg (1993) does not use the term "integration" to describe racially integrated communities because she says it is impossible to have true integration when the broader society is so segregated. Instead she uses the term "quasi-integration." Similarly, within a broader context of racism, individual teachers are always acting as intermediaries with the world outside, where racial inequality is part of the status quo. Creating an antiracist classroom requires a conscious antiracist practice. The following section describes the different actions required for building antiracist classrooms that the focal teachers discovered during their year of inquiry. I close the chapter with a vision of what an antiracist classroom might look like.

An Antiracist Classroom Requires Recognizing the Implicit Privileging of Whiteness

Antiracist inquiry requires seeing the race of all students, including White students. This particular category of students did not receive much explicit attention in the form of inquiry questions. As teachers developed the courage to ask questions about racial trends or particular student groups, they tended to ask questions about Black students as if they were the only students whom racialization might affect, rather than asking questions about how White students play into the racial dynamic as well. The following example demonstrates how much a White student's sense of centrality in the classroom can alienate students of color (Black students in these examples) and how difficult it can be to intervene with this sense of entitlement.

Ann taught special education in a suburban public high school. One of Ann's main questions was: "Do I talk to all of my students equally?" Overall, Ann was consistent in the ways that she responded to students with high expectations and humor/sarcasm. But there were a few instances when I noticed a difference in how she talked to students, a trend she had asked me to look out for. One of these instances was with a wealthy White student. On this particular day he wanted to go to the library and also wanted Ann's help on his homework; he would not stop hounding her until he got it. Ann was working with a Black student named Keisha. This is an example of allowing White students to use their privilege to assume a centrality they do not deserve:

> [For about 10 minutes, Doug read his essay out loud, trying to get Ann to help him. She had just told him that she would not help him until she finished working with Keisha, but he was sitting by himself reading in a voice that suggested that he expected her to be listening and that he was reading it for her sake.]
>
> *Ann:* What are you writing about?
> *Keisha:* Romeo and Juliet.
> *Ann:* Not just them—about what.
> *Keisha:* It's about true love.
> *Ann:* That's a true statement, but what's your essay about? . . . I picked out the four themes from *Romeo and Juliet* that are easiest to understand. If you had to pick three of those, which three would you pick?
> Keisha looks over the themes.
> *Doug:* Can I go to Ms. Gatto [the librarian]?
> *Ann:* No, I feel so left out when you say that.
>
> [Ann left Keisha and looked at Doug's work over his shoulder. She said to him, "The difference between this sentence and this sentence is that this is a 9th-grade sentence. This is the sentence of a student preparing to go to college."

She made a move as if to go back to working with Keisha, and he said, "Hold on, don't go anywhere." She went back to working with Keisha. About 30 seconds later, Doug interrupted again.]

Doug: Am I allowed to go to the library soon?
Ann: Oh honey, you're like a dog with a bone.
Doug: Okay, I really want to go to the library.
Ann: I know.
Ann (to Keisha): Okay, so you picked three out of those four—which one of those do you want to do?
Doug: I wrote this thing like five times. May I please go to the library?
Keisha: No, she said no.

[This is the first point where Keisha spoke up against him. He had been interrupting her time with Ann during the entire class.]

Doug: Can I just read you what I have so far?
Keisha: Didn't you just read that to her? Oh my God, Doug, stop, she's got to help me.
Ann (to Keisha): Just wait—let him read.

[He reads it again]

Doug: Now can I go?
Ann: Wait!
Keisha: You can't go to the library.
Ann: What are you going to do? You're going to play games, I know.
Doug: I have no math. I can work in bio.
Doug: Just, please? Come on, Harper [referring to Ann by her last name].
Ann: You can't go tomorrow—I'm going to have a sub and leave very specific instructions.
Doug: I won't go to the library tomorrow.
Ann: Oh, I know you won't.
Doug: Thank you, Ms. Harper, enjoy the rest of your day.
Ann: Okay, and I have the books for your mom.

In this scenario, Doug wanted Ann's help, and he wanted to leave the room to work in the library. He persistently interrupted Ann's work with Keisha until he got both of the things he wanted. Keisha became increasingly vocal throughout the scenario, as Ann failed to communicate to Doug that she would not listen to him. Neither Doug nor Ann intended to be hurtful or disrespectful to Keisha. However, by tacitly allowing Doug's persistent interruption, Ann lost many minutes of work with Keisha that she might have had otherwise. Keisha clearly wanted Doug to stop interrupting but did not have the power to make that happen.

This scenario played itself out in other classrooms as well, most notably during teacher–student writing conferences. The way it played out was the same as in this scenario: The teacher would be working one-on-one with a Black student, and they would be repeatedly interrupted by White students who seemed to feel entitled to the teacher's time. The behavior was barely notable, except that the reverse did not seem to happen; Black students did not seem to interrupt when the teachers were working one-on-one with White students. White students seemed to literally *white out* (Doane, 2003) their Black peers, inserting themselves in front of the teacher (both physically and in terms of attention) so that their Black peers were rendered momentarily invisible.

Another thing that stood out in this scenario was the way that Ann framed Doug's choices in his essay writing, giving him the choice between a freshman sentence and a college sentence which, in my limited observation time, she had not offered to other students. I found this assumption that Doug was college-bound ironic, given his immature behavior in contrast to Keisha's respectful behavior. But looking back, I wonder whether indeed his entitled behavior, which ultimately functioned as a form of self-advocacy with no negative repercussions (except, perhaps, damage to any relationship he had with Keisha), might ultimately be the more successful attitude within a college setting, where students must know how to self-advocate and where White males do not tend to be punished for aggressive and self-interested behavior. This just seems like one more way that behavior conditioned by social privileges such as Whiteness gets rewarded. (See Appendix A for Ann's response to this analysis.)

An Antiracist Classroom Requires Interrogating Seemingly Neutral, Culturally Loaded Terms

One critical way that teachers asked questions about themselves throughout their inquiry involved looking more closely at their personal definitions of *disruption*, a relative concept that too often gets treated as if it is an objective idea and not a culturally loaded concept.

One of Helene's "untouchable" questions[4] was: "Do I yell at my Black students too much? They make more noise than everyone else." In support of her inquiry, I suggested to Helene that she consider classroom distractions other than "noise." In my observations of her room and of other classes in the school, there did not seem to be standards for what the noise level was supposed to be; teachers simply asked students to quiet down every 10 minutes or so, and they did. I pointed out that there were some students who got in trouble a lot—every time it got loud—because they were the loudest ones. But, I suggested, if you stop and look around when you hear those students, often there were others who were contributing equally to the overall atmosphere of chaos. They were not being "louder" than everyone else—so they went unnoticed—but they were significant contributors to the general spirit of free-for-all. Seeing this was confusing to me as a visitor, and it made me wonder what the standard for behavior was. The students did not realize that noise, for Helene, was more offensive than other rude and inappropriate behaviors. As a result, to an outsider, it did seem that the loud kids got in trouble more than other students who might have been distracting the class just as much. These included typical 2nd-grade behaviors such as skipping to the sink, blowing fart noises into one's elbow, or quietly but constantly talking about a completely unrelated topic during an independent work period. And though not all of the Black students got in trouble for making noise on a regular basis, the three students who were reprimanded daily for making noise were all Black.

Helene decided to look not only at her patterns with Black students but also those with White students. She began to notice the subtle ways that her White students interrupted the class in ways that did not trigger a disciplinary response. One morning, Helene was sitting with the whole class on the rug going over the agenda for the day. One of her White students raised his hand and, changing the topic of conversation, asked if he could put up the calendar. Helene said, "Sure." A few minutes later, another White boy interrupted to ask if he could put up birthdays on the calendar because it was his birthday. Again, Helene said, "Sure."

These interruptions were characteristic of a general trend of White children seeming to feel ownership and entitlement to interrupt. Because they were doing so in a way that fit the norms of what was appropriate—by raising their hands and asking to do something that counted as a legitimate classroom interaction—they did not get reprimanded even though their behavior was potentially as distracting as talking while the teacher was talking. Their behavior had the same effect of getting the class off-task, focusing the attention on themselves, and taking up time. Given Helene's concern about telling Black students to be quiet too frequently, I suggested that perhaps she should shift her gaze away from the Black students altogether. Most teachers did not have practice examining the silent and insidious ways that they let White children have more power, centrality, or access in the classroom. Because such students assume access or belonging in ways that fit with the classroom culture, teachers might be more tolerant of their behavior, even when it constitutes a disruption. Helene might never stop reprimanding kids for making noise, but she could begin evenly distributing her reprimands by noticing all of the ways in which the class is interrupted by distractions other than "noise." One potential inquiry question is, "Do I define disruption in a way that favors the cultural styles of one racial group over another?"

An Antiracist Classroom Requires That We Talk About Language and Code-Switching

The theme of accommodating cultural style differences came up with many of the teachers and helped me to continue thinking about questions I've been asking since I started teaching. One question that repeatedly arose throughout this research was whether and how to honor the cultural styles of the students and their families when these differed from the majority of the students and the teachers themselves. Teachers felt it was their role to help students fit into the school culture and wondered to what extent they needed to correct students' language, particularly with regard to Black students who spoke African American Vernacular English (AAVE). As discussed in Chapter 2, questions about language and code-switching often fall into the category of "untouchable questions"— questions that feel racist to ask and yet need to be asked in order to build an antiracist classroom. Helene was particularly skilled at leaning into these hard questions and giving them voice and, as a result, her questions are the ones that frame this section. But she is not alone in asking them. The following quote is from Helene, who was unsure how much to intervene with a child (Wendell) in her 2nd-grade classroom who spoke AAVE:

> I mean, even my one kid who talks, I don't even know how to say it, but, in a Black dialect, if that's the way to say it. I mean . . . how much do I correct him? . . . I brought it up in a co-counseling setting and was just like, "What do I do?" and the woman I talked to was like, "You tell them that all people talk different, and that every way is great, that the way he talks is great, but there's different ways of talking in different settings." So I tried to have that conversation with him, but his way of, his thinking just wasn't there yet.

Helene was concerned about how to teach Wendell what he needed to learn to be successful, and she recognized that speech was somehow related to success. She said:

> I think the point I would want to get across is like just because more of us speak in this way doesn't make it better and just because that's . . . I don't know, there's something about that (Standard English) being expected in school and the future—jobs—that it seems important.

Wendell essentially spoke a different language, and Helene feared he needed to learn Standard English[5] to be successful in school. Language scholars (Cummins, 2000; Nieto, 2009) have demonstrated the importance of seeing dual-language learners as coming to school with more assets than single-language learners, rather than seeing the home language as a deficit that holds the student back from proficient development in the school language. But language scholar Terrence Wiley (2005) suggests that this is harder to do with AAVE because racism often finds a socially acceptable outlet in language prejudice: "Language is often used as a surrogate for more salient issues involving race and class in the USA. Consider how one often can get away with criticizing someone's language, allegedly for 'correctness,' 'appropriateness,' or 'accent.' In civil discourse, however, one cannot get away with criticizing one's race or social class" (p. 10). Because

AAVE is a denigrated language variety in the United States, creating an antiracist classroom requires modeling and teaching respect and inclusiveness for it, as Helene wanted to do. Wiley says, "Many children who come to school will be disadvantaged by the perception that they are deficient unless it is recognized that differences are quite natural" (p. 4).

The main pedagogical issues for Helene were (1) how to respond to questions from Wendell's peers about how he spoke and (2) whether and how to teach Wendell "Standard English." In "Using the Vernacular to Teach the Standard," John Rickford (2005) suggests three ways for teachers to teach the standard dialect while building on AAVE as an asset. The first is the "linguistically informed" approach, in which teachers have a deep enough knowledge of AAVE that they can recognize that students might not be miscoding words when they read but simply reading the word on the page with the pronunciation of the AAVE language variety. The second is the "contrastive analysis" approach, in which teachers explicitly teach the differences between AAVE and "Standard English," "which allows students to negotiate the line between the two much more effectively" (p. 29). The third approach is "introducing the vernacular, then switching to the standard." In this approach, students are instructed in the vernacular for a number of years and then transition into the standard. Rickford reports that students taught via this approach quickly surpassed students who were taught only in the standard throughout their schooling.

Lisa Delpit (2006) suggests some practical ways that White educators who do not speak AAVE could implement the contrastive analysis approach to help teach Standard English, which she calls "the language of power." She suggests arranging mock interviews or a mock dinner party in which Standard English is required, emphasizing the contextual nature of language. She also suggests, when a student expresses himself in a task that does not require the use of Standard English, that the teacher focus on the meaning of his words rather than the language of delivery. Failure to affirm home language, particularly with AAVE, which is so disrespected in mainstream society, can contribute to silencing children altogether.

Helene had read Delpit's book and planned to read it again. She understood much of the theory behind affirming a child's home language while also explicitly teaching him to use Standard English in particular circumstances. This felt especially challenging for her to do in a classroom in which Wendell was one of only two students who spoke AAVE regularly. She did not want to single him out, but she also did not want to neglect her responsibility to him, if indeed it was her job to teach him Standard English, which she was unsure of.

This is a question that I have long struggled with. I still remember substitute teaching in a Pittsburgh public school right after college and correcting Black students one after another as they answered a fill-in-the-blank worksheet in an English class. Each of them gave responses in African American Vernacular, which I in turn changed to Standard English, passively correcting them by citing the "right" answer after they had answered. I remembered that moment a few years later when I, red-faced with shame, read Lisa Delpit's *Other People's Children* in which she describes how and why to teach the standard while valuing and honoring the home language. I had had no idea that African American Vernacular could be a home language that tied children to their parents and grandparents; I had grown up believing it was just the wrong way of talking and needed to be corrected.

The teachers I worked with acknowledged that their students of color often had to be bicultural in a way that they themselves did not even know how to be. When there was a difference in cultural styles, it was always the children who were asked to change. At one point Helene and I imagined what it might be like if the teachers, and not the students, took on the burden of code-switching. And while that image seemed ridiculous at first, it occurred to us that code-switching is hard enough when one is consciously aware of why one is doing it; how much harder must it be for students who don't understand why it is necessary? From this conversation, I began to believe that it should be a requirement of our jobs as teacher that we be able to recognize and accommodate differences in cultural styles, including language, without demanding that children conform to our styles. And in the meantime, we should question why it is that the children, not the teacher, are usually the ones deemed unfit when the teacher–student relationship is not working.[6]

What might this look like in practice? I imagine that it would require talking with parents early on in the year to get a sense of family cultural styles and surveying parents about how they give instructions and what their expectations are for behavior. It might require learning about the ways that respect is shown to adults in family cultures and whether the school's policy for naming adults (using the formal Ms./Miss/Mr., using the appendage "teacher" as in "Teacher Ali," or simply using the teacher's first name) will be supportive of or destructive to those values. Most of all, it requires a shift in which we allow the school culture to be dynamic and malleable—shaped by all of those who are in it—rather than insisting on a static culture shaped by tradition and by the majority, which demands conformity and assimilation. This inquiry also emphasizes the importance of creating spaces to address the "untouchable questions," many of which, like this one, can be foreseen. Without the courage of teachers like Helene to ask them, however, such questions never even make it onto the table.

Envisioning an Antiracist Classroom

Throughout this chapter, I use the term "antiracist" classroom rather than "racially just" or "racially proficient" classroom because I want to emphasize that an antiracist classroom is a stance of resistance. An antiracist classroom is one in which teachers understand and take seriously that role of resistance to racism. I use the following section to begin to envision the qualities of an antiracist classroom based on my work with the focal teachers in this book, but it is hardly comprehensive. I encourage readers to engage in this exercise as well: Take 10 minutes and imagine what an antiracist classroom would look like for you. Make it a topic of inquiry: Survey parents, colleagues, and students. What makes a classroom or a school an antiracist space?

For me, an antiracist classroom is a classroom in which the teacher is aware of their own biases and the ways those biases affect how they see their students or their students' families. The teacher understands that others might have those biases as well and works to challenge or confront them when they[7] see them occurring. An antiracist classroom is one in which the teacher feels comfortable putting students in same-race groups or different-race groups according to what makes sense for students' needs and support. The teacher understands the different factors in this decision and is able to justify the decision to people who question it. It is a classroom in which equity is a priority, so teachers differentiate not only by academic skill level but by behavior and need as well. In an antiracist classroom, students learn to recognize and resist stereotypical messages that make them question their own intellect or that of their classmates, among other oppressive messages.

An antiracist classroom is one in which teachers understand that race is a part of every student's identity and that it is never all of who a student is. Teachers work to get to know students and their families, their interests and ideas. Teachers have the racial proficiency and the social skills to be able to form relationships with and ask questions of all of the students and their families. Teachers understand the value of speaking more than one language and see students' linguistic abilities as assets, whether they speak Spanish, Korean, American Sign Language, African American Vernacular English, Hindi, Haitian Creole, Arabic, Hmong, German, Portuguese, Wolof, French, Mandarin, Vietnamese, or any other language. Teachers support the ongoing development of students' languages and encourage families to do so as well.

An antiracist classroom challenges and resists structures that reinforce socially constructed racial categories such as academic tracking. I personally believe that an antiracist classroom would not have academic tracking; instead the students would be grouped heterogeneously by skill level, and teachers would have the resources and the knowledge for instructing heterogeneous groups so that students with advanced skill levels would be challenged at their level while students with lower skill levels would be challenged too.[8]

Curriculum is certainly part of an antiracist classroom. An antiracist classroom has a curriculum that portrays the historical contributions of people of color and the connections among racial groups. It goes beyond an additive holidays and heroes approach to change the entire structure of the school year so that all students develop the capacity to understand the complexity of U.S. society, to see contemporary and historical events from the perspectives of diverse groups, and then to problem-solve about current-day problems (Banks, 2009). An antiracist classroom also recognizes the hidden curriculum (Anyon, 1980; Apple, 2004) that is communicated to students every day through their environment, such as the disparities in the racial makeup of the cafeteria staff and that of the administrative council. An antiracist classroom encourages students to recognize the hidden curriculum and to critically analyze it.

In an antiracist classroom, the curriculum is rigorous in a way that demands the best of each student and holds them to high expectations, even if it's not a lesson on race. In math class students become proficient mathematicians, able to pass the tests and perform the tasks required on the life paths they choose. They might spend some time learning about great mathematicians who were of their race because that is a lesson that supports positive racial identity development. But they would also learn the concept of stereotype threat and tools for combating that psychological threat that can undermine math learning if not confronted. They would have access to math affinity support groups in which they can learn such concepts while developing relationships and their racial identities as mathematicians. The teacher would understand and use strategies for undermining stereotype threat such as making study groups mandatory and creating opportunities for students of all races to share the struggles they have with math. Most important, the students would rigorously master math concepts and skills.

An antiracist classroom recognizes the different class backgrounds and parental education levels among the students and creates structures to support students according to their needs, rather than continuing to use a structure that is based on the assumption that all students are from middle-class or upper-middle-class families and have parents with college degrees. An antiracist classroom recognizes different methods and styles of communication and validates them all as resources rather than as deficits. It uses games, activities, and intentional seating patterns and pairings to interrupt group dynamics that routinely exclude or alienate particular children.

In an antiracist classroom, the teacher is open to feedback. They hear stories about a student's difficulty or a family's discontent and use them as data from which to make change, rather than as threatening feedback that demands an explanation. In the same vein, antiracist teachers feel comfortable raising race questions, even "untouchable" ones.

Just as with the "Autonomy" status in White Racial Identity Development, this vision of an antiracist classroom is not one that most teachers find themselves in every day. Even the classrooms of most racially proficient antiracist teachers do not look like this every day. This image of an antiracist classroom is a sight to set our eyes upon so we don't get lost in the day-to-day slog of looking just one step ahead. It is also incomplete and requires the input and vision of readers, teachers, parents, and students.

CHAPTER 4

Talking About Race in the Classroom

Contrary to popular belief, the reason for educators to learn about race and racism is *not* necessarily so that they can talk about race and racism in their classrooms with students. This may seem odd, but in fact it is very normal for teachers to develop their learning in an area that never gets shared directly with students. Teachers spend countless hours learning about literacy instruction, for example, but very rarely discuss what they learn with students. Instead, when they are in their classrooms they simply employ what they learn to assess their students' skill levels and to help them learn to read. Similarly, teachers need to be able to use their understanding of race and racism to build a lens through which they can more clearly see all of the dynamics that occur in their classrooms. Depending on their students and their subject area, they may never talk about it with students. But that doesn't make it any less important.

Whenever I do trainings with teachers, the assumption from both teachers and administrators seems to be that they should learn how to talk about race with kids. Among the 25 teachers participating in the action research project at Friends Independent School, many of the White teachers started their inquiry by asking such questions as, "How do I help lead conversations about race?"

I usually try to steer people away from this question because talking about race or leading conversations about race should not be a teacher's first step when they begin to learn how to talk about race themselves. Talking about race is a skill that should be developed outside the classroom, not practiced on students. Teachers should be working to have a progressive relationship with students, in which their own racial identity is more developed than those of their students. As the opening example in Chapter 3 showed, talking about race requires a certain amount of trust that often isn't there if the teacher has a nascent racial identity. In fact, if teachers start talking about race in the classroom but do not consider the other unspoken ways that it affects their classroom, that conversation could be even more alienating or confusing to students than not talking about race at all. The first step to answering the question, "How do I talk about race with students?" is to work on one's own racial identity. The rest will follow.

That said, the ability of teachers to engage in conversations about race when it comes up, to respond to race-based insults among students, to teach lessons involving "racialized"[1] content, to teach "racialized" content, to understand accusations of racism, and to discuss racial trends is critical in any classroom. Why? For one, it breaks the racial contract, the implicit agreement among White people not to talk about race (Mills, 1997).[2] Breaking the racial contract, in turn, interrupts the status quo in which White people and White experiences are centralized and made normative. Talking about race with students also helps teachers assess what their students know and think about race, which is usually more than they expect. Also, in the same way that teaching math helps a teacher solidify her knowledge of math concepts, leading conversations about race and racism can help a teacher continue to develop her own knowledge base. But it does more than this. It makes it possible for teachers to participate in the work of racial socialization. Racial socialization involves a conscious recognition of the fact that how race is taught and talked about in school will influence students' understanding of and feelings about race, and of themselves as racialized beings.

Because racial identity development is not a linear process, making it impossible to determine when a person is ready to begin talking about race in the classroom, it seemed useful to include a chapter about how race talk came up for the teachers in this book. The rest of this chapter describes concrete examples of talking about race in the classrooms of the White teachers I observed. This includes all the ways that race talk did or could enter the teachers' classrooms, from intentional conversations about race, to the teaching of "racialized" material, to intentional racial socialization planned and taught by teachers.

CHALLENGING THE IDEA THAT TALKING ABOUT RACE IS RACIST

Over the course of the year it became clear that many White teachers had to unlearn the notion that simply talking about race is racist—and to help their students do the same. Either because their parents and teachers didn't talk about race, like mine, or because they were explicitly taught to be colorblind, people seemed to think that the best way to counteract racism was not to talk about it.

Whether it comes from feelings of discomfort, a desire for belonging in White communities, or a desire to limit White privileges, the impact of maintaining a moratorium on race talk tends to be the preservation of a racist status quo. Sociologist Eduardo Bonilla-Silva (2013) calls this "colorblind racism" to emphasize the ways in which a refusal to acknowledge race denies and exacerbates the racism that structures life in the United States. Ignoring racialized patterns in schools, for example, such as the underrepresentation of Black students in honors classes, simply perpetuates racial inequality. But within a culture of colorblindness the blame for the existence of racialized inequalities (including the racialized achievement gap) gets shifted away from structural racism and away from racializing structures and onto the individual students themselves. Because so many social and political structures in the United States are not colorblind, we cannot be colorblind in trying to address them. Regardless of the particular reasons why individual White people attempt to avoid seeing race or talking about race, the net effect is "colorblind racism," which serves to preserve racial privileges for White people.

This shift in thinking, which involved realizing the importance of naming and talking about race, may be the reason so many teachers wanted to focus their early inquiry process on that topic. However, there are countless ways that race comes up, or could come up, in the classroom without an orchestrated discussion led by the teacher. The following sections explore some examples that show how the focal teachers learned to lean into or support classroom conversations about race without simply showing up one day and demanding, "Today we will talk about race."

Leaning into Race Conversations

Throughout the course of the year, Helene shifted from asking, "How do I help 2nd-grade students talk about race honestly and critically?" to "How can I lean into more conversations about race in the classroom?" Though the shift was barely perceptible, it was significant. "Leaning into conversations" involves noticing race tangentially in a conversation, following the lead of students, and going with the flow of the developmental and cognitive needs of the students. Helene moved from a teacher-centered question to a student-centered question about race conversations.

In support of Helene's question, I noted times that race came up uneventfully in conversations in Helene's class. One morning Helene was leading a conversation with students about pioneers, asking the students to provide examples of pioneers that they read about in their biography unit. As the students named people, Helene slowly and subtly began naming race.

> *Student:* Prudence Crandall—she made a school for Black girls since there were only schools for White girls.
> *Another student:* It was in Connecticut.
> *Helene:* Was that easy for her? Did everybody agree?
> *Student:* Some people threw rocks at her. And she went to jail.
> *Helene:* So was it easy for her to be a pioneer?
> *Students in chorus:* No.
> *Helene:* Prudence Crandall was a White woman. Benjamin Banneker was an African American man. Any other people we could use for our definition for pioneers?

At the end of the discussion about Prudence Crandall, Helene took a moment to point out the races of the people they were discussing. This gesture might seem small, but it took a lot of conscious preparation and thought for Helene to get to the point where she could name people's races out loud like this. She was ready to do it because she had been talking about it for weeks with her action research group. Naming race involves breaking the unwritten standard of behavior in White culture that says we do not name race; in particular, we do not name Whiteness. Because Whiteness is normalized in mainstream U.S. society, and the lack of racial descriptors often presumes Whiteness, this choice might seem awkward. And yet, naming race, including Whiteness, is an effective way to challenge Whiteness as the default, unnamed race and to bring race into ordinary daily conversations. And though it is quite a small act, it is actually one very effective way to let race be an organic part of the classroom conversation.

During the Egypt unit in Helene's classroom, students were filling note cards with facts that they recorded about the aspect of Egyptian life they had been assigned to research. In the process, two girls discovered that hair braiding in Egypt was "an ancient and longstanding art." I suggested that this might be an organic way to connect the ancient Egyptians to Black Americans today. This is an important connection because the ancient Egyptians are often depicted as Middle Easterners, rather than Africans, thus obscuring the early contributions of Africans to the fields of mathematics and science. Africanists point out that texts referring to "wooly haired mathematicians" refer to early African mathematicians, and that a great number of early human civilization's discoveries in math and science came from Egyptian Africans (Diop, 1974). Hair braiding might be a way for students to link the great achievements of ancient Egypt to Africa, and by association to Black Americans today. Because our traditional texts scarcely acknowledge any contributions of Black people to the growth of modern civilization, small connections like this can go a long way to helping all students develop an accurate and antiracist view of history. The possibilities for bringing race into the conversation seemed many, but doing so required both the preparation to be able to say it and the consciousness of the racial links to the content teachers were working on in class.

Using One's Marginalized Identities as Teaching Resources

Helene regularly mentioned Judaism as a marginalized identity in ways that contextualized it and highlighted it but did not take over the lesson. She noted in a conversation with me that the first Jewish doll of the American Girls series was released only a few years ago, for example.

When talking with the class about President Obama as a pioneer, Helene said:

> *Helene:* So do you think that sets the road for other African Americans to be president? And what else do you think that sets the road for? Could it just be White men or African American men now? Could it be anyone else?"
>
> *Students:* Women.
>
> *Helene:* Women. We haven't had a Jewish president. So maybe he's making it possible for many other types of people to be president.

Her tangential mention of Judaism might have been barely perceptible to students who are not Jewish, but it likely provided Jewish students with a little bit of recognition and motivation. Sam did something similar:

> I mean, I think that there's a part of me that thinks wow I've been doing some of this stuff already, just like the need for everyone in the classroom to have a voice. The need for, I mean, I love it when I go, "Oh man—hey, we finally get a Jewish character and this is what they do to it!? Thanks a lot."

I encouraged Helene to take a similar stance to race—to be as aware and invested in how Blackness or Asianness are represented as she is about Jewishness. She could mention race in small, subtle ways without leading a large class-wide conversation about it. Helene answered that she agreed that being Jewish made it much easier to slip in comments here and there about Jewish people and that this was the subtle way she could and should be doing so with race. But she said with race or with African American history, it is just "so much easier to feel like I'm getting it wrong or I'm not sure." When reading a book about the slaves of ancient Egypt named Rachel and Benjamin, for example, it was easy for her to say, at the spur of the moment, "I think they might be Jewish" because she had the background knowledge required to make that connection. She says, "It's harder to say with race—it's easy to not be sure."

When it came to the histories and experiences of people of color, Helene, like most White people—myself included—did not know as much and did not have as much of a context for it, so it was harder to make assertions. This is one of the liabilities of the incomplete, Eurocentric history that most of us learn in school. It is also a reason that it is hard for White people to talk about race in general. We are often asking, "How do I bring up race here and there when I am not even sure if, or how, race fits into the picture?"

Engaging in Discussions of Race When It's Part of the Texts

In Sam's predominantly White high school English classroom I observed a conversation about identity in Zora Neale Hurston's *Their Eyes Were Watching God* in which the predominantly White class studiously avoided talking about race when a Black classmate brought it up:

> Sam called on Hakeem, who tentatively asked, "Do we have to talk about a certain thing?"
>   Sam answered, "We were talking about search for identity, but . . ."
>   "Okay, yeah," Hakeem interrupted. "Well, Janie—it's a new town and it's all Black, so she thinks it's going to be different, but men still felt superior, and she's still oppressed by men." This was the first time during the whole unit that anybody mentioned race, and Sam was thrilled. He picked up on Hakeem's

comment right away and built on it. "Yeah, I agree with you 100%. It's supposed to be different, it's supposed to be a quest. It's like if you guys took over the class and you said we were going to do things differently and we're not going to have tests, etc., etc. and it was just the same. . . . She has certain expectations because she thinks an African American town is going to provide for her."

The conversation continued for about 10 more minutes, and nobody else referenced race. The students continued to analyze the power dynamics in the novel, comparing the book to *Animal Farm* and *Mean Girls*. Sam brought it back to race again to emphasize the universality of the theme: "So suddenly she empowers them. And going back to what Hakeem and Maria said, it's like suddenly he's the man—it doesn't matter if he's Black, White, or whatever—suddenly they're willing to pull him down."

The conversation ended with a tangential, joking conversation about *Mean Girls* during which the only Black girl in the class got up to blow her nose and then asked if she could use the bathroom to wash her hands.

The avoidance of racial topics in classroom discussions is particularly harmful to racially conscious students who might be interested in engaging in a conversation about race but do not feel that there is any response or engagement from the class when they bring it up. Though not all students of color necessarily consider race an area of interest, for those that do this silence stymies their development in that area as well as their engagement with the material. It takes energy to constantly self-censor, or to cope with a stony response from classmates. Students experiencing this censorship might thus appear disengaged or bored, a façade that does not communicate the whole story. White students also miss the opportunity, both academically and personally, to think about a whole range of important issues related to race. This avoidance of racial themes affects the learning of all students, who will presumably be expected to engage in a critical analysis of literature when they go to college. One has to wonder how you can have a discussion of *Their Eyes Were Watching God* or *Beloved* without talking about race, yet I suspect this is happening in English classes all over the country.

RACIAL SOCIALIZATION

Racial socialization is broadly defined as "the transmission from adults to children of information regarding race and ethnicity" (Hughes, Rodriguez, Smith, Johnson, Stevenson, & Spicer, 2006, p. 748). Howard Stevenson (2014) describes it as "actions parents and others take to influence racial self-efficacy beliefs or the beliefs that children hold about being able to resolve the racial stressors and conflicts of the world, wherever and whenever they arise" (p. 159). It is work that "enables children to negotiate contexts characterized by high racial, ethnic and cultural diversity" (Hughes et al., 2006, p. 747). Racial socialization is a term that usually refers to the work of families, not teachers. But racial socialization processes are occurring in schools all the time. For teachers, part of the work of racial socialization involves helping students make their personal racial identities compatible with what happens in the classroom. Just as teachers of girls realize that they need to support girls in understanding that being a girl does not preclude the possibility of being a mathematician or an athlete, teachers of students of color must help students synchronize their racial identity and their student identity by interrupting misconceptions conveyed by the larger culture. Such messages can be subtle. I am reminded of my daughter's preschool teacher, who ensures there's always at least one girl team captain and usually has a girl go first when trying new games during gym. Conscious that girls can easily be overshadowed by boys in coed sports, he counters potentially negative gender dynamics in ways that are probably invisible but nonetheless significant to the children.

Similarly, although racial socialization might involve talking about race, it also involves subtle messages that might be invisible but that are significant to students. The following examples demonstrate ways that the teachers found themselves engaging in racial socialization. This included creating time for emotional processing of racialized content, proactively affirming students' racial group identities, responding to racial insults, choosing books and content with the intent of positive racial socialization, disciplining students with race in mind, and teaching the history of racism and the meaning of racial slurs.

Emotional Processing

Although teaching "racialized" content is not the ultimate goal of helping teachers to develop a racial awareness, it is an important part of the race work that teachers do, as well as a source of many of their questions. It can also be an important vehicle for racial socialization. One of the differences is in the mindset. Teachers who are aware of racial socialization processes recognize that they are constantly shaping the way that students grow up to feel about race and their racial identities. Teaching biographies of people of color and the Civil Rights Movement is not just about content—it is about introducing role models, being critical of injustice, and equipping students to recognize and confront prejudice in their own lives. Cara established three learning goals for her students that acknowledged that teaching the Civil Rights Movement was about more than content, that it could have implications for the students' lives. These learning goals were (1) the Civil Rights Movement was made up of everyday people; (2) racial inequality still exists today; and (3) young people made change. Cara approached these goals using several types of learning, including writing and performing poetry on the different perspectives of people involved in different conflicts.

Emotional processing is not typically considered a critical part of teaching the Civil Rights Movement, yet it came up multiple times in Cara's predominantly Black 5th-grade charter school classroom when her students seemed to need time to process the lesson emotionally. Ironically, there was usually not time for the emotional processing because Cara had so much content to present. She did such a thorough job presenting the content that students seemed to need more time to process it.

In Cara's case, the students read historical fiction about the bombing of the 16th Street Baptist Church in Birmingham and watched excerpts from *Eyes on the Prize*. They covered some of the most painful parts of the movement, not just the victorious moments that are usually touched on. During lessons, one or two boys laid their heads on their desks. As usual, Cara did not let them keep their heads down and would not let them check out. But I wondered if they were more than just tired. Was this an emotional reaction to painful material?

During one particularly intense read-aloud, Cara read the narration of a scene in which a young girl was being arrested by police for being involved in a protest. She read, "They called me names and cracked jokes about parts of my body." From one of the girls, I heard a sound of sympathy, "Awwwwwhhh." Students seemed to be listening particularly attentively; they were not restless. Then Cara read, "The lock shut, it was final. It said I was trapped." One student raised her hand. Cara looked up from the book and said, "That's personification."

Because this was a read-aloud book, something Cara did every day for 15 minutes, she did not have a lesson built around it, or even time scheduled to discuss it. And because she was generally trying to use every moment to teach skills, she seemed, out of habit, to identify writing techniques, such as "personification," regardless of what else was happening in the book. In this moment, however, she missed a chance to help students talk about how this passage affected them emotionally, as they heard about the arrest of a Black child only a few years older than them. Opting to focus on skills means distancing the discussion from the emotional content in order to break down a reading for its technical parts. Choosing to talk about personification meant that the students did not get to feel the full dramatic effect of what personification accomplishes, nor did they get to process what feelings it elicited for them. Talking about feelings does not have to replace technical writing conversations; in this case, had they focused on feelings first they might have developed a better understanding of how tools such as personification can be so evocative.

Part of the reason Cara did not do this processing with her students was that she thought it was not her place, which related to her own levels of confidence and self-doubt, particularly related to her racial identity as a White person. From the outside, it seemed that her students really trusted her, and I think they would have welcomed the chance to process their learning with her. But her own fears that she was overstepping her role as a White person held her back. Her hyperconsciousness of her Whiteness prevented her from taking steps that her students and their parents seemed to trust her with, denying her students the important emotion-processing aspect of racial socialization that could accompany this acquisition of new content. (See Appendix A for Cara's response to this analysis.)

From Talking About Race to Racial Socialization

Throughout the course of our work together, Todd's inquiry shifted from talking about race to focusing on proactive racial socialization. When Todd first came to the group, he was asking questions about how to respond when students insulted one another by ridiculing skin color. Throughout the year, he began to realize that he needed to be proactive, not simply reactive, to issues involving racial insults. Todd was not considering simply starting to talk about race, or to simply break norms of colormuteness. He was choosing to proactively engage in racial socialization to help his students think about themselves and one another, as Black people, more positively. This was daunting for Todd, as it likely would be for many White teachers because, as the following quote demonstrates, he often lost confidence when talking about his students' lives with them:

> I feel ignorant about a lot of aspects of my students' lives. I have a hard time feeling like I have authority to speak to them on these issues. I feel like how they view me and Whiteness in general, sometimes I think they have this idea that it's intellectual. . . . When I say things, I feel like why should they care? I feel ignorant—like I don't know what I'm talking about and it's a confidence thing.

Examples of the race-based insults that Todd was trying to address included when students were passing a note about a dark-skinned student that said she "just got off the boat" or when they said, "If we turn off the lights, we won't be able to see you." These race-based comments usually provoked a strong reaction in him and caught him off-guard. He found them extremely offensive, and he did not know what to say in response. As the comments usually came to his attention while he was in front of the class, he did not feel that he had the luxury of time to strategize a reaction. He wanted to make sure the students who were targeted by these comments knew that he noticed and that he did not think it was appropriate. But in reality his reactions usually drew more attention to the targeted student and did not stop the inappropriate comments, "So I guess my question is like how can I build my confidence around talking about those things in the class that's like . . . not fake?" Todd wanted to feel like he knew what he was going to say before entering into a conversation on race. He was afraid of responding in the moment, in part because he had tried to do so in the past and the conversations had not gone well. He said that particularly because it was middle school, he felt he needed to keep things moving in a certain direction and there was less room for doubt on his part. Yet what recourse did he have but to intervene when his students were using racially charged comments to insult one another?

> When I try to address those issues, my kids know more about it than I do. Who am I to tell them what's appropriate? They always say, "We're just playing." Usually the person who's offended backs down and says it's just

playing. So do I have a right to bring it up? The real reason I brought it up is there are certain kids that get picked on consistently for this issue and it's not addressed as much as other issues.

Todd wanted support determining the severity of the comments; they offended him but did not always appear to offend his students. The inquiry group supported Todd's hunch that such race-based comments, particularly the taunting about darkness and the disdain for Africa, were probably very hurtful to the students who were the targets of insults, as well as to all of the students, as they collectively perpetuated the notion that it is bad to be Black, worse to be dark Black, and even worse to be connected to Africa.

Sometimes discussions about skin and hair can be benign. Cara once shared that she was sitting on a school bus and listening to her students comparing different parts of the seat to one another's hair—"This smooth part is like so-and-so's hair, that rough part is like so-and-so's hair. . . ." She said that even just overhearing that conversation was very uncomfortable for her and she hoped she would not have to be a part of the conversation. This is not necessarily a situation in which she needed to intervene, but part of building racial competence is developing the ability, and the comfort level, to participate in conversations if necessary, without being paralyzed by discomfort. Racial competence can be as simple as being able to talk about skin or hair, whether White children or Black children bring it up. And it is about knowing how to intervene when students are hurting one another, by calling each other "dark" in a way that suggests it's negative or otherwise suggesting that their skin color or physical features are inferior. Most White teachers feel competent to have informal conversations about hair with White students, or have the skills to respond when White students insult each other; we need to be able to do this for all students.

Through the inquiry group's discussions of racial socialization, Todd realized that addressing race-based insults might require a more proactive strategy in order to help students critique anti-Black sentiments. The goal was not just to stop the insults but to support his students to love themselves and one another, as Black people, more authentically. Again, Todd shared discomfort with this idea, feeling that it was not his role, as a White person, to do this. And yet as a group we discussed the fact that, according to numbers gathered in 2006, 77% of new teachers hired in Philadelphia were White (Unseem, Offenberg, & Farley, 2007), whereas the student body was 85% children of color. What might change in Philadelphia schools if more White teachers were responsible for positive racial socialization in their classrooms?

Members of the inquiry group suggested starting with a small cohort of students at lunchtime and watching films about colorism (*A Girl Like Me*[3] or *Family of Skin Bleachers*) or listening to music (*Shades* by Wale) to prompt discussions about skin color. When Todd felt comfortable, he could ask the members of the small discussion group to be leaders in a wider class discussion of the same topic. Todd was excited about this idea but hesitated, feeling that as a White person he did not have the appropriate racial positioning to lead a conversation involving race:

> As a White person with lots of privileges leading the discussion—am I reinforcing that I'm better than you? I feel so unconvincing whenever I try to address something like this—because I'm not talking about personal experience. I'm just stating what I believe or what I find is inappropriate in the classroom. And they're going to say, "Oh, he's gonna give one of his speeches again"—they do need background on a lot of this stuff, but sometimes I feel like they don't care.

Todd made the previous statement in the context of the inquiry group, and Cara responded, "Sometimes I wish I could contract out and get someone who's Black to do this."

This inclination—to get support from colleagues or parents of color—is not unprecedented. Because White students and students of color will hear messages about race differently depending on who delivers them, it would make sense for Todd to partner with a Black teacher in order to have explicit conversations about race with his students. This would be particularly effective in designing proactive lessons to mitigate their race-based insults. But in the meantime, he could not realistically access another teacher every time his students insulted one another using race. Nor should he do so, necessarily, as it might have impeded him from developing his competencies and put his colleagues of color in the position of having to own the discussion when he abdicated.

To be able to lead any conversation directed toward racial socialization, Todd needed to practice talking about race outside of the classroom. Talking about race should be seen as a skill that one can develop, just like any other teaching skill. Unlike other teaching skills, however, there can be so much anxiety tied to making mistakes in talking about race, especially with 7th-graders, that it is not something that will just improve over time without practice. Arguably, over 4 years of teaching, Todd seemed to have gotten more, not less, anxious about talking about race with his students, especially after he realized that his training in African American protest studies did not easily translate into connection with or understanding of his students. He needed a space to continue to practice talking about race and to debrief his conversations with his students in ways that helped him move beyond his anxiety, rather than sitting in it and maintaining silence.

Todd also came to the realization that he did not have to address everything in the moment. When Todd intercepted the note that said a student "just got off the boat," he could have taken the note away, told students to get back to work, and ignored the comments altogether, or waited to address the issue later, after he had time to think about it. He could also begin thinking about potential responses now that he realized he needed a plan for when this happened again.

Talking about race with students can help a teacher understand a whole aspect of his students' racial identity that usually remains invisible. At the end of the year, Todd invited me into his predominantly Black 8th-grade public school classroom to support him in presenting a lesson about media analysis with his students.[4] This hour-long exercise was incredibly valuable for helping Todd learn some of the beliefs and values that his students held about race, which very likely affected their learning. The following points are realizations Todd had about his students' racial knowledge while listening to their participation in this lesson.

First, some of his biracial students were censored by other students who felt being lighter complexioned meant they could not authentically talk about being Black:

> One of the students more or less questioned another student's ability to speak on an issue based on the fact that he was biracial, and one of them said they were 100% Black—it's hard to generalize, but clearly they know there's differences and people are treated differently based on that.

Second, his students seemed to think that kids who attend predominantly White suburban schools were better than kids who attend predominantly Black urban ones as they did:

> . . . they have almost an inferiority complex about race and it's surprisingly not that negative toward—in some cases it is—negative toward White people. But it's also like, oh, White schools are better. And I don't think somebody necessarily told them that, but I think they have this idea of White schools, from things like media and things like that, are better and I think it can kind of be extrapolated onto a lot of things that they consider like White, like clothing, things like that.

Third, rather than critique the structural racism that influences the differences between urban and suburban schooling, students seemed to blame urban Blacks for their problems, as if films that stereotyped urban schools as violent and unruly were accurate portrayals:

> Well, that's what worries me, like there's like a little bit negative view of White people, but they're much more negative about themselves and other Black people. . . . They were like, "They are more violent, look at them. . . . " They don't think like, "Well, what's wrong with public education?" They think like, "What's wrong with me that I'm not successful?" And I think you get those messages in a lot of ways, like if you're not successful—it's not your school, your principal, your teacher—it's you and your family. Like what aren't you doing?

Fourth, as a result of this incomplete critique, his students might not have the negative feelings toward White people that Todd expected them to have, based on his own knowledge of structural racism:

> And I don't get the sense that my kids are really, like I think they have a sense of injustice between White and Black, but it's not like overtly negative, there's not like a ton of animosity . . . I was a little surprised.

Fifth, his students did not seem to have a sense of the many different ways that Black people are economically successful:

> We were doing a debate—and one kid said suburban schools have more money and there was some correlation that it was better. And one kid said, well, rappers' and R&B artists' kids' go to those schools too. . . . They didn't say doctor or lawyer—like if you're going to have money, that's the only way. Like why is that what happens in your mind? It's interesting to me that that's what pops into your head. Like when I was little, thinking about things that I could do to make money, like I would never think I'll be a famous musician, I thought like I'll be a doctor or a lawyer, that's how I thought you were successful.

Todd realized he needed to support his students' racial identities by expanding the notion of Black culture for his students to include images of wealthy Black professionals and other forms of success typically associated with Whiteness:

> Rich schools, White schools. My students call a lot of things White and that typically means with money. Like, "Do you live in a White neighborhood?" If so, it's a rich neighborhood. . . . It's weird—I feel like it's important to be a part of Black culture, but at the same point, there's all these things that they don't see as part of their culture that they think are good . . . so like it's not good for somebody to call you White, but in a way it kind of is because it's kind of implying that you have certain things that other kids don't that are things that you might want to have.

The 1-hour media analysis workshop that Todd and I led for his students helped him begin to get a picture of how his students thought about race and what he could do to help them cultivate more positive images of themselves and their communities. If we don't ask what they think, how will we know how to support their developing racial identities? For students, just like teachers, their racial identities are their toolboxes. Without a strong toolbox, it is hard to carry many tools for navigating a mainstream culture that regularly misunderstands, misrepresents, and assaults their racial group. In this way, positive racial socialization is intimately connected with academic confidence and success. If Black students like Todd's connect academic success, wealth, or traditional career pathways with being White, they will only aspire to those things to the detriment of their self-image and belonging. But if they have a strong racial identity and a broad sense of possibility for Black people, they will not feel the same pressure to reject those pathways that they typically associate with Whiteness. (See Appendix A for Todd's response to this analysis.)

Racial Microproficiencies

Sometimes teachers can be so paralyzed by conflicts involving race that they forget the skill they would regularly invoke in other, nonracialized situations. It might be useful to realize that even though the comments are about race, the response does not necessarily have to be. Teachers can respond to race-based insults as they would any other insult. In the following excerpt from Ann's interview, she describes how she handled insults based on skin color between two students in her class. Picking on skin color, she said, was a way that they "go for the jugular":

> *Ann:* She has this great relationship with Aaron because they're like siblings. They like pick on each other and stuff. I think sometimes he does go to the extreme, and I think it does hurt her feelings, but it is often about their skin color.
> *Ali:* The way that they joke with each other?
> *Ann:* Uh huh, like, "What do you know, you're so light skinned? What do you know, you're . . . ?" He calls her chocolate and stuff and makes her very angry. I never hear her talk back, but to that she'll shut him up.
> *Ali:* Do you ever wonder if you should be intervening with that or . . . ?
> *Ann:* Well, I do at times, and I'll say to him, "You've offended her, she is your friend." And he'll be like, "Oh, she doesn't care." And I'm like, "No, clearly she cares because she told you to shut up." And I'll say, "Why do you have to take it to that level? It hurts her feelings." So I handle it more as a put-down as I would with any other situation because I know that's the motivation behind it, but I do think it's interesting that . . . I mean, I understand how kids fight and how they go for the jugular, you know, but I think that for other teachers that would look at that and say, "How's a Black kid gonna pick on another Black kid for being Black?" but I know that in their minds that's a disparaging remark to make. . . .

Watching Ann solve conflicts as in the scenario above inspired me to coin a term for actions that are the opposite of racial microaggressions. When I was in Ann's classroom, I saw her doing many barely perceptible things that signified a comfort with her students of color and a facility with race issues. Ann had many microproficiencies about race that made it possible for her to do things that many other White teachers found challenging. I call these "microproficiencies" because, like microaggressions, they are small and barely perceptible but can make a big difference to the lives of individual students as they navigate our educational system. Ann was receptive to learning these microproficiencies because she was willing to learn from, and ask questions of, Black colleagues; her self-image was not significantly threatened when she realized there were things she needed to learn; and she continuously pursued professional development opportunities on race, such as the cultural competency group and the teacher reading group at her school.

Ann felt comfortable talking about race with her students in many small ways, but that did not mean that responding in the moment to troubling racialized conversations was easy for her—it was not. It is not easy for anyone to know how to respond in the moment when students are going off-course, and that is particularly true with regard to addressing racialized content as a White person. In the following story, Ann was not sure what to say or that her students would trust her enough to listen to her.

Ann introduced the following story to me by saying that she had had a very interesting exchange with some of her Black students and telling me, "You are going to be proud of me." She told me that she had been at a mentor reception with some of her Black students, and three of them were passing around the computer and laughing. She asked them, "What's so funny?" They showed her a picture of a Black teenaged boy with an afro, hat sideways, holding a bucket of chicken with a t-shirt that said "Jigaboo Jones." Ann responded, "I can't believe you think it's funny. It makes me sad to think you would laugh at that." One student said, "What, are you being racist?" Ann answered, "Are you kidding me? Look at his t-shirt. What does it say?" They looked at the shirt, but they did not know what Jigaboo meant. She said to them, "Let me tell you how wrong this is and for many reasons. This is a derogatory term. It's not a nice way to talk." One of the students said, "I think I've heard that before." Another student looked it up online. She said then they realized what it meant. Ann asked, "Do you get why that's not okay?" She said she was so proud of herself because in the past she would have been completely dumbfounded and not known what to say:

> A year ago I would have said, "That's inappropriate, put that away." I felt like I had grown to the point to be comfortable enough to sit down and go through it with them and tell them why it is wrong.

Notably, Ann was confident enough in her own racial identity that she was not undone by the initial student response, asking her, "Are you racist?" This vignette demonstrates how difficult it can be for White teachers to engage in even a simple exchange without freezing up or ignoring something that is problematic. Ann's excitement after it was over indicates the extent to which this was indeed an achievement for her. Successful interactions like this one will help her to expand her comfort zone so that her capacity to intervene in the future will increase. Because of her relationship with her students, she was able to be trusted throughout this intervention (if not immediately), although she was not Black herself. This is powerful for many reasons. First, it shows that growth is possible. A conversation that Ann would not have previously felt comfortable with became something she could do in the moment. Second, she was able to support students to stop laughing at racist material that was meant to mock them. In doing so she helped support positive racial identity development in her students.

In psychologist Howard Stevenson's work with Black youths, he teaches young people skills so they can reframe stressful racial experiences as mountains to climb rather than tidal waves that will drown them—hurdles, not dead-ends. It seems a testament to the strength of Ann's microproficiencies that she was able to frame the conversation just described as a challenge for her (a mountain to climb) rather than as a tidal wave. (See Appendix A for Ann's response to this analysis.)

Using "Racialized Content" for Racial Socialization

In spite of her reservations about her role as a White teacher, Cara did say that she used the Civil Rights Movement as an opportunity to do some racial socialization with her students. Sometimes this was explicit; other times, she might not even have realized she was doing it. While watching a segment on the Little Rock Nine, in which White students were trying to get Black students expelled by making them angry, Cara said to her students, "So if you didn't want to get expelled, what did you do?" They answered her, "Keep cool." Helping students to notice the strategies young people had to use to fight for justice while protecting themselves is a form of racial socialization.

Understanding Race While Offering Rebuke

When Cara disciplined her students, she did so with the knowledge that she was preparing her students to be successful in a society that can be dangerous to Black boys. She kept this in the back of her mind while disciplining them, even if she did not mention race:

> Bringing race up in general, like I mean, it's tricky and I'm not sure I always do it the right way, but I was sitting outside of my classroom with one of my students the other day who had reacted really angrily to something. . . . I had asked him to sit in his seat. We were at the carpet and he had been talking to someone he wasn't supposed to or something and I calmly was like, "Well, you're talking so that's why I'm asking." And he had this angry face and said, "Well, I didn't do nothing." He stayed angry about it for a really long time. So finally when I had time I had him sit outside with me for a little while and I talked to him about it and I said, "Do you understand why I'm out here talking with you right now?" and he said, "But I didn't do nothing."

And I said, "It's not about, like what you did wasn't even a problem, it was how you reacted to it." And I said, "I have time to talk with you and I care about you and I'm gonna keep talking to you, but you know because of what we've learned about . . ." and it didn't jump right from there to there, but I said, "I need you to develop better ways to handle it when you don't like something or when you think something isn't fair and I want you not to forget that you don't think it's fair and I want you to be able to explain your side of the problem, but you need to find ways to do it that people will be open to listen to. We know that the world's not a very fair place and some people will be really ready to say you're just a bad kid that's angry and bad. You need to find a way to calm yourself down before you respond to something." I always tell them, "I'm learning to do it too and I'm way older than you so you still have a lot more time."

Cara conveyed this lesson without explicitly talking about race, but she did so with the consciousness that it was a critically important lesson for her Black male students to learn because of the way their anger would be perceived outside of her classroom.

Books

One of the most straightforward forms of racial socialization that teachers found, particularly at the elementary level, was through choosing books to read with students. Teachers struggled with how to choose books, whose experiences to represent, and how to determine whether or not a book was a stereotypical representation.

Cara read aloud to her Black 5th-grade charter school class every day for 15 minutes. All but one of the read-aloud books that she read that year had Black protagonists. Cara wondered aloud during an interview if it was overkill to have almost all Black protagonists. I laughed when she said this. I acknowledged that it is probably a good question because all kids need diversity. But White teachers routinely read almost all books with White protagonists and do not ask that question. Having a wide range of Black protagonists gives her students many ways to connect to characters and to literature. Do they really need diversity in the free-reading selections? Don't they get enough of other races in the history books, the mandated curriculum, as well as from the teachers they had before Cara and the ones they would have after her? Again, at a school like the independent school where Helene and Laurie taught, this might be a harder question because there are so many different races represented in each classroom, and each child should have the chance to see themselves reflected by the protagonist. But when all of your students are Black, it seems like the choice is less fraught.

One way to think about this decision might be to go back to the reasons Cara used free-reading time in the first place:

1. To help students learn to love reading and being read to
2. To give students exposure to more books
3. To calm students down after lunch

None of these objectives is compromised by having only Black protagonists. In fact, the first might even be accomplished more effectively if most of the books have Black protagonists.

Teaching Racism in Context

When Helene and her co-teachers taught a biography unit that included teaching biographies of people from a diverse range of racial backgrounds, they consciously avoided a common tendency to teach about people of color only from the perspective of oppression, as if oppression is the singular defining aspect of life for people of color.

> We were making it, you know, intentionally diverse. And trying to put in African Americans who didn't have an oppression as the main issue in their life. Some athletes and artists and scientists. (Helene)

This illustrates one strategy of racial socialization. They were increasing student exposure to the lives and stories of Americans of color who did things besides fight for civil rights and, in doing so, were providing students with examples and role models of successful people of color. The stories do not have to be focused on racism or resistance.

The choice to teach about the lives of Americans of color who did things besides fight for freedom does not have to preclude including some perspective on their struggles with racism. In reality, very few people of color in U.S. society have been successful without knowing how to navigate racism and prejudice. Including this aspect of their lives can be a contextualized, comprehensible way to present racism to young children through the lives of real people. Racial socialization involves helping students learn to navigate a world in which racism operates, and learning how others have done so is a great way to do it.

In research on the impact of curriculum on racial attitudes psychologists have found that White children had more positive racial attitudes when they learned not only about Jackie Robinson as an athlete but when they learned a small piece about his experiences with discrimination as well (Bigler, 1999; Hughes, Bigler & Levy, 2007).[5] A contextualized understanding of racism helps children make sense of the world around them, one that is and has been shaped by systems of racism. In his critique of textbooks that erase the true history of racism in the United States, James Loewen (2008) wrote that the ignorance that comes from a sugar-coated history leaves students "hamstrung in their efforts to analyze controversial issues in our society" (p. 8). Giving children an accurate understanding of history, and of their current social and political context, requires a contextualized, age-appropriate understanding of racism.

Racial Socialization in Multiracial Schools

Racial socialization takes place in schools regardless of whether teachers intentionally engage in it. Not talking about race sends a message about race, just as talking about race does (Michael & Bartoli, 2014). With issues of race and racism, it is impossible for teachers to be neutral, which is one of the reasons the topic merits attention and skill development for all teachers.

Racial socialization is not only a process that occurs for students of color. White students are constantly being socialized into Whiteness by their school experiences. Preliminary studies of White racial socialization in families show that it tends to take the form of an adherence to colormuteness and colorblindness with an emphasis on the idea that all people are equal (Michael & Bartoli, 2014). These lessons are usually taught at home and reinforced by the supposed neutrality of schools on race issues, a neutrality that perpetuates a racist status quo. This often leads to students developing negative racial identities because they become delusional about the racial reality in the United States, unquestioningly believing racial stereotypes and generally feeling paranoid that they don't know how to engage when the topic of race comes up. This process of White racial socialization tends to leave White students without the opportunity to develop skills of racial competence (Michael & Bartoli, 2014).

Racial socialization is different from merely teaching "racialized" content, although there is significant overlap in the two processes. Racial socialization involves the conscious realization that how one talks and teaches about race will affect not only students' cognitive development but their attitudinal, emotional, and social development as well. As the stories from the teachers in this chapter demonstrate, one thing that distinguished intentional racial socialization from the mere introduction of "racialized" content was teachers' awareness of the racism their students would likely have to face in their lives. Teachers who were more familiar with the racialized obstacle course their students would have to master were better able to prepare students for it. Notably, this also seemed easier for Cara, whose students were all Black, than for teachers who had large numbers of White students in their classrooms.

Although it might seem that racial socialization must be race specific, in fact there is a tremendous amount of racial knowledge, skills, and competencies that can be taught in schools to students of any race. Racial knowledge includes some ideas that have been covered in this book, such as talking about race is not racist, race is an essential part of one's identity, race is not negative and should not come up only when there's conflict. Content knowledge includes critical media analysis and the history of oppression in the United States. Skills include managing racial

stress, intervening with racisn
tic relationships with student:
and awareness of the larger ra
for recognizing and debunkin
accurate perception of the racia
dents of color to reject ideas tha

A racial socialization persp
race is not only about what th
schooling: how people treat one
their families fit into the larger
other students' homes for birthda
cial context, how much they have t
how often they must confront mist
er they are able to build personal
and whether they feel they have a r
school—or if they are simply percei
tion perspective acknowledges that c
the classroom, not simply from the cu

From Th
Facili

.om every aspect of

.....

...eory to Practice to Theory:
...ating Inquiry

This chapter is an inquiry into my own role as a facilitator[1] of race inquiry. I focus the chapter specifically on locating the strategies I used that were effective in helping teachers deepen and persist with their inquiry process. To do this I have looked at two sets of data. First, I have combed my interviews and observations for moments when teachers touched on difficult questions or moved from a place of fear and silence to a place of safety from which they could voice questions with which they struggled. I tried to locate what I did in those moments as a facilitator and interviewer to contribute to that shift. Second, because I sometimes struggle to recognize in myself the things I do that help people feel safe and move forward, I have asked some colleagues, workshop participants, and the teachers themselves to share their observations of my facilitation. Using their responses, I have assembled and described strategies they deemed effective. This chapter is not meant to be a complete inquiry into my practice but rather an accounting of useful strategies that might be helpful to readers who are (or want to be) involved in race inquiry of their own. I hope that this chapter will also assist teachers, professors, teacher educators, and other professionals whose role it is to facilitate race conversations.

KEEPING THE FOCUS ON RACE

This might seem like an obvious, or even unnecessary, strategy for facilitating race dialogues. But I notice as I look back at my process, much of what I seemed to be doing was simply helping people stay focused on race. Because White people are so unaccustomed to seeing with a racial lens or talking in racial terms, it can be easy to lose the focus on race. Sometimes we jump to explanations of class because it seems more logical and easier to talk about than race. Sometimes conversations about race bring up our own feelings of marginalization, so we change the conversation to one about the ways we are marginalized by gender, sexuality, or religion. And although these aspects of identity should never be absent from conversations about race—because all of our identities are intersectional—it is also useful to notice when those conversations end up replacing our conversations on race rather than adding to them. Sometimes keeping the focus on race is just a matter of showing up; when teachers saw me or talked to me they remembered the many disparate moments that had happened the day before that they'd meant to write down but hadn't. Sometimes it means pointing out the racialized aspects of things that are not obviously race related, such as suggesting that the Oregon Trail game encourages students to identify with the European American pioneers and that there might be a way to have them identify with Native Americans as well. Similarly, when teachers have conflicts with colleagues or students, I have always tried to ask, "What part of this might be racial?" Often just asking this question gave people permission to think racially about a relationship that they had trained themselves to deracialize.

I was struck as I compiled this chapter on facilitation by how facilitator-centric the processes of the different inquiry groups were. At no time did our groups simply gather to discuss a reading without someone taking on the role of facilitator. Inquiry groups tend to distribute leadership roles differently. Some rotate each time they meet, and others have one or two members who take the lead at each meeting. Some groups have no leader. I was not always the leader in our groups, but we always had a leader. When I am the leader I tend to be directive and structured because I want the group to stay focused on their stated goal, which, through no malice of any individual, a group can very easily collaborate to abandon. Especially when race is the topic it can be easy to drift into conversations about everything else. I am hopeful that the following strategies will be useful to any group because, no matter what the leadership structure, each member of an inquiry group has the opportunity to facilitate the growth of their colleagues. I invite inquiry group participants to see themselves as always already facilitating each other and themselves. I offer these suggestions as resources for everyone in the group, regardless of their role.

STORYTELLING

As I look back on my notes as both a facilitator and interviewer, I see that I was constantly telling my own story. The first thing I did when I introduced myself to these inquiry groups, before citing my degrees or my research, was to share that I grew up in a predominantly White suburb of Pittsburgh where we never talked about race. This is not always easy to do. Especially as a White person talking about race, it is tempting to start out by announcing all the things that make me qualified to do this work. I want everyone to see me as credible, and I know some of them are wondering, "How can you do this work? You're White." But I've found that White people trust me and open up more with me if they can relate to me. They need to know that I have not always been able to talk about race. Similarly, people of color trust me more if they know I'm aware of my own biases than if I went to this school or have that degree. So I share my personal background in order to begin to connect with groups, to break norms of not talking about race or Whiteness, to remove the shame of an experience of colorblindness and ignorance about race that is quite common for White people, and to begin to connect to people personally. As we build our relationships, I continue to share stories from my childhood, questions I still have, and things I have recently realized or learned.

Interviewing

I also told stories in the one-on-one interviews I conducted for this book. Conventionally, interviews are thought of as one-sided conversations in which the interviewer does nothing more than ask questions. But that is beginning to change as people realize that interviews are never just a product of the interviewee but are rather a co-construction of the interviewer and the interviewee, in which both are responsible for what gets said and how it gets said. Because of the racial contract that exists in White communities (Mills, 1997), if I ask questions about race and reveal nothing about myself, I might get only cursory answers. The final product will be vastly different if I share some of my own experiences with race and break the racial contract within that relationship.

I told stories about being the only White person on a research team of 8 and seeing how differently the team functioned from my research team where I was one of 10 White people. I told stories about my reading group that I had with other White people in which we tried to educate ourselves about race so that people of color wouldn't have to. I told stories about the other teachers I was working with and other schools I had worked with. Storytelling—much like I've tried to do in this book—helps ground the big ideas we learn about race in the daily here and now. It humanizes the theory and helps people connect to it. Beyond that, hearing a story about someone else's anxiety helps us put our own anxiety into perspective.

I constantly told teachers stories about the ways that I've messed up or gotten things wrong in an attempt to balance the vulnerability that they brought to our work together. When Helene said she got her conviction from a Black leader in her community, I interjected, "That's where I get most of my information, too." Later in the conversation, when she expressed her fear of asserting those convictions in a conversation with Black parents, I told her about a time that I repeated something I heard from my Black principal to my 8th-grade class. I will share that story now. In a private meeting, in order to motivate me to be a stronger disciplinarian, my principal reminded me that the KKK prevented Black children from getting an education. "You would never let the KKK stop you from educating your students. Why would you let the students themselves interrupt one another and stop you from educating them?" Impressed with this example, and motivated to make change, I returned to my classroom. I then naively repeated what he had said to me in confidence to my class of Black and Latino students. I knew as soon as I said it that it was completely inappropriate and felt baffled that I hadn't realized this before I shared it. They were rightly furious that I compared their behavior to the KKK and it took time to repair our relationship. Helene responded to this confession of a stupid thing I said as a new teacher by connecting, understanding, laughing, and shaking her head. We were allying to one another throughout the interview, acknowledging that we both made mistakes, that we both had a lot to learn, and that we both had done things we wished we hadn't. It doesn't make what I said okay, but sharing it opens up space for all of us to make stupid mistakes— and to own and learn from those mistakes. I believe that this is part of why Helene was able to ask untouchable questions in this interview and has been open to difficult conversations throughout her inquiry. Although her capacity to be vulnerable has a lot to do with her own racial identity and skills development, I believe her willingness to share her stories with me—while the recorder was running—was a result of our mutual vulnerability.

Self-Disclosure

When I facilitate, I plan for and model self-disclosure for every exercise that I lead. I think about the stories I want to tell ahead of time and practice telling them. I push myself to think about stories that are current so as to model my ongoing personal struggle and the authentic vulnerability that comes from exposing our current flaws rather than focusing on things we have overcome or learned in the past.

I also use self-disclosure to help normalize the experience of the people in the room. It's not uncommon to work with people who have never had a conversation about race with anyone other than close family or friends and thus do not have practice seeing themselves or their experiences as part of a common pattern in a racialized society. With largely White groups I try to emphasize stories of omission—how my family did not talk about race or how I did not know many people of color—and how those absences influenced my learning and my story. Because so much race learning in White families happens through this type of omission, many White people struggle to identify their own racial stories. For White facilitators, telling others one's own stories can help White people begin to identify their own.

A Caution About White Privilege and Storytelling

A lot of my strategies are general enough for people of any race to use them. However, I have a clear bias as a White facilitator who focuses on the learning and growth of White participants. My colleague Chonika, who is Black, challenged me to see the way that my use of storytelling, particularly in regard to my style of introduction, which prioritizes my racial story above my professional credentials, works especially well because of racial privilege. If I were Black, people would not accept stories about how ignorant I once was as a sign of my credibility. Beyond that, as a Black woman, if Chonika were not to list her professional credentials people might not listen to her. After our conversation, I have changed the way I introduce myself when I cofacilitate with people of color. Now I state my professional qualifications so that there is a parallel style of introduction from my cofacilitator and me. But it's not just the introductions I change; when I cofacilitate I try to be mindful that storytelling is more risky for people of color overall. They have to navigate the burden of representation, the risk of confirming stereotypes, and the constant possibility that people will not believe them or will think they are complaining, speaking in their own self-interest, or trying to play the race card. When I share stories I do so in a conscious and strategic use of privilege, and I honor the decisions of colleagues of color about whether they will share, knowing that my colleagues of color have a much more accurate gauge for when and how it makes sense. I encourage inquiry group members and facilitators to think about stories as precious currency, and to honor and respect the decisions that group members make about whether and when to share them. Like currency, group members need to give some to get some. It is important not to let the storytelling become a one-sided process whereby the people of color share their stories in exchange for sympathetic nods from their White colleagues. It may take extra work to help the White participants recognize and tell their racial stories, but every person has a story and the group will be stronger if each person shares theirs.

TRACKING—BOTH INTERNAL AND EXTERNAL

Tracking is a term that comes from diversity educator Elsie Cross (2000) and refers to noticing without judgment. It is about noticing patterns by group identity, including who is present in a given class and who is absent, who talks and who is silent, who gets represented in the curriculum and how they get represented, who makes the rules and who follows them, and who engages and who leaves. Noticing these things aloud can help a group see things about itself that might otherwise stay invisible to some or all members of the group. Tracking also involves noticing and being conscious about what is happening for oneself internally without judging the feelings and reactions.

External Tracking

Tracking is what I did when I noticed that Sam's AP English class was all White. It's what I did when I told Cara that some of her characterizations of students seemed to align with common stereotypes. Sometimes I tracked non-race-related things, such as when I observed to Todd that his students were genuinely funny, or when I mentioned that because of the acoustics in his classroom it was almost impossible to understand him from the back of the room. Tracking is noticing without judgment so that the group or individuals can see and discuss a phenomenon or group dynamic that is occurring. I also use tracking when I witness people using different racial skills. Sometimes people speak from an "I" perspective or ask authentically curious questions, and I try to point out that these are skills and track their impact on the conversations. This helps individuals see the skills they already have and helps the group recognize strategies that work to help them be productive.

Internal Tracking

Tracking is also something we can do internally with our own feelings and reactions. During one inquiry group meeting, I found myself stumbling over how to refer to "Standard English." I said, "We don't teach kids to love themselves, but we teach them correct English. It's really messed up—we think our job as teachers is to teach Standard English or something, and we don't know how to teach our children to love themselves." I felt uncomfortable with the word "correct" because it was so loaded with judgment and the assumption that there is one right way to speak English. I didn't want to say "standard" for the same reason. As the conversation continued, I sat there tracking my discomfort and then brought it up to the group. Tracking my discomfort out loud did not necessarily help us decide on a right answer for how to talk about "Standard English," but it gave us a chance to recognize and practice sitting with the discomfort of uncertainty. I reminded the group of our Four Agreements for Courageous Conversations (namely "lean into discomfort" and "expect and accept a lack of closure"), which helped us avoid getting mired in the common roadblock of frustration that comes from feeling that there are no right answers. We certainly left with a greater understanding of the nuances of the different terms that commonly get used. And then, despite not reaching consensus or fixing my discomfort, we finished the meeting and continued our conversation the next month. Tracking can help make the group dynamics become part of the inquiry. If individual discomfort and problematic group level discomfort is not tracked out loud, it remains under the surface and over time can subvert the work and cohesiveness of the group.

Track When the Four Agreements Are Needed

Our groups came back to the four agreements again and again in moments such as this one when either the discomfort or the lack of closure could have been an impasse. Just knowing that such moments were to be expected and were not a sign that we were doing something wrong was enough to help us keep moving rather than get caught up in the discomfort. Similarly, when people share their truth or when White people tell their racial stories, I track out loud that they are doing so. This is particularly important when someone shares their truth, and another group member attempts to question or dispute it. Noting how hard it is to share a truth and how everybody's truth is indisputable usually helps the group to return to a place of honoring stories and one another.

SUPPORT AND CONFRONT

Support and confront is a general strategy for confronting racist remarks, engaging in conflict, or encouraging people to think or act differently. The general idea is to support the person and confront the behavior or the comment, to disassociate the person from the comment. If a person makes an ignorant comment, for example, a support-and-confront strategy would support the person and their intention while confronting the comment. I find this strategy especially useful when people say hurtful things because they're nervous or unpracticed in race conversations. When a student says "colored people," for example, rather than "people of color," I might say, "I am so glad you are stepping into this conversation (honoring the effort) and taking some risks to talk about this. I just want to check in because I know you want to respect people (intention) and I know the term "colored people" can be offensive because of its history. Have you heard the term 'people of color'?"

Support and confront works broadly as a feedback mechanism, but I would not suggest that this should be everybody's method for interacting. It is my personal belief that people of color should not have to temper their feelings or comments for the effective education of White people. But support and confront works particularly as a strategy for White people talking to other White people because it does two things. First, it challenges a call-out culture in which White people try to one-up one another or shame one another, a culture that ultimately alienates more people than it persuades. Call-out culture is rooted in individualism and competition, two aspects of White culture that do not necessarily further antiracist goals. Second, because so many White people are averse to conflict, we often do not engage in conversations that might take us in that direction. A strategy like support and confront gives White people a way to engage conflict that does not lead to more conflict. If White people do not have such strategies, we often just avoid difficult conversations. When working with other White people in an inquiry group, White people require strategies they can use for addressing problematic things that come up so they don't revert to the White racial subcultural trend of being "nice" and then discussing people behind their backs or becoming passive-aggressive.

Another way to think about support and confront is join and share. When participants share problematic stories or statements, I often join them by sharing the ways that their statements connect to something I once believed or was taught. Then I talk about what I have learned or changed in the interim. Constantly grounding ourselves in the humility of our own journeys can create momentum for the group rather than dividing and shaming.

Avoid the R-Word

Someone once asked me the worst thing you can call a White person. "Is it a 'cracker'?" the person asked. I thought for a moment. "No. It's 'a racist.'" People are terrified of the word and go to extensive lengths to try to demonstrate they are not one. They (we) spend so much energy trying to not look racist or sound racist that they (we) are afraid to do or say anything. I generally find that it is not productive to label individual people or actions "racist." It perpetuates this paranoia as well as a racist/nonracist binary. It makes people feel unsafe and insecure, which pushes their biases deeper into their subconscious mind, making these harder to reckon with. Systems, on the other hand, are "racist," and it is useful to recognize them as such, particularly by citing racially disparate outcomes and circumstances.

Safety Versus Comfort

When creating group norms for talking about race, people often ask for things like "safety." My mentor, Sarah Halley, usually asks groups to differentiate between "safety" and "comfort." When uncomfortable things happen, we often say we're unsafe. In reality, we are perfectly safe. We are physically and emotionally unharmed, but we are uncomfortable. It's hard to promise "safety" to a whole group because what makes one person feel safe makes another person feel unsafe. Talking about race, for example, might make someone feel unsafe. But when it's part of the story of one's life, it feels unsafe not to be able to talk about it. White people are accustomed to having conversational norms that align with our racial subgroup culture, which usually includes not having to talk about race if it makes us uncomfortable. Having open and honest conflict can feel unsafe or uncomfortable to many people, whereas silence and subverted conflict can feel unsafe to others. Whereas trust and relationship are prerequisites for raising race questions, the demand for "safety" is one that can sometimes abort conversations rather than cultivate them.

Nonthreatening Accountability

One of my goals as a facilitator is to create a climate of nonthreatening accountability so that group members can hold themselves and one another accountable to the stated goals of working toward racial justice. There are countless ways to reach this goal, but I will list a few of the strategies I use.

From the beginning, find out what people's individual and collective goals are for being there and remind them of these throughout the process. Acknowledge the challenges of the discussion upfront so people know what they are getting into. Share the four agreements as a way of offering people concrete steps they can take for managing those challenges. Legitimize people's fears, discomforts, and uncertainties by sharing your own and creating space for the members of the group to share theirs; continuously emphasize that uncertainty is okay and that we are all here to learn and inquire together.

Connect with people in the group. Like them. Help them get to know and like each other. We really only engage in difficult relational work when we feel safe and value our partners in that work enough to take risks with them.

Finally, hold people accountable in a nonthreatening way. Holding people accountable in a way that feels threatening or intimidating makes the group, and the individuals in it, less effective. Similarly, a group or a facilitator that is nonthreatening but does not hold people accountable does little to help the individuals in the group advance their goals. Hold yourself accountable as well; this sets high standards for self-monitoring and ownership in the group.

Avoid Dichotomous Thinking

Dichotomous thinking is either/or thinking, sometimes called black-and-white thinking, such as the idea that you can either be nonthreatening or you can hold people accountable, but you can't do both. The shift this requires is to change either/or to both/and. The tendency to think in dichotomous ways is pretty widespread in our society even outside conversations of race. It has its roots in a Eurocentric worldview and is much less common in non-European cultures. When you add fear and anxiety about saying the wrong thing or being racist to a tendency to think dichotomously, this can contribute significantly to a block caused by the fear that saying the wrong thing will make one permanently and irrevocably a racist. Sometimes my role as a facilitator involves tracking dichotomous thinking and suggesting a reframe. I have found that it's not useful to spend time deciding whether somebody or some action is racist, for example. The term itself just blocks people from taking risks (and having a "growth mindset"). So when teachers start to question whether they or their practice or another teacher is racist, I often point out the dichotomy implicit in that question and ask, "What is the impact of the action? How can we address that instead?"

White People Need Allies Too

The concept of allyship typically gets framed as people from privileged groups being allies to people from oppressed groups. I tend to think about allyship more broadly, as support that anyone challenging individual and systemic racism requires to keep going. Because breaking the racial contract can be socially isolating, White people need allies for support. Facilitators, regardless of their race, can consider themselves allies to White people and should encourage every member of the group to act as allies to one another. Group members should all have somebody they can go to with questions or reflections without fear that they will be judged or lectured. Every member of the group, including the facilitator, should be in the struggle together. I try to support teachers by joining them in their struggle and inquiry. Allyship might include offering warmth and acceptance as well as guidance and reality checks.

STRENGTHEN YOUR OWN TOOLBOX

Just as in teaching and counseling, facilitators should continuously work to develop a positive racial identity so they do not have regressive relationships with their group in which members of the group with a well-developed racial identity feel unsupported or even unwelcome. This includes continuing to learn, read, watch movies, read blogs, have conversations, attend workshops, and participate in community forums to keep learning about race, the myriad manifestations of racism, and what it means to be White in this society.

Recently I stopped referring to antiracism as "work" and started referring to it as a "practice." Antiracism is a life practice that I need to do every day in order to stay engaged and aware of how it affects me and my relationships. I continue this practice because I feel more free when I am doing it. I have always had teachers and mentors who helped me learn about race in a way that felt liberating and life-giving. I would come away from class or conversations with a new lens for seeing the world through, so I could look beyond stereotypes and see individuals that I had not fully seen before. I was invited to look at myself and my life in a way that helped me see the impact of a racist national history, without it denigrating me as an individual. This is a practice I choose to continue because I can see the ways it makes me more whole as a human being, not just as a professional.

Facilitators of antiracism need to figure out what sustains them to make this more than a job, to make it a life practice, and to continue the work of developing their own racial identity outside of the group.

Cofacilitation

I sometimes struggle with cofacilitation, particularly with cofacilitators of color, because my internalized sense of superiority often manifests in these relationships. I tend to think I know best how to reach White people or how to structure a workshop. I erroneously see my ways of organizing, planning, and facilitating as better. Our workshops and relationships are always more successful when I can defeat this wrong thinking. I have to remind myself that our diversity of styles enriches a group, that my cofacilitator has ideas, experiences, and ways of communicating that will reach some participants who I cannot or will not reach. To avoid this trap, track the differences in styles without judgment and create space for each facilitator to play to their strengths and bring their whole selves to the group. Be aware of the possibility that White facilitators or group members may have an internalized sense of superiority about whose ideas count or how the process should go, which gets in the way of healthy collaboration. The dynamics of racial superiority and inferiority, if unrecognized, will erode the power of the multiracial group model and further alienate colleagues from one another.

LEARNING FROM CONFLICT

There are a couple of things I do to support groups to move past difficult issues without getting railroaded by them. To illustrate these I will share a challenging moment from a recent workshop in which two White women used the "N-word" in consecutive comments during a whole-group session. They were not actually using the term—they were referring to it—but they both said the word without abbreviating it. A few minutes later, another White woman tracked what had happened and tracked her own emotional response, sharing that she was uncomfortable and wondering aloud if we were creating a new norm as a group that made it okay to say the N-word. She asked others to share their feelings. A Black woman shared that when she heard the word she immediately shut down and was no longer able to engage in the conversation.

This discussion triggered an impasse for many in the group. The original use of the word shut down many people of color, including the one Black woman who shared. When she shared that impact on her, many White participants began to shut down because they felt they were being called racist (even those uninvolved in the conflict shut down because of the vicarious experience of seeing other White people get negative feedback). The conversation played out for several minutes but ultimately had little fuel because so many people were shutting down emotionally and could not find the words to verbalize their feelings.

The group did not let go of the issue nor did we insist that we solve the issue at that moment. We used multiple strategies for engaging this conflict. At the close of the session in which it occurred, my cofacilitator (who was Black) and I talked to each participant involved in the conflict to gauge how they were feeling and what they needed. One of the White women who said the word was angry and hurt and wanted to say something in the next large-group session; I encouraged her to wait and process some of her anger and hurt in a White affinity group before expressing it to the large group. I took time throughout the day to listen to her discomfort and anger while also challenging her to do the following: (1) Own the impact of her statement; (2) let go of her intent; and (3) remember that the woman who had been offended said very clearly that she knew there was no bad intention and that she was not angry at her personally, but that she simply shuts down when she hears that word. Although the White woman understood all of this intellectually, she could not let go of her anger and continued to assert that her intentions were being misread. It was clear that she could not hear me, so I switched tacks and told her a story. I tried to remember a story that had evoked deep feelings of shame, defensiveness, and a sense of victimization in me.

I told her the story of my first year in graduate school when I went to the multicultural student orientation thinking, "Hey, if they want to be multicultural they're going to need some antiracist White folks in the mix." When I arrived at the orientation, there were no other White folks there and on the chalkboard was a handwritten greeting, "Welcome to the Students of Color Orientation." I quickly realized that this was an affinity space I did not belong in, but I didn't want people to think I was afraid to be the only White person in the room, so I didn't leave. Afterward I confessed to a classmate that I really didn't belong there and shouldn't have stayed, and she agreed. I asked her to tell me more about what she thought, and when she told me I shouldn't have been there and that antiracist White allies support affinity groups by staying out of them, and so on, I became more and more panicked. I left that interaction unable to look that classmate in the eye for 3 years. I had asked her for her thoughts, but when she gave me critical feedback, it completely paralyzed me. I told this story in the workshop while continuously emphasizing how bad I was at taking feedback even after asking for it, how hard it was to hear negative feedback even when it only confirmed what I already knew and believed, and how damaged my relationship with this classmate had been as a result of my incapacity for feedback. I shared my feelings of panic and shame that led to this 3-year estrangement and the opportunities for collaboration and action that had been lost because of my lack of skills.

At that point in the workshop we broke into affinity groups as we had planned to do from the beginning of the workshop, but now both groups (the people of color group and the White group) had some specific work to do. Affinity groups can be an incredibly powerful tool for multiracial groups, particularly when there's conflict. Both intergroup (cross-racial) dialogue and intragroup (same race) dialogue are tools for growth, and we employ them both at different times. When the White group gathered, in our first and only affinity meeting, I asked everyone to participate in an anonymous feelings share. Feelings included confusion and discomfort, the challenge of hearing that they had hurt someone, and a self-defensiveness that surprised the whole group with its depth. People found themselves saying things like, "I did not own slaves. I don't even know why I'm saying that, but that's what's coming up for me." Meanwhile in the people of color affinity group, people were able to process the depth of their pain over the N-word and the common pattern of Whites practicing self-defense and logical argument rather than just owning the impact of their words.

When I realized how many White people in the White affinity group were experiencing vicarious trauma through the White women who felt they had been called "racist," I retold my grad school story. I also encouraged others to share times when they had done things they had been ashamed of in regard to race. It's counterintuitive, but when we share our mistakes, it helps us all open up to one another in a way that overcomes the alienating effects of shame. We need to be able to connect and to support each other emotionally so we can hold each other accountable. And when we do both of those things well, it takes the burden off of people of color to hold us accountable and support us emotionally when we can't take the heat.

I use the word "trauma" here because of the shock and denial that situations like this induce in people, and the deep and lasting effects that remain well past the conflict scenario. I hesitate to use it because it feels minimizing of the experience of

Black people in the group to label the experience of White people in this scenario "trauma." And yet, I think we need to get away from the binary thinking that says only one party can be traumatized by a conflict like this. Affinity groups are particularly valuable because they create a space to honor the trauma that White people experience without forcing people of color to put aside their trauma to support the White people. One cautionary note: White affinity groups need to help White people both deal with this trauma and to take responsibility for the impact of their actions. The groups are a place to process and move beyond the trauma; they are not a place for criticizing people of color or forming oppositional arguments.

In the case of our workshop, people left the group feeling open, recharged, and able to think. We asked group members from each affinity group to find a partner in the other group and share their experience of being in the affinity group. In this case the teachers who had been central in the conflict were able to connect with one another and talk things through in a way that left them both feeling a sense of resolution. The rest of the group also got to process their experience of the affinity group—and of the conflict—with someone of another race and reach some kind of balanced closure. After that we came together as a large group, and each person shared one sentence about how they were feeling before breaking for the end of the day.

I share this scenario with great detail to give an example of ways to help a group avoid getting stymied by difficult issues. In this case, we worked with the individuals involved in the conflict, we did not insist on solving the conflict immediately, we created opportunities for everyone to learn from it, we used affinity groups strategically, I shared a story and related to participants who were feeling a sense of shame, and we intentionally reintegrated the group after affinity group time.

GROUP DYNAMICS

Every group has mainstreams and margins that are formed by the particular dynamics of the group. Sometimes extroverts are in the mainstream and introverts on the margins. On school faculties men are often marginalized while women set the mainstream norms for communication style and in-group membership. But mainstreams and margins also correspond to social identity and social power in the broader society. Being White in the United States is a mainstream racial identity, whereas being a person of color is a marginalized racial identity. Although men are often marginalized on school faculties, they still bring social power into school with them from the society outside and can tend to exhibit privileged behaviors such as talking first or interrupting others even if they are the only man in the room. Diversity educator Rev. Dr. Jamie Washington says, "We tend to live in the pain of our marginalized identities and act out of the arrogance of our mainstream identities." In other words, most people are aware of the ways they themselves are oppressed or marginalized. These are the parts of one's life that are not easy or smooth. Often they are also parts that define one's uniqueness. But although people have a heightened consciousness in regard to their marginalized identities, they usually take their mainstream identities for granted. As a heterosexual person, for example, I take it for granted that I can kiss my partner in public. As a middle-class person, I took it for granted that my parents and grandparents paid for me to go to college. When we end up hurting people because of unconscious use of privilege, it is usually related to those taken-for-granted aspects of our mainstream identities. When conversations get stuck, it's sometimes because people cannot get out of the pain related to their marginalized identities.

Take Time to Honor the Margins

Sometimes race conversations are stymied by the pain that everyone feels from their oppressed or marginalized identities. When people are sitting with their own pain it can be hard to access the empathy required to hear the pain of others. It can also be hard to acknowledge one's mainstream privilege. If this is a significant stumbling block to the race conversation, I usually take the time to allow the group to share their own experiences of marginalization. I am explicit about what I am doing and why so that the group doesn't think I am abandoning the race conversation or changing the subject. I verbalize the importance of honoring our own pain and marginality so that we can be allies around race. I usually require that everyone share because this is a moment that can make everyone vulnerable and reveal more of each person's story, which in turn brings the group closer together.

Push Everyone to Recognize Their Mainstream or Privileged Identities

Diane Goodman (2011), a White diversity educator, writes that we have to know how to educate people from privileged groups because if we left out people with privilege, there would be nobody left. Her point is that almost everyone has some form of privileged, or mainstream, identity. I encourage everyone in the group to think about the ways their identities are privileged and what they take for granted as a result. When people act out of a sense of internalized superiority, this action is often related to mainstream identities they are not conscious of. When mainstream privilege is acknowledged across multiple identities (e.g., when a Black woman in the group ackwnowledges her Christian privilege or when an Asian American teacher acknowledges his male privilege) the whole group can better see the power and agency that exists in them. It highlights the many different ally relationships that are possible in the group, and it shows that the White people are not the only ones who need to deal with their privileged identities. This acknowledgment should not detract from the focus on race, but should help create a supportive base in which the group is well versed in power dynamics and the complex interplay of intersectional social identities.

NUTS AND BOLTS

There are countless small things I try to do to create a productive atmosphere for race inquiry.

Plan Activities That Help Individuals Engage and Grow

This is related to staying focused on race. Without engaging activities that help people focus on race, they will change the subject.

Use Humor to Help the Group Integrate

I swore off any kind of racial humor a long time ago because it does not, as you might guess, diffuse tension. It's too confusing to people who are in different places in their racial identity and requires too much sophistication and nuance to do it in a way that does not end up being or seeming racist. But joking with people about innocuous topics can help them relax and engage. In a recent workshop focused on teaching the Civil Rights Movement, I asked a group to keep moving because they were getting sidetracked, saying, "Let's keep going everybody. We've got to keep our eyes—am I really going to say it?—on the prize." This was a ridiculous, obvious reference and yet it (and my self-mockery) amused everybody. Laughing together can help a group deepen its capacity for emotion, which can support the group to do the hard emotional work involved in personal reflection.

Listen to People with My Whole Self

I maintain eye contact with participants, give facial cues, ask relevant questions, and share stories that demonstrate that I am focused on the individuals in front of me and not on stereotypes or assumptions.

Treat Each Individual as an Individual

I make an effort to learn people's names and use them within the first hour of the workshop. I try to affirm the experiences and truths of the people in the room, reminding group members and myself that everyone's truth is indisputable.

Provide Localized Closure

While asking participants to expect and accept a lack of closure (Singleton & Linton, 2005), it can be supportive to provide localized closure in time and space. Every inquiry group session must end, just as every school year does. And while the learning continues, I try to take time at the end of sessions or workshops to give everyone a chance to share final thoughts, next steps, or feelings. Localized closure helps everyone in the group feel they have a sense of how the rest of the group is doing and where they fit into that. It helps the group take ownership for the ongoing life of the group. Sometimes this involves inviting each member of the group to share one thing they've learned or describe how they are feeling. It could involve writing next steps or newly raised questions on Post-its and posting them in a common place. Whole-group participation in any activity is an important aspect of creating closure that supports the group development.

CONCLUSION

I recently experienced two meetings that demonstrated for me how profound and transformative the practice of race inquiry can be for a school. The first meeting was a typical faculty meeting at a school where the racial contract still shaped what was and was not said out loud. To my knowledge, they had not engaged in any kind of race inquiry or any racial competency training. The math department was hiring a new algebra teacher. They brought in three candidates, and not one of them was a person of color. A White faculty member who had been developing her racial competency skills tracked this and brought it up: "I really appreciate all of the work you've put into this search so far, but I just need to name that none of the candidates are people of color. I thought we were committed to hiring more candidates of color." A White man on the search committee responded, "Are you calling us racist?" Another White woman who was not involved in the search said, "I'm getting very uncomfortable with where this conversation seems to be going." The group returned to the agenda, and the matter was dropped. A White candidate was hired for the position. This scenario might sound familiar to readers because it regularly repeats itself in schools across the country. It demonstrates the way that the racial contract and White people's fears of talking about race obstruct pathways to change. The group was unable to even engage a conversation about the race of the candidates because of the automatic defensiveness and fear reactions of White people on the faculty, which silenced the conversation before it could go anywhere. As a result, one of the stated goals of that faculty, to diversify their teaching staff, was left unmet.

In contrast, I recently attended a reunion of teachers from Friends Independent School who had been engaged in our inquiry group 5 years ago. The 10 teachers talked about current problems at the school, including the need to hire more faculty of color and a Black boy pipeline that starts in lower school and funnels Black boys away from the highest math and science classes. I was amazed at how fluidly they debated strategies for hiring more faculty of color and redirecting the pipeline. They didn't all agree, but they were not intimidated by the disagreement or conflict. What struck me also was how many assumptions they had in common: that student failure is an indication of a flaw in the system, that hiring faculty of color would help them meet all of their goals (not just diversity goals), and that they needed to continue to shift their school culture in order to support students and faculty of color. In the 5 years since we started that inquiry group, their school has become known as a place where both teachers and students are racially competent. Both groups lead workshops at diversity conferences and astound participants with their expertise and fluidity on topics of race and oppression. The teachers at the reunion were quick to point out how far they still had to go and how much they still needed to learn. They now knew what they don't know, and they had incredibly high standards. But it was amazing for me to sit back and listen to how different their conversation was 5 years later, how willing and able they were to name race, to examine the structures of a system that they had built (many of them had been at the school more than 15 years), and how nondefensively they were able to question their own practice and ask what they still needed to know.

The contrast of these two meetings was a result of many things (including the nature of the meetings), but it highlighted for me the value of creating spaces for teachers to engage in an inquiry process about race together. Individual inquiry is valuable to each classroom, but group- and schoolwide inquiry supports a cultural shift. This is necessary not only for changing school systems and structures but also for creating a supportive community in which teachers who are working to have an antiracist practice can thrive. Creating an antiracist practice has been compared with swimming upstream. When a critical mass of teachers are doing this, the currents actually start to shift in the local environment. And though that doesn't mean that anyone can then be antiracist by standing still (the racism of the external environment is still very much intact and rushing downstream), it does mean that there's not the same resistance and isolation that most people experience when they resist racism.

Pursuing equity in schools is not just about individual classrooms—it's about changing systems. It is incredibly difficult to transform a system while it is in operation, particularly because students within the system manifest the symptoms and skills of their placement within the system. Students do not necessarily stick out as obviously misplaced in "regular education," for example, because they are always already being shaped by their location in the system. They might have the potential to be honors students, but they are currently not honors students—not necessarily because of their capacity, but because of their skill level and their current level of challenge, their current "regular education" peer group expectations, and their self-perception as "regular education" students. Raising race questions involves looking beyond the taken-for-granted roles of the present and imagining what else is possible. It's about acknowledging that, as teachers, we are simultaneously gatekeepers and advocates, reformers and maintainers of the system.

This book was truly an inquiry project for me. I started out wanting to know how to better support White teachers to recognize and understand racial dynamics. I wanted to know what holds people back and what questions people have. I wanted to know how inquiry about race can change a teacher's practice. I did not start out knowing what I have written here, but rather co-constructed all of these ideas with teachers and colleagues of different races over the past few years. Today the lessons shared here have become the foundation of the workshops that I lead. These include the following ideas: The goal of an antiracist practice is to build more whole people and more whole communities—it's not about tearing people down. We need to support the positive racial identity of our students and we as teachers cannot do that without having a positive racial identity ourselves. Our racial identities are our toolboxes, and if they are not strong, we will not be able to hold or use any other tools. A multicultural curriculum is not sufficient for creating an antiracist classroom. Racial competence can be learned. Talking about race is not racist. Teachers must engage in learning about race for reasons other than talking about race with students. Some of the questions we most need to verbalize are the most "untouchable."

All these lessons crystallized as I watched teachers trying to change themselves and their practice. Change requires a depth of engagement that cannot be broached without a sustained process. It is my hope that the lessons recorded here, lessons that emerged from my own process of inquiry over the past many years, will support, challenge, and accompany teachers as they journey on their own process of inquiry and change.

Responses from Teachers

Teachers shared so much of themselves to help make this book possible. For that reason I have communicated with them throughout my process of research and writing, keeping them abreast of new ideas and interpretations of my observations, and requesting updates on their classrooms. I never held back my thoughts out of a fear of offending (although I did often fear that I would offend them), but I took steps to make sure that the teachers themselves would benefit from and appreciate what they read in these pages. Whenever I had critical feedback, I gave it to them directly, using strategies I describe in Chapter 5 and framing it in a way that I thought they could hear. I wanted the words in this book to describe, resonate with, and affirm the struggles of the teachers portrayed here. As I finished the book, I asked each teacher to read it and write a response so they could update readers on their progress and have the final word on their own stories. The following pieces were written by the teachers themselves in response to reading this book.

SAM

1. How did you see your teaching and your thinking about race change over the year that you were involved in this race inquiry group?

I became involved in this type of work—focusing on race in the educational realm—for two reasons. I have always been interested and concerned about my African American students' successes and failures in my classes over the years. I wanted to learn how other researchers and institutions were addressing the performances of these students. And to be honest, I wanted to see how my own school community was going to spend the 2-year period of research. For years I had watched the more influential individuals of my community either ignore the educational challenges for students of color or make decisions that were based solely on skin color and not on ability. I wanted to see if this technique was going to be encouraged or exposed in other communities.

From the start, however, I have found this work to be invigorating, exciting, and enlightening. The notion of becoming more and more aware of my own Whiteness and other folks' "color" has expanded how I consider my curriculum, enter my classroom, and interact with students. It has also (obviously . . . it seems) influenced how I experience the world around me, and my own understanding of what I have, get, and expect, and what other people do *not* have, get, or expect. I have had epiphanies time and again in which my learning in this area has exposed new truths for me, such as what privilege really looks like in a classroom, the ways in which privilege opens certain doors, and how the lack of it seals off entire metaphoric buildings. So I am much more aware of how Whiteness and color function beyond the simple, superficial notion of skin.

And this last comment, obvious though it might be, is at the heart of this work for me. I am now asking and reading about how the racial situation has developed from the inception of this country. I am now monitoring how I react to people of color who live in poverty and those who have the same or more than me. I am now cognizant of how television, movies, catalogs, and advertisements work to maintain stereotypes on multiple levels. And throughout all of this work, I have been asking myself, if I were a student of color, where would I find myself in this curriculum? This particular honors class? This school? In what ways am I represented, and in what ways am I not invited? These questions continue, and most important, I have learned that I must ask them all the time, every day.

I have also learned that there are things all teachers need to do when we teach students of color, when we engage our students, and when we work one-on-one with them. These 2 years of work and the two conferences I was lucky enough to attend—POCC and WPC—showed me that just putting students of color in classes or sections was more often than not unsuccessful; rather, I began to see that while there is enormous amounts of work to be done, the true charge of this type of work is considering how best to support students of color, how best to push them to do and learn more, and how best to include them in the process of learning. I never read one article that suggested we just hug our Black kids and give them a pass for not doing their homework simply because they are Black. I have learned that high expectations for all students is the best method for encouraging excellence and getting it. Then again, the home life, educational experience, and work life of parents affect students significantly. So I have to make myself more available to meet with these students and also encourage, or force, some of them to meet with me even when they don't want to do so.

2. How have you grown or changed since then with regard to race?

I have tried to expand my curriculum to include more writers and poets of color. I try to consciously balance the number of texts I read based on genre and on who the writer is. This means I need to read beyond the canon and even push beyond the "private school canon" to find writers that will "work" for high school students. This approach benefits both my White students and students of color. Hearing new voices, witnessing new vantage points, and expanding perceived experience benefits all of my students and provides them with opportunities to make connections, articulate differences, and celebrate commonalities.

I have tried to engage with students of color in a more honest and relaxed manner. I am learning daily who I am more and more, and I try to share this awareness with my all of my students. I talk about race in the texts, about race in my city of Philadelphia, and race in America. I make race a constant theme that is always pertinent to the discussion. For example, I have become more aware of how the transcendentalists were all referring to the notion of slavery and expanded this to include my own readings about the institution of slavery's impact on the life of Southerners and Northerners during the 19th century. Even the "black man in the forest" who wanders through Hawthorne's *The Scarlet Letter* gained new life and vitality when we considered how in 1850 this entity would have certainly been more than Satan. This figure has also made me more aware of my own students of color who are reading this text. They read "black man in the forest" in a very different way from the White students. I talk about this; I bring it up; I don't have the answers, but I am much more likely to address these issues and ideas such as "who is invited" and "who is not" in these texts than I used to be.

I also am more aware of who talks and seems to dominate the class. I created a grid to help all students monitor who participates and who does not in class, and we did this for about 2 weeks. The idea was to see what the students "see" in class, but also to get them to stop for a second and consider who is doing the talking and who feels empowered to do it. And in many ways, this is what this work—race work—is really about: becoming more aware of who is talking, who is telling their stories, and who is responding to the stories. This dynamic plays out in an English classroom every day.

3. What questions do you still have? Where do you still get stuck?

I could make this response 300 pages, but I'll just limit myself to a few huge questions:

- What are the best techniques for engaging students of color in an English classroom?
- What are the best techniques for aiding students of color in becoming better readers and writers?
- How do we hire more faculty of color?
- How do we use texts written by people of color if the topics are often about oppression and racism? Do we embrace these texts or look for different ones?
- Now a few years later at my school, after the 2-year program focusing on race, we the participants are not sure what has happened to our work or if this is work that should still be a priority.
- Does all work focusing on students of color or diversity work need to be done through the campus office of diversity?
- How do you deal with folks who are not yet at your stage in the journey? How do folks deal with me when they are ahead of me in the journey?
- Can we engage older colleagues and make them see the importance of this work?

- What do we, White teachers, do if there are few to no Black colleagues? Do we act? Do we wait?
- How do we deal with programs that seem to promote "old school racism" in an environment that is "committed to creating a new culture of inclusion and respect"?

Dr. Chonika Coleman-King, who worked with my group, was adamant that the educational state for many students of color is an emergency; I agree now, but what are the next steps?

4. How do you agree or disagree with Ali's analysis? What would you like to add?

I have to admit that it was tough reading some of Ali's suggestions, but they are all spot on. We do need to create new opportunities and avenues for success for these students, *but* when they don't work or don't work well enough, we can't just raise our hands and mutter, "Well . . . we tried."

We have to keep attacking this problem, keep working to figure out what could work and what will work, and keep focused on making all students excel in our classes. To put it another way, we have to be sure that the only thing holding a student back is a lack of effort and nothing more.

I want to thank Ali for giving me the opportunity to be involved in her research and her work. Our conversations have kept me committed, and just when I think I might be getting tired, an email will pop up in my inbox from Ali, and I'll get re-ignited, again. Thanks, Ali!

HELENE

Over the course of the year I worked with Ali, I developed a real comfort and trust in her that helped me, maybe for the first time, really be honest about where I struggle and have room to grow as a White teacher. I felt validated and supported in a way that made the important feedback Ali provided me with much easier to hear, take in, and respond to. Ali mentions that I was able to ask "untouchable" questions; I believe that this is because it was such a relief to finally find a space where I could talk about topics that seemed too scary to bring up elsewhere for fear of being seen as clueless or, worse, racist.

One area that I gained a lot of clarity in was the use of African American Vernacular English (AAVE) by some of my Black students. The idea of correcting my students of color who were not speaking "proper" English seemed like part of my job as a teacher—in the same way that I would correct a student of any race who used the word "brang," by telling them that brang is not a word and instead they should use brought. At the same time, I had an unease that I couldn't quite place with correcting the way my Black students spoke, and I was wary of the imbalance of negative and positive feedback a student would get if I corrected him or her too frequently.

Through conversations with Ali and, more recently, from reading what she has written in this book about AAVE, I gained insight into how to think about some of my Black students' use of language. I began to understand that my unease was not necessarily a bad thing, because there *is* something inherently problematic in telling a child that the way they speak is "wrong." I learned that there is a time and place for correcting AAVE and that, as teachers, we do have a responsibility to help our students be as successful as possible in the world outside of school; part of that success is knowing how to code-switch. I also learned that a lot of the conversations about code-switching that needed to take place with students of color were not necessarily appropriate for my 2nd-graders and would be more useful when they were a bit older. I was able to find an answer to the question of whether I should correct my students' use of AAVE, and that answer, most of the time, is "no." At such a young age, it seems most important to validate the children for who they are and, as Lisa Delpit suggests, to listen to the meaning of their words and not the specific language. When they are older and more able to recognize and articulate their own code-switching, I hope that they will have a kind teacher or other adult who helps them understand that the way they speak is great but that there is a different, equally valid way that they will likely need to speak in certain work and academic situations.

During my time with Ali, I recognized how much I didn't know I didn't know. One particular area that Ali helped me think about was the noise level that I preferred to have in my classroom. I had not thought to question my rigidity about the noise level and instead felt that I had clear expectations about noise. I was, however, often frustrated that despite my clear expectations year to year, there were always children who needed constant reminders about volume control, and often these children were Black or Latino. Ali suggested that I look at distractions present in the classroom that did not involve noise, and that consequently might be sliding under my radar. I found that there were other ways that kids interrupted or distracted from a whole-group lesson or from my work with an individual student, and because they were quieter, I would not even notice them as distractions. Often these types of distractions came from White children. This awareness is something that has stayed with me and that I continue to try to pay attention to. I had not looked at the idea that my expectations for a quiet classroom were truly a personal preference related to my own race and cultural upbringing and that quiet might not be as necessary to a productive learning environment as I had originally thought. I still find that I get frustrated and distracted by noise during work time, but because I can now see this as a personal preference rather than the way a classroom "should" be, I respond in a different, and I hope less exasperated, manner.

One area that I continue to struggle with, and that I still don't feel that I have a real grasp on, is the issue of parents physically reprimanding their children. Reading over the section that Ali wrote about my two students who had gotten a "whooping" felt very emotional because although on one hand I feel that I should respect discipline procedures that are more normative in some communities, I also felt—and still feel—strongly that using physical force, even just spanking, to teach a lesson is counterproductive and hurtful. I believe that physically reprimanding a child makes him or her fearful, angry, and powerless.

Reading Ali's analysis of physical punishment in some families was helpful, but it was also hard. I felt that her points made sense, specifically about it being the parent's right to choose how to parent, the idea that physical punishment needed to be looked at in the context of a family and a culture, and how my views about the right way to reprimand children could be alienating to some families. At the same time, as I was reading, I just kept feeling, "No, no, no, this just can't be right." It seems to me that there are certainly some things that, despite a person's cultural background, are definite "no's" in terms of raising children, but I cannot say for sure that this is one of them. I know that we all need to do a better job of having respect for other cultural norms, but do we do that even when it goes against our deeply held beliefs about how to treat children? Again, I cannot say for sure; it's a tough dilemma, and I still have some thinking, learning, and growing to do.

ANN

1. How did you see your teaching and your thinking about race change over the year that you were involved in this race inquiry group?

When I was introduced to Ali and asked to participate in her study, I was eager to have a guest in my classroom who would be able to assess my style of teaching in terms of methods of communicating with, and providing instruction to, my students of color. Having Ali with me was like having a light switch with a dimmer; at the outset the lights were on, but they grew brighter as the year progressed. After this experience, I read Ali's comments and felt validated by the term she used, "microproficiency;" at the same time, I wondered if this meant I was on the right track. It was uncomfortable to read about the scenario of my two students who had vied for my attention. The memory of that scenario is vivid in every detail because I learned two valuable lessons that day. First, teachers should always be mindful that the frenetic lives of high school teenagers will sometimes spill over into our classroom space; and, second, individualized instruction can be very messy.

Ali's visits throughout the year were concurrent with my experience working with our district's Cultural Proficiency Cadre. I was completely engaged in the program, so I felt obligated to speak my truth and hold all stakeholders accountable; however, that policy did not always serve me well, personally or professionally. For instance, in one meeting I commented on the "tone" of our committee and questioned the progress related to our goal. Despite the mission of our committee, after only several meetings our three teachers of color stopped attending our meetings; the reason for disengaging was never shared. Although those of us that remained continued to work on program development and strategic planning, the three teachers met separately and circumvented the intended process by reviewing our meeting notes and engineering the program to their own design. Lesson learned: Sometimes speaking your truth is easy, but explaining your truth is not.

The result of the changes to our group dynamic and three teachers abandoning the committee was that the White female teacher, who had led the building Achievement Gap program, was replaced. This teacher is a strong, extremely bright, and hardworking person who was responsible for the design and implementation of the program. She had worked tirelessly with both students and parents in order to address the needs of students of color. In less than 1 academic year, she was replaced by a Black male teacher, who was no less dedicated, but the point was resounding: A White teacher is unable to work effectively with students of color. Despite vehement protests regarding the replacement of the White teacher by respected members of our community, and the parents who served on the committee (whose children participated in the program), the decision was final.

This decision secured the perception that the members of that "inner circle," of our larger group, were "experts" on all matters involving race. This was made clear as they dominated the conversations at subsequent meetings, and thwarted any attempt to explore race as it might pertain to new opportunities for students of color. Although the White teachers fulfilled their obligation to the cadre for the remainder of the school year, they chose not to continue after that, opting instead to participate in another activity in the building, or an extracurricular activity in support of students. Prior to this incident, I believe that we, as part of the district initiative, were making great strides in our effort to understand issues of race and culture. The actions of my colleagues in this matter undermined my confidence and my sense of pride. Until this incident, I truly believed participating on a committee of mixed race could lead to progress. I walked away from a role in that collaborative but have continued the journey on my own.

Since this experience, I have become more aware of racial inconsistencies in our school, especially when it comes to permissiveness. When teachers allow students to be late; leave class for nonessential reasons (usually they have texted a friend to meet in the bathroom); fail to discipline students for disrupting the educational process, affecting their education as well as others'; or make excuses for students who do not perform academically because they expect less of them, it is unprofessional and just plain wrong. If students are not provided with expectations of behavioral and academic performance, they are not being educated. The world outside of high school is demanding; we need to prepare them for it in every way.

A confession: I am not perfect. The student who asks for extra help easily sways me. I will advocate for a student to have a second attempt at a paper or an exam if she needs that opportunity to prove to herself, and her teacher, that she can do better. When asked, I will read students' papers before they are submitted for a grade, and gladly provide comments for revision. Over lunch, or after school, I will read with them, discuss and clarify assignments, quiz them, and help with note cards. Of course, providing water and granola bars is great incentive—food is a great motivator for hungry teens. Whatever it takes to help students who are trying to make it in a highly competitive academic setting works for me—I'm all in.

2. How have you grown or changed since then with regard to race?

I believe that I have evolved more in a spiritual way (do unto others) rather than in a Darwinian way (survival of the fittest). In the past, I might have asked questions because I felt that others needed to hear the answers; but now, I have learned to ask the questions that I need answered. My teaching practice has become much more reflective and more focused on student learning. I not only challenge myself, but I also challenge all of the people in my life, a testament to which my students, my boss, and my family would attest. I continue to educate my own children in matters of race; this is perhaps partly a byproduct of their own maturation as well as their mother's growing, sage-like wisdom. Feedback from every source is essential to how I learn; I highly value the authentic thoughts and opinions of others. I have become acutely aware of the need to understand race and racial factors while working with my students. I have learned to push through moments of racial discomfort with students and parents, colleagues and friends, because it is what is best for kids: theirs, mine, and ours.

3. What questions do you still have? Where do you still get stuck?

I get stuck whenever I try to understand the "achievement gap." Of course, many educational and academic gurus from all levels of academic strata continue to struggle with this conundrum, so I guess I am in good company. One aspect of this issue is what I call the parent trap. To me, this term refers to the idea of a student whose parents or guardians may or may not be able to support and engage their child on a daily basis to ensure academic success. Parent support coupled with the financial wherewithal to provide private tutoring is largely associated with our White students. A greater number of parents of our White students also tend to have a postsecondary education, and they personally support their children in their pursuit of academic success. As a result, these students appear to have an advantage, specifically with homework completion, preparedness, and ultimately overall grades. Students without this financial and familial support system can easily fall behind. The dilemma is how do we fix this parent trap? Do we provide parent involvement opportunities at school? Tutoring? Homework clubs? Mentors? What is the best way to level the playing field when money and family support are the variables? I believe that innovative educational programs and policies that challenge students and help prepare them for a productive life are worthy of our collective focus.

CARA

1. How did you see your teaching and your thinking about race change over the year that you were involved in this race inquiry group?

Over the year that I was involved in the race inquiry group, I found myself coming to terms with the concept that I could and should teach Black history, even as a White woman and even though there were aspects of my civil rights curriculum and instruction that felt deeply uncomfortable. It became clearer to me that as a teacher of any children, especially children of color, I needed to seek out and learn from resources about the history of people of color in order to support my students in developing a more accurate understanding of American history and their place in it. Learning about the framework for Racial Identity Development, and the range and flux involved in it, has helped me better understand my students of color and myself. Finally, I was able to reinterpret some of the mannerisms and behaviors of some of my students as neutral expressions rather than targeted disrespect. All of this growth has continued to inform my practice and has made it easier for me to build relationships with some of my students.

2. How have you grown or changed since then with regard to race?

I have become more comfortable talking about race with my colleagues, students, family, and friends in the years since my participation in the inquiry group. It feels like a small but powerful move to break the unwritten code of race-muteness. This has allowed me to increase my own sense of integrity with regard to antiracist work. I have become more sensitive to the choices I make in how I relate to colleagues and parents of color, especially in regard to interrupting (a marker of the culture of White supremacy). My relationship with my husband, who is Black, and his family has allowed me to advance my learning about race to some extent. When reflecting on my perceptions of my students and their families, I have often thought about how my husband's White teachers might have viewed and judged his family's cultural differences. Since the inquiry group, I have attended a training entitled Whites Confronting Racism and have done more reading by authors such as Howard Stevenson and Lisa Delpit in order to build and refresh my understanding of the implications of race in the classroom. In the years since my initial work with Ali, I have learned about, accepted, and become more comfortable with my racial identity as a White person. I am literally more comfortable in my own skin, which helps me relate more authentically to my students, their families, and my colleagues at school. To a large extent, feelings of fear, shame, and guilt do not stymie me in the ways they did during my first 5 years of working with children of color in school settings.

3. What questions do you still have? Where do you still get stuck?

I still have questions about how to systematically modify my curriculum to better suit the needs of my students of color (which is all of them). This includes incorporating more content about people of color, more real-world application of math skills and concepts, and adding more elements of verve and cooperative learning to the lessons I teach. All of this is made challenging by the pace and scope of the curriculum that my school (and my state) expects me to teach.

I also have questions about instruction. My classroom is an extremely structured place, which helps many of my students to focus on learning. Many of my students, however, would benefit from more opportunities to collaborate on projects and discuss ideas with one another in the course of the school day, rather than spend the bulk of their independent practice working by themselves. I understand this prioritization of quiet, independent assignments and practice to be a function of my cultural bias, based on my racial identity. I want to push myself to step outside of my comfort zone and relinquish some control in order to create a learning environment that engages and respects the needs of my students of color.

It was helpful for me to revisit Ali's analysis of my interactions with the boys in my class whom I had characterized as pouty and unable to accept responsibility for their actions. I continue to struggle with the best ways to support and to discipline boys who have maladaptive reactions to consequences. I have become more flexible and empathetic in the ways I approach boys who exhibit these behaviors, but I still catch myself getting frustrated. I want to build up my toolbox so that I am better able to understand and teach them.

4. How do you agree or disagree with Ali's analysis? What would you like to add?

I agree with Ali's analysis. The work I did during and since the inquiry group has been invaluable to my personal and professional development. Even though I have a lifetime of learning and antiracist work ahead of me, I don't have reservations about pursuing it. Instead, I have tools and resources for dealing with unhelpful feelings of guilt or shame and the lack of confidence that sometimes arises. I'm familiar with research and authors whose work can support me in understanding the ways race affects my professional work and social relationships. I am glad that some of my experiences and questions are included in this book. They are a testament to the complexity involved in building racial and cultural competence. I hope other teachers who struggle with similar questions and challenges can use this book to find a starting point for working through them.

LAURIE

In the years since I worked with Ali, I have moved to 1st grade and have continued to develop my practice step-by-step. The following is a list of the things I have done and continue to do to keep myself in this work. I have found colleagues as allies to have ongoing and honest conversations with. I continue to use teachable moments to allow conversations about race. I provide tools and opportunities for children to notice and name race. I provide tools for children to express emotions in a safe environment. I have found that it is useful to foreground the conversation with parents and teachers about how topics regarding race come up in the classroom, and to keep that door open for ongoing opportunities to engage. This can happen on an individual basis during conferences and in a group setting on Back to School Night. On Back to School Night I also present my intention of an antibias classroom in which we notice and name race as it authentically comes up and provide opportunity for discussion through literature, videos, conversations, and lessons. I invite families to share questions and concerns and provide insight and feedback regarding their children and culture. I continue to search for and provide excellent literature in which every child can see themselves or their family represented in an authentic and genuine way that honors their culture. I seek to share other cultures that are not represented in our classroom population through literature and video and in person.

I have also learned to prioritize learning from students. I have attended upper-school student discussions, when invited, to hear what conversations about race are like for them in order to be informed about how students coming from the lower and middle school, or who are new to our school community, address race-related topics. Some opportunities for this were at a student-led discussion at the People of Color Conference, and in an upper-school assembly in which students presented a town forum style of discussion on race. Recently, I was asked to present how I approach race in the classroom for a faculty inservice (panel discussion). I continue to read books and articles to further develop my awareness and sensitivity and become culturally competent. I also continue to attend workshops and discussions on race. I am currently part of a teacher-led monthly discussion group on race and a city-wide discussion series hosted by the Multicultural Resource Center. The next discussion in the series will be "The Politics of Hair."

This work never ends for teachers or for students. I have found how important it is for conversations to be ongoing across grade levels. As our students and teachers deepen their own identity and cultural sensitivity, they need space to engage in conversation with adults, peers, and parents in safe, supportive, and honest ways.

I appreciated Ali's response to our time together and her observations, which provided another perspective to help me see where I can and need to change and grow. In direct response to Ali's reflections, I have read Lisa Delpit's *Other People's Children,* a gift from a former parent, and [Denton and Kriete's] *The First Six Weeks of School,* both of which provide insight and tools into creating a classroom that is nurturing and supportive, that builds every child up, and that addresses bias. They talk about how to confront stereotypes and prejudice when we see them as well as how to communicate with my students with consistency, explicitly naming what I expect from each of my students and providing examples on the expected behavior, such as "When we come to circle time (morning meeting) we sit like this. . . ."

I am open and eager for more feedback from colleagues on how they see my teaching, how I can improve, and if they see biases, microaggressions, inequalities, or misuse of power, which will perpetuate the system of racism that exists in every institution on various levels. I ask for this of my allies and colleagues.

TODD

Over the course of the year that I met with Ali and the other members of the inquiry group, I felt that for the first time, I had a place where I could speak honestly and openly about race in my classroom. From my first day teaching, race seemed like the elephant in the room. I was not confident enough to talk about it or ask the questions I needed answered in order to feel like I was doing a good job and giving my students the education they deserved. My classroom and my school seemed like a microcosm of the district I worked in. The lack of acknowledgment of race on all levels seemed to permeate everything.

While working with Ali and the other teachers, I was able to identify where I was failing to infuse my teaching with multicultural elements. Like so many other teachers starting out, I was clueless about what multicultural education truly meant. I bought posters showcasing African American scientists, but I never planned any lessons or discussions to give those visuals context and meaning. Unfortunately, they became decorations rather than a foundation for a realistic portrayal of non-White contributors to the sciences. By working with Ali and the group, I felt challenged to do more and make it my priority to develop the skills I would need to improve my craft. What kinds of examples did I use in class? How would I connect my content to the life experiences of my students? To answer these questions, I had to invest time in learning about my students on a different level. What challenges did they face when entering the classroom? What were their strengths and weaknesses, passions and interests? I knew that I had to open myself up to learning more and also sharing more about myself. I realized that by ignoring the racial differences in my classroom, I was silencing my students in a way and taking away their agency. Instead of helping to normalize racial discussions, my silence was promoting and condoning negative stereotypes that my students had already ingrained in their minds about themselves and aspects of their culture and background.

I had to confront my own mindsets about my students as well. Although I didn't mean to, in reflecting now, I know that my expectations were affected by my thinking. Although not featured prominently in this book, many of the discussions I had with Ali centered around my struggle to determine expectations for my students. I constantly felt that my expectations were inconsistent at best, and I had trouble finding a way to problem-solve and hold high expectations for my students. I tried to find good examples of how to maintain high expectations, but most of the time, I came up with nothing. It was hard for me to picture how I could change and grow as a teacher, and unfortunately as budget and testing crises loomed, professional development for teachers was on the back burner.

At the same time, I was regarded as one of the best teachers in my school. My classroom was not out of control and, for the most part, I had a positive rapport with my students. It was always ironic to me that I secretly felt like I was doing such a bad job while at the same time receiving positive praise from my administration. After trying for a few more years, I became increasingly disheartened at the lack of progress I saw and the continual obstacles to education that I felt were beyond my control. Ultimately, I left the public schools in search of a setting where I could develop into a stronger instructor. I moved to a charter network and carried with me my experiences and desire to grow. I learned so many important lessons from working with Ali and the focus group. Although I still don't feel like I've reached my goal, I do believe that the first step is opening up the discussion and being receptive to the vulnerability that comes from reflecting about privilege and race in education. I know that I will carry these questions with me to any classroom I enter and hopefully learn and grow along the way.

Resources for Use in Race Inquiry

Books

Articulate While Black: Barack Obama, Language and Race in the U.S. (Alim & Smitherman, 2012).

Beyond Heroes and Holidays: A Practical Guide to K–12 Antiracist Multicultural Education and Staff Development, 2nd ed. (Menkart, Okazawa-Rey, & Lee, 2008)

Beyond the Bake Sale: The Essential Guide to Family/School Partnerships (Henderson, Mapp, Johnson, & Davies, 2004).

Black Male(d): Peril and Promise in the Education of African American Males (Howard, 2013).

Categorically Unequal: The American Stratification System (Massey, 2008).

Colorblind (Wise, 2010).

Critical Race Theory: An Introduction (Delgado & Stefancic, 2012).

Crossing over to Canaan: The Journey of New Teachers in Diverse Classrooms (Ladson-Billings, 2001).

Culturally Responsive Teaching: Theory, Research and Practice (Gay, 2010).

Detracking for Equity and Excellence (Burris & Garrity, 2008).

A Different Mirror: A History of Multicultural America (Takaki, 2008).

Dreamkeepers: Successful Teachers of African American Children (Ladson-Billings, 2009).

The Education of Black People (DuBois, 1973).

Everyday Antiracism (Pollock, 2008b).

The Everyday Language of White Racism (Hill, 2008).

The First R: How Children Learn Race and Racism (Van Ausdale & Feagin, 2001).

Forty Ways to Raise a Nonracist Child (Mathias & French, 1996).

Foundations of Critical Race Theory in Education (Taylor, Gillborn, & Ladson-Billings, 2009).

The Gift of Black Folk: The Negroes in the Making of America (DuBois, 2009).

Inquiry as Stance: Practitioner Research in the Next Generation (Cochran-Smith, & Lytle, 2009).

Keeping Track, 2nd ed. (Oakes, 2005).

Killing Rage: Ending Racism (hooks, 1995).

Lies My Teacher Told Me (Loewen, 2008).

The Miseducation of the Negro (Woodson, 1933).

Multiplication Is for White People: Raising Expectations for Other People's Children (Delpit, 2012).

The New Jim Crow: Mass Incarceration in the Age of Colorblindness (Alexander, 2012).

Open Minds to Equality (Schniedewind & Davidson, 2006).

Other People's Children: Cultural Conflict in the Classroom (Delpit, 2006).

Playing with Anger (Stevenson, 2003).

The Possessive Investment in Whiteness: How White People Profit from Identity Politics (Lipsitz, 2006).

Practice What You Teach: Social Justice Education in the Classroom and in the Streets (Picower, 2012).

A Promise and a Way of Life: White Antiracist Activism (Thompson, 2001).

Promoting Racial Literacy in Schools (Stevenson, 2013).

Race in the Schoolyard: Negotiating the Color Line in Classrooms and Communities (Lewis, 2003).

Racial Proficiency in Schools: Difference That Makes a Difference (Stevenson, 2014).

Racism without Racists: Colorblind Racism and the Persistence of Inequality in America (Bonilla-Silva, 2013).

Readings for Diversity and Social Justice (Adams, Blumenfeld, Castañeda, Hackman, Peters, & Zúñiga, (2013).

Recruiting and Retaining Culturally Different Students in Gifted Education (Ford, 2013).

The Skin That We Speak (Delpit, 2008).

Starting Small: Teaching Tolerance in Preschool and the Early Grades (Teaching Tolerance Project, 1997).

Stickin' to, Watchin' over, and Gettin' with: An African American's Guide to Parenting (Stevenson, Davis, & Abdul-Kabir, 2001).

Subtractive Schooling: U.S. Mexican Youth and the Politics of Caring (Valenzuela, 1999).

Talking Race in the Classroom (Bolgatz, 2005).

Teaching/Learning Anti-Racism: A Developmental Approach (Derman-Sparks & Phillips, 1997).

There Is a River: The Black Struggle for Freedom in America (Harding, 1993).

The Trouble with Black Boys: And Other Reflections on Race, Equity and the Future of Public Education (Noguera, 2009).

To Remain an Indian: Lessons in Democracy from a Century of Native American Education (Lomawaima & McCarty, 2006).

Up Against Whiteness: Race, Schooling and Immigrant Youth (Lee, 2005).

Uprooting Racism: How White People Can Work for Racial Justice, 3rd ed. (Kivel, 2011).

We Can't Teach What We Don't Know (Howard, 2006).

What Does It Mean to Be White?: Developing White Racial Literacy (DiAngelo, 2012).

What If All the Kids Are White? Anti-Bias Multicultural Education with Young Children and Families, 2nd ed. (Derman-Sparks & Ramsey, 2011).

Whistling Vivaldi and Other Clues to How Stereotypes Affect Us (Steele, 2010).

White by Law (Haney-López, 2006).

White Like Me:Reflections on Race from a Privileged Son (Wise, 2007).

White Privilege: Essential Readings on the Other Side of Racism, 4th ed. (Rothenberg, 2011).

White Teachers, Diverse Classrooms (Landsman & Lewis, 2011).

White Women, Race Matters: The Social Construction of Whiteness (Frankenberg, 1999).

Why Are All the Black Kids Sitting Together in the Cafeteria? (Tatum, 2003).

Why Race and Culture Matter in Schools (Howard, 2010).

You Mean There's Race in My Movie?: Understanding Race in Mainstream Hollywood (Gooding, 2007).

Articles

"Becoming an Antiracist White Ally" (Michael & Conger, 2009).

"From the Achievement Gap to the Education Debt: Understanding Achievement in U.S. Schools" (Ladson-Billings, 2006).

"Just What Is Critical Race Theory and What's It Doing in a *Nice* Field like Education?" (Ladson-Billings, 1998).

"My Class Didn't Trump My Race" (DiAngelo, 2006).

"Niggers No More: A Critical Race Counternarrative on Black Male Student Achievement at Predominantly White Colleges and Universities" (Harper, 2009).

"Questioning Your Collection" (Rajput, 2009).

"Racial Micro-Aggressions in Everyday Life" (Sue, 2007).

"Straight Talk on Race" (Perkins, 2009).

"A Talk to Teachers" (Baldwin, 1963).

"Uncertain Allies" (Cochran-Smith, 1995).

"The Unexamined Whiteness of Teaching: How White Teachers Maintain and Enact Dominant Racial Ideologies" (Picower, 2009).

"What White Children Need to Know about Race" (Michael & Bartoli, 2014).

"White Privilege: Unpacking the Invisible Knapsack" (McIntosh, 1998).

Workshops

Beyond Diversity Resource Center, www.beyonddiversity.org
Border Crossers, www.bordercrossers.org

The People's Institute for Survival and Beyond, Undoing Racism, www.pisab.org
The Race Institute for K–12 Educators, www.raceinstitute.org
Seeking Educational Equity and Diversity, The National SEED Project on Inclusive
    Curriculum, www.nationalseedproject.org
Social Justice Training Institute, www.sjti.org
Whites Confronting Racism, www.whitesconfrontingracism.org
Witnessing Whiteness, www.witnessingwhiteness.com

Conferences

Facing Race: A National Conference, facingrace.raceforward.org
National Association of Multicultural Education Annual Conference, www.
    nameorg.org
National Conference on Race and Ethnicity in American Higher Education, www.
    ncore.ou.edu
People of Color Conference, www.pocc.nais.org
White Privilege Conference, www.whiteprivilegeconference.com
Winter Roundtable on Cultural Psychology and Education, www.tc.columbia.
    edu/centers/roundtable/

Films and Videos

Cracking the Codes of Racial Inequality by Shakti Butler for World Trust, www.
    crackingthecodes.org
The Danger of a Single Story by Chimamanda Ngozi Adichie, www.ted.com/talks/
    chimamanda_adichie_the_danger_of_a_single_story
A Girl Like Me by Kiri Davis for Reel Works Teen Filmmaking, www.mediathat
    mattersfest.org/films/a_girl_like_me
Mirrors of Privilege: Making Whiteness Visible by Shakti Butler for World Trust, www.
    world-trust.org/shop/films/mirrors-privilege-making-whiteness-visible
Race: The Power of an Illusion produced by California Newsreel, www.pbs.org/race
Speaking Truth to Privilege by Ali Michael, www.alimichael.org/film
Teens Talk Racial Privilege by Ali Michael for TRTaylor Consulting LLC, www.ali
    michael.org/film
Traces of the Trade by Katrina Browne for California Newsreel, www.tracesofthe
    trade.org
The Way Home by Shakti Butler for World Trust, www.world-trust.org/shop/films/
    way-home-women-talk-race-america/

Websites

EdChange is a team of educators committed to equity and social justice founded
    by diversity educator Paul Gorski. They collaborate to develop resources and
    workshops, many of which are available on their website. www.edchange.org

Ground Spark creates visionary films and dynamic educational campaigns that move individuals and families to take action for a more just world. www. groundspark.org

The Microaggressions Project "is a response to 'It's not a big deal.'" It's a collection of microaggressions that individuals have experienced in regard to race, sexuality, religion, gender, class, body type, education level, and more. www. microaggressions.com

Race: Are We So Different? helps individuals of all ages better understand the origins and manifestations of race and racism in everyday life by investigating race and human variation through the framework of science. www.under standingrace.org

Rethinking Schools advocates the reform of elementary and secondary education, with a strong emphasis on issues of equity and social justice. www.rethink ingschools.org

Teaching for Change provides teachers and parents with tools to transform schools into centers of justice where students learn to read, write, and change the world. www.teachingforchange.org

Teaching Tolerance is a place for educators to find thought-provoking news, conversation, and support for those who care about diversity, equal opportunity, and respect for differences in schools. www.tolerance.org

Welcoming Schools offers tools, lessons, and resources on embracing family diversity, avoiding gender stereotyping, and ending bullying and name calling in elementary schools. www.welcomingschools.org

Research Methods

RESEARCH QUESTIONS

1. How do teachers translate race learning into classroom practice?
2. How do teachers use their conversations on race and racism to make pedagogic and curricular decisions?
3. What questions do teachers ask about race and racism as they try to apply their learning to their classrooms?

I addressed all three of my research questions through close ethnographic fieldwork with six focal teachers, which consisted of two formal interviews, four classroom observations, observations of inquiry group participation, and informal interviews. In the tradition of action research, both the observations and the interviews were co-constructed, based on the questions teachers were asking about their practice. From the very first interview, I worked with the teachers to find out their questions on race and racism, and then we tracked those and how they changed throughout the year. In sticking to an action research model, I wanted my observations to be based on these questions, so that the observations would be oriented around the teachers' concerns. The only complication in this collaboration was that the teachers also seemed to be aware of the fact that they couldn't know what they didn't know. They all shared their questions, but then they asked me to share what I saw in the classroom, giving me free rein to focus the observations on whatever caught my eye. This shifted my framework for observations, which was still based on teachers' questions but was also shaped by all that I have learned from the academic literature on race and education. In informal follow-up interviews, I asked what information, knowledge, or skills were helpful to them as they tried to apply their learning.

To answer my second question, I also asked teachers to tell me about the pedagogic and curricular choices they made throughout the year and to explain changes they made. Curriculum and pedagogy cannot be decoupled from questions of culture. As anthropologist of education Ruth Landes (1965) has written,

> Since cultural considerations are intrinsic to human processes of communication and learning, educators must choose materials, modes and paces of instruction in accordance with pupils' backgrounds. (p. 51)

To answer my third question, I continuously pushed teachers to vocalize the questions that they had. To contextualize the questions that the focal teachers asked, I also gathered questions from all of the teachers in the three inquiry groups. I gathered these questions via a number of methods. First, I attended all of the meetings of each of three inquiry groups as a participant observer, audio recording and manually recording the questions that teachers asked about race and racism. Each group met monthly, and I attended each of three groups every month of the school year, which meant that on average I attended one inquiry group meeting per week. Second, I tracked the questions that emerged during interviews and observations with the focal teachers. Third, I used an online survey site to distribute two questionnaires to all inquiry group participants (about 40 teachers total from all three inquiry groups), asking them about their emergent questions throughout the school year.

At the beginning of the inquiry process, Laurie asked, "Isn't race socially constructed? Isn't it not real? If so, then how do we incorporate that into what we're doing here [referring to the inquiry group on race] and what we teach our students?" Although every racial project must ask how it continues to perpetuate notions of race as biological or fixed, the fact that race is socially constructed does not mean that it is not real. As anthropologist Troy Duster (2001) has written in *The Making and Unmaking of Whiteness*, race—and Whiteness—is constantly morphing. Just as water changes form, from gas to liquid to solid, so too does race have features that are "fluid . . . and ever-changing," while simultaneously being "deeply embedded, structural, hard, enduring" (p. 113). Though there might be moments in which race seems to have little salience in the classroom, there is no time when racial dynamics (both current and historical) do not shape the relationships, curriculum, resources, speech patterns, group dynamics, and personal histories of all the members of that classroom. On this local level, race had already been constructed. And although race is constantly being constructed, an overemphasis on its social constructedness can diminish the urgency of addressing its real effects in the present.

RESEARCH SITES

At Friends Independent School, the faculty was engaged in a 2-year inquiry project on race that involved 25 teachers (broken up into four smaller inquiry groups) conducting inquiry research on their own classroom practices. This was the purest form of inquiry research in the three groups with which I worked. And even this group was not solely inquiry based. They had an average of four outside speakers or professional development sessions on race (some of which were led by me as a consultant to the project) throughout the year. The entire project was funded by a grant, which provided computers for all the teachers in the group as well as food for meetings. It was an inquiry group, but the teachers were constantly aware that they were being funded by an outside grant and that they were going to be accountable to the administration at the end of the project. The administration constantly tried to alleviate the image that they were controlling the project, to let leadership come from teachers, to free up their time so that they could work on the project, to give them resources on how to conduct inquiry, and to use the consultants as much as possible. But it was ultimately a project organized and driven by the administration. This does not change the fact that it was an inquiry group, but it means that it was different in tone and structure from an inquiry group formed independently by teachers for the sake of their own learning. One advantage to this structure was that teachers knew they had the administration's support. The disadvantage was that teachers who were unhappy with the process did not have an easy way to opt out.

The Philadelphia Urban Public School District inquiry group was a group that I started so that I could find teachers from the urban public school district who would be involved in my research. We structured it on an inquiry group design, but teachers did not undertake individual inquiry projects the way they were required to do at Friends Independent School, where it was a stipulation of their participation in the schoolwide project. Instead, teachers came to the group each month with questions, and the facilitators recommended research articles and books that attempted to address their questions. Each month we would read articles and discuss them in reference to the earlier questions, and then we would proceed by examining new questions that arose from classroom circumstances or from the responses to the readings.

The third group, in St. Clair Suburban Public School District, was the least like an inquiry group. Teachers gathered monthly for an optional districtwide professional development on cultural competency with a Black facilitator who was an expert on both professional development for teachers and race issues in education. The facilitator invited me to be her assistant, and as such I took notes during the meetings and participated in all of the meetings. This group focused heavily on sharing personal stories among teachers of different races, discussing aspects of cultural competency, and applying those aspects to education. Although the teachers were not asked to develop inquiry projects, as they did at the independent school, they were constantly encouraged to think about how this work applied to their classrooms, and many of the teachers had forms of inquiry projects that they were working on throughout the year. Through their observations and interviews with me, each teacher conducted a form of inquiry over the course of that year.

FACILITATION

My role as an inquiry group facilitator and an antiracism educator ultimately played a prominent role in this book. Although I had initially intended not to focus on my role, it quickly became apparent that my interactions with teachers became pivotal moments for their learning and application. This happened in part because of how our interactions created the space and time for teachers to focus on their questions and the application of their learning. It was also always a generative time, when we would cycle through the inquiry process together, often taking questions one level deeper. I was able to direct teachers to resources that helped them continue to pursue their questions without stagnating. For all of these reasons, my interactions with teachers became an important focal point for reflection.

Mutually Beneficial Research

As a participant in the process of change and learning that the teachers in this book were going through, I did not hesitate to share my opinion when teachers asked. I was not interested in recording teachers' beliefs as they were but in recording the process of change that the teachers themselves were going through. And so I frequently added ideas and resources that I felt would support them in reaching their learning goals; and in the meantime, that gave them more to work with in their change process, which gave me more to watch. The partnerships were mutually beneficial in this way as the teachers really sought time with me to find more resources and ideas. And each time we met was an opportunity for me to gain greater insight into their individual processes.

The interviews that I conducted with teachers were loosely structured by a general list of questions that I tailored to each individual teacher based on the questions they were asking in their classrooms. We co-constructed both the interviews and the observations through our conversations, building on what one another said. I knew that to have a conversation that broke local norms of color-blindness, I would have to share my own thoughts and experiences as a White person. As a facilitator, it has been my experience that when I model vulnerability and self-reflection, it makes it possible for others to open up as well. This hypothesis seemed to be supported by the ways that teachers continuously opened up, sharing increasingly more risky questions as the year went on.

Throughout our work together, I tried to be completely transparent with the teachers in this book. I did not want them to be surprised by any of the ideas that I thought I might present in the final book form. I hoped that they could read the final product and feel that my analysis of their situation was both fair and helpful. And yet I wanted to be honest and incisive so as to honor their desire to improve. It would not be respectful of their hard work and their commitment to antiracism if I did not honestly analyze the racial dynamics of their classroom, both one-on-one with them and also here in the book.

To accomplish these intentions, I gave teachers feedback throughout our process of working together. During interviews, I would respond if they asked me what I thought, and after observations I usually emailed them or called to discuss my reflections. I also frequently shared stories of my own questions and confusion about race.

After observations, teachers often wanted feedback in person, but I found that I usually had very little to say. While sitting in the classroom, everything that happened seemed to be a normal and integral part of the whole. Cause and effect seemed obvious, and I could provide an explanation for everything I saw. Rather than analyze, I spent my time in classrooms simply writing down every single thing that I saw, describing rather than interpreting, and trying to note the races of the students as I wrote. At the end of an observation, I had little to say and, in fact, often feared that I would have no feedback for the teachers—and thus no material to write about.

Afterward, however, I would go home and spend hours fleshing out my skeletal fieldnotes within a day or 2 of each observation. And as I did so, I began to see patterns and questions that did not arise for me while I was in the classroom. It was in these reflections that I found questions and ideas that could support teachers' growth. This phenomenon was so consistent that I now encourage teachers to journal about racial dynamics at night, when they are away from the specious logic of the intact environment of the classroom and they can focus on just one scenario, or one child, more thoughtfully.

Sharing Feedback with Teachers

After I had time to write and think about what I saw in the classroom, I usually composed an email to the teachers in which I shared my thoughts, sometimes directly pasting whole paragraphs from my fieldnotes into the communication. In giving feedback, I tried to use the effective methods that my teaching mentors had used with me. I remembered how in my first teaching job, my middle school principal would observe me every 6 weeks. After each observation, we would meet in her office for half an hour, and she would give me gentle feedback on observations. She started by asking me what I thought I did well and what I might do differently the next time. She would give lots of positives accompanied by just one or two things to work on that she often reflected back to me from my own critical evaluation of my teaching. This remains one of my most positive experiences of professional development, yielding the most growth and self-confidence for me as a teacher. Later, as an adult educator, I had the privilege of being observed by a highly talented staff developer, who was also a friend. He only observed me once and, at the end of the observation, he gave me a long list of things I should do differently, many of which were impossible to do given my experience and skill level. The evaluation left me feeling defensive and angry because so many of his suggestions weren't even things I was capable of at that time; it required too much personal change, which, as teachers know, happens slowly. In giving feedback to my focal teachers, I tried to mirror the strategies of my middle school principal.

In spite of the genuine requests for critical feedback I got from teachers, I understood that it is very hard to hear feedback about one's teaching, particularly when it is about race. It can feel like nitpicking. It can be embarrassing and feel shameful. The teachers in this book were working so hard to be antiracist that feedback that said otherwise could feel devastating. And even though they volunteered for this research in order to get feedback, and even though they tended to be very self-critical, I knew they would receive my feedback more openly if I used my skills for delivering effective feedback. First, I asked a lot of questions. I wanted to acknowledge that although I know a lot about race, I was also in the process of learning how this knowledge gets applied to education. I tried to remember that I was not an expert on the developmental stages of their students, whereas they were. Second, I gave them lots of positive feedback on all of the things that I felt were effective in their classrooms. I usually sandwiched any critical feedback within layers of affirmation, all of which was genuine. Indeed all of these teachers were probably more critical of themselves than I could ever be. And yet our critiques did not always match; there were times that I felt they were spending energy on one topic while neglecting one that might matter more. Finally, I tailored my observations, feedback, and the resources I shared to the specific inquiry questions with which the teachers were already engaged.

Notes

Introduction

1. The notion that positive racial identity development for both teachers and students is foundational to any antiracist project in schools was first introduced to me by Marie Michael, PK–12 chair of equity and instruction at the Blake School.

2. I use the terms "colorblind" and "colormute" (Pollock, 2004) liberally throughout the book because these terms are currently used to refer to individual and societal avoidance of recognizing or discussing race. I have great respect for the theorists who helped popularize these terms—Mica Pollock (2004) and Eduardo Bonilla-Silva (2013)—and quote their work frequently in this book. I also want to acknowledge that the use of these terms reflects an ableist description, and I hope other terms will soon emerge to replace them.

3. While people of color in our institutions tend to be the most knowledgeable about racism, when we expect them to be teachers for everyone else, it places an undue (and unpaid) burden on them. I tried to write this book in a way that would be accessible to Whites without requiring a person of color to represent or mediate the content.

4. This refers primarily to Ashkenazi Jews who immigrated from Eastern Europe and Russia. There are many Jews of color in the United States who are still seen as—and identify as—people of color. So conflated are Jewish and Ashkenazi identities, however, that many Jews of color struggle to be recognized as Jewish, both within and outside of the Jewish community.

5. In their book *Critical Race Theory: An Introduction*, Richard Delgado and Jean Stefancic (2012) lay out six tenets of Critical Race Theory. Among these are the two tenets that lead me to assume that racism is present in most school classrooms: first, that racism is "ordinary, not aberrational" (p. 7) in our society and, second, that most White people don't have a material interest in ending racism, according to the principle of interest convergence.

Chapter 1

1. According to the U.S. Census Bureau, "Hispanic" is an ethnicity, not a race. Many academics and activists, however, tend to consider "Latinos" a racial group separate from Black-, White-, Asian-, Native-, Pacific Islander-, or Arab-Americans. Racial identity scholars Ferdman and Gallegos (2001) explain why racial identity is so complicated for Latinos and Hispanics (both terms are widely used—sometimes interchangeably—by individuals to describe themselves) writing: "Because they span the color spectrum, Latinos cannot be racially categorized in a simple manner" (p. 44). They go on to say, "[M]any Latinos choose to see themselves as White, while others place themselves in a distinct Latino racial category . . . while some Latinos reject the label 'person of color,' because they see it as lumping them together with other groups that they would rather not compare themselves to; others are very proud of this denomination and use it for precisely the same reason that others reject it" (p. 45). It is not surprising that Latino teens sometimes have trouble deciding how they identify or where they fit.

In the novel *Americanah*, author Chimimanda Adichie (2014) writes that "Hispanic" is "an American category that was, confusingly, both an ethnicity and a race" (p. 105). The novel's protagonist, Ifemelu, writes a blog post on this confusion entitled "Understanding America for the Non-American Black: What Hispanic Means":

Hispanic means the frequent companions of American blacks in poverty rankings, Hispanic means a slight step above American blacks in the race ladder, Hispanic means the chocolate-skinned woman from Peru, Hispanic means the indigenous people of Mexico. Hispanic means the biracial-looking folks from the Dominican Republic. Hispanic means the paler folks from Puerto Rico. Hispanic also means the blond, blue-eyed guy from Argentina. All you need to be is Spanish-speaking but not from Spain and voila, you're a race called Hispanic. (p. 105)

2. We regularly think of students in terms of gender (dividing them into boys and girls groups to use bathrooms, noticing who plays with whom, creating gender-balanced groups and classes, etc.). I suggest that thinking in terms of race should become just as comfortable to us as thinking in terms of gender. At the same time, as educators we need to be mindful that gender is a spectrum and some students don't fit into the "boy" group or the "girl" group. So while we should continue to be notice and name gender dynamics, we need to be able to think beyond the girl/boy binary. Similarly, as we develop a consciousness of racial dynamics, we need to recognize all of the complicated manifestations of racial background, and honor the ways that students do not fit neatly into racial categories.

Chapter 2

1. While the model designed by Helms and popularized by Tatum is the best known, there are other models of White racial identity development. Tema Okun (2006) wrote an activist-oriented identity model called the Ladder of Empowerment. La Fleur et al. (2002) proposed a White Racial Consciousness model.

2. In the 1970s the National Association of Black Social Workers issued a statement that said White people should not be allowed to adopt Black babies because they would not be able to racially socialize the children adequately. Though I do not believe that White people are incapable of raising healthy Black babies with strong positive racial identities, I do believe that, just like White teachers, White parents of Black children must work hard to build their own racial identities and to support their children's racial identity. I also agree that most White people do not have the background knowledge or experience required to do this effectively.

3. *Indígena* scholar and professor of education, Sandy Grande (2003) coined the term "whitestream" to more accurately describe "mainstream" feminism, which "is not only dominated by White women, but also principally structured on the basis of White, middle-class experience" (p. 330). I use the term here to describe norms that are similarly "structured on the basis of White, middle-class experience."

4. Many of my Black colleagues have asked me to encourage White people to think critically before using the term "antiracist" or "allies" because they have experienced so many White allies as oppressive or unhelpful. In Becky Thompson's (2001) amazing research on White antiracists, which she published in a book called *A Promise and a Way of Life*, she points out that many White people who have spent their lives trying to be antiracist do not self-identify as such but rather see it as a goal for which they are constantly striving.

Chapter 3

1. The concept of windows and mirrors is widespread in multicultural education. Though it's not clear where the term originated, it can be traced to an article by Emily Style (1996) called "Curriculum as Window and Mirror."

2. This quote is paraphrased from my observation notes as I did not record the conversation.

3. Fear of creating an all-Black or predominantly Black support class should not preclude the provision of support for students who want to advance into AP or honors classes. However, if a class is framed in terms of remediation and it is all Black, it will likely serve to reinforce negative perceptions (self and otherwise) of Black students rather than supporting students to build academic confidence and skills. Framing such classes in terms of challenge, excellence, and advancement can help avoid this type of stigma and, subsequently, will draw more students.

4. See Chapter 1 for more explanation. "Untouchable" questions are those questions that teachers were hesitant to ask because they feared that asking them made them sound racist, and yet not asking them might mean that racist patterns continue unquestioned.

5. Terrence Wiley refers to Standard English as "so-called American English Standard" (2005) to emphasize that the language that is often called "Standard English" is not standard at all. Within the United States, "there is no academy of experts as there is in some countries with the authority to define all of the characteristics of the standard" (p. 5). I agree with him and, for the ease of this discussion, I continue to use the term "Standard English," just as he does throughout most of his chapter. Conversations about race and language can be stymied by a fear of using problematic terms. I want to acknowledge the problems with the term "Standard English," but not let those problems preclude a discussion about it.

6. Recently I was challenged to think even more broadly about this question when I heard Dr. Eddie Moore Jr., founder of the White Privilege Conference, speak about the irreparable harm of making Black children give up parts of themselves to fit into predominantly White schooling standards. The worst part, he said, is that after they give up parts of themselves to assimilate—their speech, their hair, their relationships with families, etc.—they still don't fit in. Eddie challenges educators to keep asking questions about what it would look like to honor and use nonstandard languages in schools.

7. Whenever possible, I use the term "they" rather than the singular "he or she" to refer to an anonymous third person. While I realize this is not grammatically correct, it is inclusive of individuals who do not identify as male or female.

8. In a review of literature on detracking, Beth C. Rubin and Pedro Noguera (2004) warn of the possible dilemmas created by unstrategic detracking. In detracked classrooms, teachers sometimes teach to the middle, depriving all students of academic rigor. At other times, teachers retrack the class by assigning different work to students based on skill level. Simply sitting together in the same classroom with "advanced" students did not necessarily increase the educational opportunities of formerly "remedial" or "regular" students. In fact, students often resegregated themselves within the classroom, sometimes even finding evidence for their racial stereotypes of one another through their interactions. Rubin and Noguera argue that tracking must not simply redistribute students but resources as well:

> If detracking is to achieve its primary aims—providing the opportunity for all students to engage with high-level teaching and a rich curriculum, we argue, it must be part of comprehensive reform aimed at the more equitable distribution of resources and opportunities within schools. (2004, p. 92).

Schools that have been effective at detracking—that is, schools that have raised the scores and graduation rates of all students while maintaining a challenging and rigorous curriculum by using heterogeneous grouping—attribute their success in detracking to a philosophy of "leveling up" rather than teaching to the middle (Burris & Garrity, 2008). These schools provide support classes to any student whose grades fall below a certain standard, or to students who simply opt to take those support classes. But the support class does not replace the challenging class; it merely gets added on to a student's schedule until it is no longer necessary. These schools have demonstrated that detracking is politically and logistically possible, though not easy, and that it can have positive social and academic results.

Jeannie Oakes (2005), one of the best-known researchers (and opponents) of academic tracking, suggests that tracking is hard to dismantle because it is not just a system of schooling that needs to be restructured but a reflection of a deep national belief in education as a sorting mechanism:

> Indeed, the social consequences of tracking—sorting students according to preconceptions based on race and social class and providing them with different and unequal access—are part of the core logic of schooling. It is that logic, far more than specific organizational structures or pedagogical practices that leads Americans to cling to this type of sorting. (p. 706)

Chapter 4

1. I put "racialized" in quotes because, in fact, all content is racialized, but mainstream society tends to construe "racialized content" as content involving only people of color. Because White people are often not seen as having a race, history that only covers White people is often seen as "neutral" or nonracialized history.

2. Some theorists have described silence about race as requisite for membership in many predominantly White communities. According to philosopher Charles Mills, in order to fit into White communities White people must follow certain rules of engagement including not naming race, not noticing or naming Whiteness, and not embracing difference (Mills, 1999; Thandeka, 2000). Mills (1999) calls this the "racial contract." White people and people of color in predominantly White communities risk real social—and sometimes economic and political—sanctions if they break the racial contract, which serves to maintain privileges for White people.

3. www.mediathatmattersfest.org/films/a_girl_like_me/

4. I brought in a slide show that portrayed movie posters from movies that depict urban schools (*Dangerous Minds, Lean on Me*, etc.) and others that depict suburban schools (*The Breakfast Club, Juno, Ferris Bueller's Day Off*, etc.). We analyzed the covers in terms of the messages they sent about urban and suburban schooling, as well as about race. I developed this lesson based on the article by James Trier* (2005) called "Sordid Fantasies: Reading Popular 'Inner-City' School Films As Racialized Texts With Pre-Service Teachers."

5. This and other research on talking about race with White children has been written about in one highly readable and accessible chapter in *Nurture Shock* by Bronson and Merryman, 2010.

Chapter 5

1. I struggle to acknowledge my sources in this chapter because so much of my learning has been through workshops and mentorship relationships that are not easy to cite. Although I use this chapter to trace and write about my own practice as a facilitator, I am really documenting the tools and strategies I have learned as a trainer for Whites Confronting Racism and Training for Change. When I know the reference for a certain strategy, I cite it. But so much of what we do is passed down through the oral tradition, cofacilitation, and observation; even if I cited the person who taught me, it would very likely not be the original source. At the beginning of the chapter, I want to generally acknowledge my mentors Sarah Halley, Lorraine Marino, Antje Mattheus, and Molly McClure for all they have taught me. Sarah Halley, in particular, has spent hundreds of hours sharing her wisdom, creativity, and knowledge of group dynamics. Thank you, Sarah, for all that you have taught me and all that you contribute to this chapter.

References

Adams, M., Blumenfeld, W. J., Castañeda, R., Hackman, H., Peters, M. L., & Zúñiga, X. (2013). *Readings for diversity and social justice.* New York, NY: Routledge.

Adichie, C. N. (2014). *Americanah.* New York, NY: Anchor Books.

Ahram, R., Fergus, E., & Noguera, P. (2011). Addressing racial/ethnic disproportionality in special education: Case studies in suburban districts. *Teachers College Record 113*(10), 2233–2266.,

Alexander, M. (2012). *The new Jim Crow: Mass incarceration in the age of colorblindness.* New York, NY: The New Press.

Alim, H. S., & Smitherman, G. (2012). *Articulate while Black: Barack Obama, language and race in the U.S.* Oxford, England: Oxford University Press.

Anyon, J. (1980). Social class and the hidden curriculum of work. *Journal of Education 162*(1), 67–92.

Apple, M. (2004). *Ideology and curriculum.* New York, NY: Routledge Falmer.

Aronson, J., Lustina, M. J., Good, C., Keough, K., Steele, C. M., & Brown, J. (1999). When white men can't do math: Necessary and sufficient factors in stereotype threat. *Journal of Experimental Social Psychology, 35,* 29–46.

Baldwin, J. (1965). A talk to teachers. In *The price of the ticket: collected non-fiction 1948–1985* (pp. 325–332). New York, NY: St. Martin's Press.

Banks, J. A. (2009). Multicultural education: Characteristics and goals. In J. A. Banks & C. A. McGee Banks (Eds.), *Multicultural education: Issues and oerspectives* (7th ed.). (pp. 3–26).

Beauboeuf-Lafontant, T. (1999). A movement against and beyond boundaries: "Politically relevant teaching" among African American teachers. *Teachers College Record, 100*(4), 702–723.

Berthoff, A. E. (1987). The teacher as researcher. In D. Goswami & P. R. Stillman (Eds.), *Reclaiming the classroom: Teacher research as an agency for change* (pp. 28–39). Upper Montclair, NJ: Boynton/ Cook.

Bigler, R. S. (1999). The use of multicultural curricula and materials to counter racism in children. *Journal of Social Issues, 55*(4), 687–705.Blanchett, W. (2006). Disproportionate representation of African American students in special education: Acknowledging the role of white privilege and racism. *Educational Researcher 35*(6), 24–28.

Bolgatz, J. (2005). *Talking race in the classroom.* New York, NY: Teachers College Press.

Bonilla-Silva, E. (2013). *Racism without racists: Colorblind racism and the persistence of racial inequality in the United States* (4th ed.). Lanham, MD: Rowman & Littlefield.

Bowles, S., & Gintis, H. (2002). Schooling in capitalist America revisited. *Sociology of Education 75,* 1–18.

Brodkin, K. (2001). Comments on "discourses of whiteness." *Journal of Linguistic Anthropology 11*(1), 147–150.

Brodkin, K. (2004). *How Jews became White folks and what that says about race in America.* New Brunswick, NJ: Rutgers University Press.

Bronson, P. O., & Merryman, A. (2009, September 14). See baby discriminate. *Newsweek, 52–60.*

Bronson, P. O., & Merryman, A. (2011). *Nurtureshock: New thinking about children.* New York, NY: Twelve.

Burris, C., & Garrity, D. (2008). *Detracking for excellence and equity.* Alexandria, VA: Association for Supervision and Curriculum Development.

Butler, J. (1993). *Bodies that matter: On the discursive limits of "sex".* New York, NY: Routledge.

Child Welfare Information Gateway. (2014). *Mandatory reporters of child abuse and neglect.* Washington, DC: U.S. Department of Health and Human Services, Children's Bureau.

Cochran-Smith, M. (1995). Uncertain allies: Understanding the boundaries of race and teaching. *Harvard Educational Review, 65*(4), 541–571.

Cochran-Smith, M. (2004). *Walking the road: Race, diversity, and social justice in teacher education.* New York, NY: Teachers College Press.

Cochran-Smith, M., & Lytle, S. (2009). *Inquiry as stance: Practitioner research in the next generation.* New York, NY: Teachers College Press.

Cohen, S. (2001). *States of denial: Knowing about atrocities and suffering.* Cambridge, UK: Polity.

Coleman-King, C. (2014). *The (re-)making of a Black American: Tracing the racial and ethnic socialization of Caribbean American youth* (Vol. 51). Peter Lang.

Creswell, J. W. (2003). *Research design: Qualitative, quantitative and mixed methods approaches* (2nd ed.). Thousand Oaks, CA: Sage.

Cross, E. (2000). *Managing diversity: The courage to lead.* Westport, CT: Quorum Books.

Cummins, J. (2000). *Language, power and pedagogy: Bilingual children in the crossfire.* Bristol, UK: Multilingual Matters.

Cunningham, R. T., & Boykin, A. W. (2004). Enhancing cognitive performance in African American children: Infusing afro-cultural perspectives and research. In R. Jones (Ed.), *Black Psychology* (4th ed.). Hampton, VA: Cobb and Henry.

Danius, S., Jonsson, S., & Spivak, G. (1993). An Interview with Gayatri Chakravorty Spivak. *boundary 2. 20*(2): 24–50.

DeCuir, J. T., & Dixson, A. D. (2004). "So when it comes out, they aren't that surprised that it is there": Using critical race theory as a tool of analysis of race and racism in education. *Educational Researcher, 33*(5), 26–31.

Delgado, R., & Stefancic, J. (2012). *Critical race theory: An introduction.* New York, NY: New York University Press.

Delpit, L. (Ed.) (2003). *The skin that we speak.* New York, NY: W. W. Norton.

Delpit, L. D. (2006). *Other people's children: Cultural conflict in the classroom* (2nd ed.). New York, NY: The New Press.

Delpit, L. D. (2012). *Multiplication is for White people.* New York, NY: The New Press.

Denton, P., & Kriete, R. (2000). *The first six weeks of school.* Greenfield, MA: Northeast Foundation for Children.

Derman-Sparks, L., & Ramsey, P. (2011). *What if all the kids are White? Anti-bias multicultural education with young children and families* (2nd ed.). New York, NY: Teachers College Press.

Devos, T., & Banaji, M. R. (2005). American = White? *Journal of personality and social psychology, 88*: 447–466.

Diamond, J. B., Randolph, A., & Spillane, J. P. (2004). Teachers' expectations and sense of responsibility for student learning: The importance of race, class, and organizational habitus. *Anthropology and Education Quarterly, 35*(1): 75–98.

DiAngelo, R. (2006). My class didn't trump my race. *Multicultural Perspectives, 8*(1), 52–56.

DiAngelo, R. (2012). *What does it mean to be White?: Developing White racial literacy.* New York, NY: Peter Lang.

Diop, C. A. (1974). *African origin of civilization . . . myth or reality?* Chicago, IL: Chicago Review Press.

Dixson, A. D., & Rousseau, C. K. (2005). And we are still not saved: Critical race theory in education ten years later. *Race, Ethnicity & Education, 8*(1), 7–27.

Dixson, A. D., & Rousseau, C. K. (2006). *Critical race theory in education: All god's children got a song.* New York, NY: Routledge.

Doane, W. (2003). Rethinking whiteness studies. In W. Doane E. Bonilla-Silva (Eds.), *White out* (pp. 3–20). New York, NY: Routledge.

Donaldson, M., & Johnson, S. (2011). Teach for America teachers: How long do they teach? Why do they leave? *Phi Delta Kappan, 93*(2), 47–51.

Dovidio, J. F., & Gaertner, S. L. (2000). Aversive racism and selective decisions: 1989–1999. *Psychological Science, 11*, 315–319.

Dovidio, J. F., Gaertner, S. L., Kawakami, K., & Hodson, G. (2002). Why can't we all just get along? Interpersonal biases and interracial distrust. *Cultural Diversity and Ethnic Minority Psychology, 8*, 88–102.

Dovidio, J. F., Kawakami, K., Johnson, C., Johnson, B., & Howard, A. (1997). On the nature of prejudice: Automatic and controlled processes. *Journal of Experimental Social Psychology, 33*, 510–540.

DuBois, W.E.B. (1961). *The souls of Black folks.* Greenwich, CT: Fawcett Publications Inc.

DuBois. W.E.B. (1973). *The education of Black people.* New York, NY: Monthly Review Press.

DuBois, W.E.B. (2009). *The gift of Black folk: The negroes in the making of America.* Garden City Park, NJ: Square One Publishers.

Duster, T. (2001). The morphing properties of Whiteness. In B. B. Rasmussen, E. Klinenberg, I. J. Nexica, & M. Wray (Eds.), *The making and unmaking of Whiteness* (pp. 113–137). Durham, NC: Duke University Press.

Dweck, C. (2007). *Mindset: The new psychology of success.* New York, NY: Ballantine Books.

Ferdman, B. M., & Gallegos, P. I. (2001). Racial identity development and Latinos in the United States. In C. L. Wijeyesinghe & B. W. Jackson (Eds.), *New perspectives on racial identity development* (pp. 32–66). London, UK: NYU Press.

Ferguson, R. F. (2003). Teachers' perceptions and expectations and the Black-White test score gap. *Urban Education, 38*(4), 460–507.

Fine, M. (1997). Witnessing Whiteness. In M. Fine, L. Weis, L. Powell & L. Wong (Eds.), *Off White: Readings on race, power, and society* (pp. 163–172). New York, NY: Routledge.

Fine, M., & Ruglis, J. (2009). Circuits and consequences of dispossession: The racialized realignment of the public sphere. *Transforming Anthropology 17*(1), 20–33.

Fine, M, Weis, L., Powell, L., & Wong, L. (1997). *Off white: Readings on race, power, and society.* New York, NY: Routledge.

Ford, D. (2011). *Multicultural gifted education,* (2nd ed.). New York, NY: Teachers College Press.

Ford, D. (2013). *Recruiting and retaining culturally different students in gifted education.* Waco, TX: Prufrock Press.

Foster, M. (1997). *Black teachers on teaching.* New York, NY: The New Press.

Frankenberg, R. (1999). *White women, race matters: The social construction of Whiteness.* Minneapolis, MN: University of Minnesota Press.

Frankenberg, R. (2001). The mirage of an unmarked whiteness. In B. B. Rasmussen, E. Klinenberg, I. J. Nexica, & M. Wray (Eds.), *The making and unmaking of whiteness* (pp. 72–96). Durham, NC: Duke University Press.

Gay, G. (2010). *Culturally responsive teaching: Theory, research, and practice.* New York, NY: Teachers College Press.

Giroux, H. (1997). White squall: Resistance and the pedagogy of Whiteness. *Cultural Studies 11*(3), 376–389.

Goffman, E. (1986). *Stigma: Notes on the management of a spoiled identity.* New York, NY: Simon and Schuster.

Good, T., & Brophy, J. (2002). *Looking in classrooms* (9th ed.). Boston, MA: Pearson Education.

Gooding, F. (2007). *You mean there's race in my movie?: Understanding race in mainstream Hollywood.* Silver Springs, MD: On the Reelz Press.

Goodman, D. (2011). *Promoting diversity and social justice* (2nd ed.). New York, NY: Routledge.

Grande, S. (2003). Whitestream feminism and the colonialist project: A review of contemporary feminist pedagogy and practice. *Educational Theory 53*(3), 329–346.

Greene, J. P., & Winters, M. A. (2006). The effect of residential school choice on public high school graduation rates. *Peabody Journal of Education, 81*(1): 203–216.

Hamm, J. (2001). Barriers and bridges to positive cross-ethnic relations: African American and White parent socialization beliefs and practices. *Youth and Society, 33*(1), 62–98.

Haney López, I. (2006). *White by law: The legal construction of race.* New York, NY: New York University Press.

Harper, S. (2009). Niggers no more: A critical race counternarrative on Black male student achievement at predominantly White colleges and universities. *International Journal of Qualitative Studies in Education, 22*(6), 697–712.

Harding, V. (1993). *There is a river: The Black struggle for freedom in America* (reissue edition). Boston, MA: Mariner Books.

Helms, J. (1984). Toward a theoretical explanation of the effects of race on counseling: A black and white model." *Counseling Psychologist, 12,* 153–165.

Helms, J. (1990). *Black and White racial identity: Theory, research and practice.* Santa Barbara, CA: Praeger.

Helms, J. (2008). *A race is a nice thing to have.* Hanover, MA: Microtraining Associates.

Henderson, A. T., Mapp, K. L., Johnson, V. R., & Davies, D. (2007). *Beyond the bake sale: The essential guide to family/school partnerships.* New York, NY: The New Press.

Hernstein, R. J., & Murray, C. (1996). *The bell curve: Intelligence and class structure in American life.* New York, NY: Free Press.

Hill, J. (2008). *The everyday language of White racism.* Hoboken, NJ: Wiley Blackwell.

Holbrook, C. (2006). Low expectations are the worst form of racism. In J. Landsman & C. W. Lewis (Eds.), *White teachers/Diverse classrooms* (pp. 243–253). Sterling, VA: Stylus.

hooks, b. (1995). *Killing rage: Ending racism.* New York, NY: Henry Holt and Company.

Howard, G. (2006). *We can't teach what we don't know: White teachers, multiracial schools.* New York, NY: Teachers College Press.

Howard, T. (2010). *Why race and culture matter in schools.* New York, NY: Teachers College Press.

Howard, T. (2013). *Black male(d): Peril and promise in the education of African American males.* New York, NY: Teachers College Press.

Hughes, D., Rodriguez, J., Smith, P., Johnson, D., Stevenson, H., & Spicer, P. (2006). Parents' ethnic-racial socialization practices: A review of research and directions for future study. *Developmental Psychology, 42*(5), 747–770.

Hughes, J. M., Bigler, R. S., & Levy, S. R. (2007). Consequences of learning about historicalracism among European American and African American children. *Child Development, 78*(6), 1689–1705.

Ignatiev, N. (1995). *How the Irish became White.* New York, NY: Routledge.

Ignatiev, N. (1997, April). *The point is not to interpret Whiteness but to abolish it.* Talk given at the The Making and Unmaking of Whiteness Conference, University of California, Berkeley.

Jabulani, S. M. (2008). *Cultural slant and mathematical achievement.* (Unpublished dissertation). Wayne State University, Detroit.

Kailin, J. (2002). *Antiracist education: From theory to practice.* Lanham, MD: Rowman & Littlefield.

Katz, J. (1978). *White awareness: A handbook for anti-racism training.* Norman, OK: University of Oklahoma Press.

Kim, C. J. (2004). Imagining race and nation in multiculturalist America. *Ethnic and Racial Studies 27*(6), 987–1005.

Kivel, P. (2011). *Uprooting racism: How White people can work for racial justice* (3rd ed.). Gabriola Island, BC: New Society Publishers.

Kugler, E. G. (2002). *Debunking the middle class myth: Why diverse schools are good for all kids.* Lanham, MD: Scarecrow Publications.

Ladson-Billings, G. (1995a). Toward a theory of culturally relevant pedagogy. *American Educational Research Journal 32*(3), 465–491.

Ladson-Billings, G. (1995b). But that's just good teaching! The case for culturally relevant pedagogy. *Theory into Practice 34*(3), 159–165.

Ladson-Billings, G. (1998). Just what is critical race theory and what's it doing in a *nice* field like education? *Qualitative Studies in Education 11*(1), 7–24.

Ladson-Billings, G. (1999). Preparing teachers for diverse student populations: A critical race theory perspective. *Review of Research in Education 24,* 211–247.

Ladson-Billings, G. (2001). *Crossing over to Canaan: The journey of new teachers in diverse classrooms.* San Francisco, CA: Jossey-Bass.

Ladson-Billings, G. (2006). From the achievement gap to the education debt: Understanding achievement in U.S. schools. *Educational Researcher, 35*(7), 3–12.

Ladson-Billings, G. (2009). *The dreamkeepers: Successful teachers of African American children* (2nd ed.). San Francisco, CA: Jossey-Bass.

Landes, R. (1965). *Culture in American education.* New York, NY: Wiley Publishing.

Landsman, J., & Lewis, C. W. (2011). *White teachers, diverse classrooms.* Sterling, VA: Stylus Publishing.

Landry, D., & MacLean, G. (1996). Introduction. In D. Landry & G. MacLean (Eds.), *The Spivak reader: Selected works* (pp. 1–14). New York, NY: Routledge.

Lee, S. (2005). *Up against Whiteness: Race, schooling and immigrant youth.* New York, NY: Teachers College Press.

Lewis, A. (2003). *Race in the schoolyard: Negotiating the color line in classrooms and communities.* New Bruswick, NJ: Rutgers University Press.

Lewis, A. E. (2004). "What group?" Studying Whites and Whiteness in the era of "color-blindness." *Sociological Theory, 22*(4), 623–646.

Lipsitz, G. (2006). *The possessive investment in Whiteness: How White people profit from identity politics.* Philadelphia, PA: Temple University Press.

Loewen, J. (2008). *Lies my teacher told me: Everything your American history textbooks got wrong.* New York, NY: The New Press.

Lomawaima, K. T., & McCarty, T. L. (2006). *To remain an Indian: Lessons in democracy from a century of Native American education.* New York, NY: Teachers College Press.

Luft, J., & Ingham, H. (1950). The Johari window, a graphic model of interpersonal awareness. *Proceedings of the Western Training Laboratory in group development.* Los Angeles: UCLA.

Marshall, P. (2002). Racial identity and challenges of educating White youths for cultural diversity. *Multicultural Perspectives 4*(3), 9–14.

Marshall, C., & Rossman, G. (1999). *Designing qualitative research* (3rd ed.). Thousand Oaks, CA: Sage Publications.

Marx, S. (2006). *Revealing the invisible: Confronting passive racism in teacher education.* New York, NY: Routledge.

Massey, D. (2008). *Categorically unequal: The American stratification system.* New York, NY: Russell Sage.

Matthias, B., & French, M. (1996). *Forty ways to raise a nonracist child.* New York, NY: William Morrow.

Maxwell, J. A. (2005). *Qualitative research design* (2nd ed.). Thousand Oaks, CA: Sage Publications.

McIntosh, P. (1998). White privilege: Unpacking the invisible knapsack. *Race, class, and gender in the United States: An integrated study, 4,* 165–169.

Menkart, D., Okazawa-Rey, M., & Lee, E. (2008). *Beyond heroes and holidays: A practical guide to K–12 antiracist multicultural education and staff development* (2nd ed.). Washington, DC: Teaching for Change.

Michael, A., & Bartoli, E. (2014, Summer). What White children need to know about race. *Independent Schools Magazine,* 56-62.

Michael, A., & Conger, M. (2009, Spring). Becoming an antiracist White ally. In *Perspectives on Urban Education* (pp. 56–60). University of Pennsylvania Graduate School of Education.

Mills, C. (1999). *The racial contract.* Ithaca, NY: Cornell University Press.

National Alliance for Public Charter Schools. Retrieved from http://dashboard.publiccharters.org/dashboard/students/district/PA-39/year/2012.

National Center for Education Statistics. (2014). *The condition of education.* Washington, DC: Grace Kena, Susan Aud and Frank Johnson.

Neal, L., McCray, A. D., Webb-Johnson, G., & Bridgest, S. (2003). The effects of African American movement styles on teachers' perceptions and reactions. *The Journal of Special Education 37*(1), 49–57.

Nieto, S. (2009). *Language, culture and teaching* (2nd ed.). Mahwah, NJ: Lawrence Earlbaum Associates.

Noguera, P. (2008). *The trouble with black boys: And other reflections on race, equity and the future of public education*. San Francisco, CA: Jossey-Bass.

Oakes, J. (2005). *Keeping track: How schools structure inequality* (2nd ed.). New Haven, CT: Yale University Press.

Oakes, J. (2008). Keeping track: Structuring equality and inequality in an era of accountability. *Teachers College Record 110*(3), 700–712.

Okun, T. (2006). From white racist to white antiracist: The life-long journey. Retrieved from http://www.cwsworkshop.org/pdfs/CARC/White_Identity/4_Life_Long_Journey.PDF. Accessed July 1, 2014.

Omi, M., & Winant, H. (1994). *Racial formations in the United States: From the 1960s to the 1990s*. New York, NY: Routledge.

Omi, M., & Winant, H. (2002). Racial formation. In P. Essed & D. T. Goldberg (Eds.), *Race critical theories*. Oxford, UK: Blackwell.

Palmer, P. (1999). *The courage to teach: Exploring the inner landscape of a teacher's life*. San Francisco, CA: Jossey Bass.

Pennsylvania Department of Education. (2014). Enrollment statewide by county, race and grade. Retrieved from www.portal.state.pa.us/portal/server.pt/community/enrollment/7407/public_school_enrollment_reports/620541

Perkins, M. (2009, April). Straight talk on race: Challenging the stereotypes in kids' books. *School Library Journal*, 28–32.

Perry, P. (2002). *Shades of white: White kids and racial identities in high school*. Durham, NC: Duke University Press.

Picower, B. (2009). The unexamined whiteness of teaching: How white teachers maintain and enact dominant racial ideologies. *Race Ethnicity and Education, 12*(2), 197–215.

Picower, B. (2012). *Practice what you teach: Social justice education in the classroom and in the streets*. New York, NY: Routledge.

Pollock, M. (2004). *Colormute*. Princeton, NJ: Princeton University Press.

Pollock, M. (2008a). *Because of race*. Princeton, NJ: Princeton University Press.

Pollock, M. (2008b). *Everyday antiracism: Getting real about race in school*. New York, NY: The New Press.

Rajput, T. (2009). Questioning your collection. *Knowledge Quest, 38*(1), 62–69.

Reason, P., & Bradbury, H. (2006). *Handbook of action research*. Thousand Oaks, CA: Sage.

Reinharz, S. (1992). *Feminist methods in social research*. New York, NY: Oxford University Press.

Rickford, J. R. (2005). Using the vernacular to teach the standard. In J. D. Ramirez, T. G. Wiley, G. de Klerk, E. Lee, & W. E. Wright (Eds.), *Ebonics: The Urban Education Debate* (2nd ed.)(pp. 18–40). Clevedon, UK: Multilingual Matters Ltd.

Roediger, D. (1994). *Towards the abolition of whiteness*. London, England: Verso.

Roediger, D. R. (1998). Introduction. In D. R. Roediger (Ed.), *Black on white* (pp. 1–28). New York, NY: Schocken Books.

Rothenberg, P. (2011). *White privilege: Essential readings on the other side of racism* (4th ed.). New York, NY: Worth Publishers.

Rubin, B. C., & Noguera, P. A. (2004). Tracking detracking: Sorting through the dilemmas and possibilities of detracking in practice. *Equity & Excellence in Education 37*, 92–101.

Schniedewind, N., & Davidson, E. (2006). *Open minds to equality: A sourcebook of learning activities to affirm diversity and promote equity*. Milwaukee, WI: Rethinking Schools Publications.

Singleton, G., & Linton, C. (2005). *Courageous conversations*. Newbury Park, CA: Corwin.

Singleton, G. E., & Hays, C. (2008). Beginning courageous conversations about race. In M. Pollock (Ed.), *Everyday antiracism: Getting real about race in school* (pp. 18–23). New York, NY: The New Press.

Sizer, N. F., & Sizer, T. (2000). *The students are watching: Schools and the moral contract*. Boston, MA: Beacon Press.

Sleeter, C. E. (1993). How white teachers construct race. In C. McCarthy & W. Crichlow (Eds.), *Race, identity, and representation in education* (pp. 157–171). New York, NY: Routledge.

Sleeter, C. E. (1995). Teaching whites about racism. In R. J. Martin (Ed.), *Practicing what we teach: Confronting diversity in teacher education* (pp. 117–130). Albany, NY: State University of New York Press.

Smitherman, G. (2005). Black language and the education of black children: One mo once. In J. D. Ramirez, T. G. Wiley, G. de Klerk, E. Lee, & W. E. Wright (Eds.), *Ebonics: The urban education debate* (2nd ed.). (pp. 49–61). Clevedon, UK: Multilingual Matters Ltd.

Spencer, M. B. (2008). Lessons learned and opportunities ignored since *Brown v. Board of Education*: Youth development and the myth of a colorblind society. *Educational Researcher 37*(5), 253–266.

Spencer, M. B., & Tinsley, B. (2008). Identity as coping: Assessing youth's challenges and opportunities for success. *The Prevention Researcher (15)*4, 17–21.

Spivak, G. (1990). Criticism, feminism, and the institution with Elizabeth Grosz. In S. Harasym (Ed.), *The post-colonial critic* (pp. 67–74). New York, NY: Routledge.

Staiger, A. (2004).Whiteness as giftedness: Racial formation at an urban high school. *Social Problems 52*(2), 161–181.

Steele, C. (2010). *Whistling Vivaldi and other clues to how stereotypes affect us.* New York, NY: W. W. Norton.

Steele, C., & Aronson, J. (1998). Stereotype threat and the test performance of academically successful African Americans. In C. Jencks & M. Phillips (Eds.), *The Black-White test score gap* (pp. 401–427). Washington, DC: Brookings Institute Press.

Stevenson, H. C. (2014). *Promoting racial literacy in schools: Difference that makes a difference.* New York, NY: Teachers College Press.

Stevenson, H. C., Davis, G., & Abdul-Kabir, S. (2001). *Stickin' to, watchin' over and gettin' with: An African American parent's guide to discipline.* San Francisco, CA: Jossey Bass.

Stevenson, H. C., Davis, G. Y., Herrero-Taylor, T., & Morris, R. (2003). "An hour of play": Theoretical frames for the PLAAY project. In H. Stevenson (Ed.), *Playing with anger: Teaching coping skills to African American boys through athletics and culture* (pp. 1–20). Westport, CT: Praeger Publishers.

Style, E. (1996). Curriculum as window and mirror. *Social Science Record*, 35–38.

Sue, D. W. (2004). Whiteness and ethnocentric monoculturalism: Making the "invisible" visible. *American Psychologist 59*(8), 761–770.

Sue, D. W. (2007). Racial microaggressions in everyday life. *American Psychologist 62*(4), 271–286.

Sue, D. W. (2011). The challenge of white dialectics: Making the "invisible" visible. *The Counseling Psychologist, 39,* 415–422.

Takaki, R. (2008). *A different mirror: A history of multicultural America.* New York, NY: Little, Brown.

Tatum, B. (1994). Teaching white students about racism: The search for white allies and the restoration of hope. *Teachers College Record 95*(4), 462–476.

Tatum, B. (2003). *Why are all the Black kids sitting together in the cafeteria?* New York, NY: Basic Books.

Tatum, B. D. (2007). *Can we talk about race?* Boston, MA: Beacon Press.

Taylor, E., Gillborn, D., & Ladson-Billings, G. (2009). *Foundations of critical race theory in education.* New York, NY: Routledge

Teaching Tolerance Project and the Southern Poverty Law Center. (1997). *Starting small: Teaching tolerance in preschool and the early grades.* Montgomery, AL: Teaching Tolerance.

Technical Assistance Center on Disproportionality. Retrieved from http://steinhardt.nyu.edu/metro center/programs/TACD/publications.html.

Thandeka. (2000). *Learning to be white.* New York, NY: Continuum.

Thomas, W. P., & Collier, V. P. (2001). *A national study of school effectiveness for language minority students' long-term academic achievement.* Report prepared with funding from the Center for Research on Education, Diversity & Excellence (CREDE), a national research center funded by the Office of Educational Research and Improvement (OERI) of the U.S. Department of Education, under Cooperative Agreement No. R306A60001–96 (July 1, 1996–June 30, 2001).

Thompson, B. (2001). *A promise and a way of life: White antiracist activism.* Minneapolis, MN: University of Minnesota Press.

Thompson, C. E., & Carter, R. (2012). An overview and elaboration of Helms' racial identity development theory. In C. E. Thompson & R. Carter (Eds.), *Racial identity theory: Application to individual, group and organizational interventions* (pp.15–32). New York, NY: Taylor and Francis Group.

Thompson, C. E., Neville, H., Weathers, P. L., Postin, W. C., & Atkinson, D. R. (1990). Cultural mistrust and racism reaction among African American students. *Journal of College Student Development 31*, 162–168.

Trier*, J. (2005). "Sordid fantasies": Reading popular "inner-city" school films as racialized texts with pre-service teachers. *Race Ethnicity and Education, 8*(2): 171–189.

Tyson, K. (2011). *Integration interrupted: Tracking, black students, and acting white after Brown.* New York, NY: Oxford University Press.

Unseem, E., Offenberg, R., & Farley, E. (2007). *Closing the teacher quality gap in Philadelphia: New hopes and old hurdles.* Philadelphia, PA: Research for Action.

U.S. Department of Education, National Center for Education Statistics, Common Core of Data (CCD). (2000). *Percentage distribution of enrollment in public elementary and secondary school jurisdiction: Fall 2000.*

U.S. Department of Education, National Center for Education Statistics, Common Core of Data (CCD). (2010). *Percentage distribution of enrollment in public elementary and secondary school jurisdiction: Fall 2010.*

U.S. Department of Education Office for Civil Rights. (2014). *Civil rights data collection.* Data Snapshot: School Discipline. Issue Brief No. 1: March, 2014

Valenzuela, A. (1999). *Subtractive schooling: U.S.-Mexican youth and the politics of caring.* Albany, NY: State University of New York Press.

Van Ausdale, D., & Feagin, J. (2001). *The first R: How children learn race and racism.* Lanham, MD: Rowman and Littlefield.

Ware, F. (2006). Warm demander pedagogy: Culturally responsive teaching that supports a culture of achievement for African American students. *Urban Education, 41*(4), 427–456.

Watson, S. (2001). Recruiting and retaining teachers: Keys to improving the Philadelphia public schools. Consortium for Policy Research in Education. Retrieved from http://www.cpre.org/images/stories/cpre_pdfs/children01.pdf. Accessed July 1, 2014.

Wetherell, M. (2003). Racism and the analysis of cultural resources in interviews. In H. van den Berg, M. Wetherell, & H. Houtkoop-Steenstra (Eds.), *Analyzing race talk* (pp. 11–30). New York, NY: Cambridge University Press.

Whaley, A. (2001). Cultural mistrust: An important psychological construct for diagnosis and treatment of African Americans. *Professional Psychology, Research and Practice 32*(6), 555–562.

Wiley, T. (2005). Ebonics: Background to the current policy debate. In J. D. Ramirez, T. G. Wiley, G. de Klerk, E. Lee, & W. E. Wright (Eds.), *Ebonics: The urban education debate* (2nd ed.) (pp. 3–17). Clevedon, UK: Multilingual Matters Ltd.

Wimsatt, W., West, C., & Ignatiev, N. (1997). I'm Ofay, You're Ofay. *Transition 73*, 176–203.

Winant, H. (1997). Behind blue eyes: Whiteness and contemporary U.S. racial politics. In M. Fine, L. Weis, L. C. Powell, & L. Mun Wong (Eds.), *Off White: Readings on race, power and society* (pp.40–56). New York, NY: Routledge.

Winant, H. (2001). White racial projects. In B. B. Rasmussen, E. Klinenberg, I. J. Nexica, & M. Wray (Eds.), *The making and unmaking of Whiteness* (pp. 97–112). Durham, NC: Duke University Press.

Wise, T. (2010). *Colorblind: The rise of post-racial politics and the retreat from racial equity.* San Francisco, CA: City Lights Publishers.

Wise, T. (2011). *White like me: Reflections on race from a privileged son* (2nd ed.). Berkeley, CA: Soft Skull Press.

Woodson, C. G. (1933). *The miseducation of the Negro*. New York, NY: SoHo Press.

Yosso, T. (2005). Whose culture has capital? A critical race theory discussion of community cultural wealth. *Race, Ethnicity & Education, 8*(1), 69–91.

Yosso, T. (2002). Toward a critical race curriculum. *Equity and Excellence in Education, 35*(2), 93–107.

Zeichner, K. (2009). *Teacher education and the struggle for social justice*. New York, NY: Routledge.

Index

About the Author

Ali Michael is director of K–12 consulting and professional development for the Center for the Study of Race and Equity in Education at the University of Pennsylvania. She is also the director and cofounder of the Race Institute for K–12 Educators.

Ali earned her BA in political science and African studies at Williams College, her MA in anthropology and education from Teachers College, and her PhD in teacher education from the University of Pennsylvania. She received her education as an activist and a facilitator from Training for Change and Whites Confronting Racism. She and her partner, Michael, live in Philadelphia, where they grapple with questions of race, education, and the parenting of two small children.